D1478453

# The Politics of Management Knowledge in Times of Austerity

# The Politics of Management Knowledge in Times of Austerity

Ewan Ferlie, Sue Dopson, Chris Bennett,

Michael D. Fischer, Jean Ledger,

and Gerry McGivern

OXFORD
UNIVERSITY PRESS

# OXFORD

UNIVERSITY PRESS

Great Clarendon Street, Oxford, OX2 6DP,
United Kingdom

Oxford University Press is a department of the University of Oxford.
It furthers the University's objective of excellence in research, scholarship,
and education by publishing worldwide. Oxford is a registered trade mark of
Oxford University Press in the UK and in certain other countries

First Edition published in 2018

Impression: 1

Published in the United States of America by Oxford University Press
198 Madison Avenue, New York, NY 10016, United States of America

British Library Cataloguing in Publication Data

Data available

Library of Congress Control Number: 2018945109

ISBN  978-0-19-877721-2

Printed and bound by
CPI Group (UK) Ltd, Croydon, CR0 4YY

# CONTENTS

# ■ ABBREVIATIONS

| | |
|---|---|
| CCG | clinical commissioning group |
| CEO | chief executive officer |
| CLAHRC | Collaboration for Leadership in Applied Health Research and Care |
| CQC | Care Quality Commission |
| EBM | evidence-based medicine |
| EBMgt | evidence-based management |
| GP | general practitioner |
| ICT | information and communications technology |
| IHI | Institute for Healthcare Improvement |
| IPPR | Institute of Public Policy Research |
| KPI | key performance indicator |
| NDPB | non-departmental public body |
| NGO | non-governmental organization |
| NHS | National Health Service |
| NHS IQ | National Health Service Improving Quality |
| NICE | National Institute of Health and Care Excellence |
| NPM | New Public Management |
| PCT | primary care trust |
| PDSA | Plan Do Study Act |
| QIPP | Quality, Innovation, Productivity, and Prevention |
| RBV | resource-based view |
| SHA | strategic health authority |
| TDA | Trust Development Authority |
| UK | United Kingdom |
| USA | United States of America |

# ABOUT THE AUTHORS

**Ewan Ferlie** is Professor of Public Services Management at King's College London. He has published widely on themes of change and reorganization in public services settings, especially in health care and higher education. He is also interested in the tension between the logics of professionalism and managerialism in these settings. His work seeks to characterize high-level narratives of public services 'reforming', including New Public Management and post-NPM narratives of reform, which include political, ideological, and technical components. He was elected as an Academician of the Social Sciences in 2008 and a Fellow of the British Academy in 2016.

**Sue Dopson** is the Academic Director of the Oxford Diploma in Organizational Leadership, a Fellow of Green Templeton College, Oxford, and Visiting Professor at the University of Alberta, Canada. She is a noted specialist on the personal and organizational dimensions of leadership and transformational change. Her research centres on transformational change and knowledge exchange in the public and health care sectors, and she currently represents the University of Oxford as Non-Executive Director of the Oxford Health NHS Foundation Trust.

**Chris Bennett** is an independent research psychologist. She was previously employed by the Medical Research Council, and as a Senior Research Fellow at the Centre for Corporate Strategy and Change, University of Warwick. Most of her research and publications have explored different aspects of change within the NHS and other public-sector bodies.

**Michael D. Fischer** is Professor in Organizational Behaviour and Leadership at Australian Catholic University, an Associate and Programme Director at Melbourne Business School, and Visiting Scholar at the Saïd Business School, University of Oxford. Trained as a business school social scientist and clinical group analyst, his research has a strong empirical focus on the practice-level microsociology of organizational change in research-intensive settings, especially in health care. He specializes in ethnographic and comparative case studies, analysing intersubjective relations, emotions, and power, and their potential to mobilize organizational change. He is an elected member of several international learned societies, including Fellow of the Royal Society of Medicine, Fellow of the Royal Anthropological Institute, and Fellow of the Higher Education Academy.

**Jean Ledger** is currently a Research Associate in the Department of Applied Health Research, University College London. She previously worked on the project reported in this book as a Research Associate in King's College London.

**Gerry McGivern** is Professor of Organizational Analysis in the Organization and Human Resource Management (OHRM) Group at Warwick Business School. His research focuses on understanding professionals' knowledge, practice, identity, leadership, and how they are affected by systems of regulation and organization, primarily within health care systems. He has led Economic and Social Research Council, General Medical Council, National Institute for Health Research, and General Osteopathic Council funded research projects, published in leading international social science and management journals, and co-authored *Making Wicked Problems Governable? The Case of Managed Networks in Health Care*.

# 1 Introduction

## Exploring the politics of management knowledge in times of austerity

This book explores the production and consumption of management knowledges and associated texts within English health care organizations. This broad theme is of interest because since the 1980s there has been a significant expansion internationally, and certainly in England, of what can be called the 'management knowledge production system' in the sphere (which is of special interest here) of public/health management as well as more widely in private-sector firms.

This introductory chapter outlines the overall positioning of the book and then provides some signposts to later chapters. The management knowledge production system we refer to consists, in our view, of a self-reinforcing nexus of individual and institutional actors (Ferlie et al. 2016) including influential management consultancies (e.g. McKinsey & Co., PWC), think tanks, and business schools and their faculty (notably Harvard Business School and other elite schools in America but also a few English business schools, such as Warwick Business School, that have also been influential in the public management field). The English business school sector has expanded considerably since the 1980s to become more influential in management practice. In addition, some business and management-orientated media (e.g. the *Financial Times*) are influential components of the nexus and take an interest in key management ideas.

From the 1980s onwards, high-profile management 'gurus' popularized key management ideas in best-selling texts (a key example in relation to American public-sector management is Osborne and Gaebler 1992). Publishers' lists of management books have expanded substantially over the last thirty years or so, both of best-selling and popular texts but also of more scholarly works. Harvard Business School, in particular, has developed an internationally influential publishing brand, both in books published by the Harvard Business School Press and in short and accessible articles in the *Harvard Business Review*. This press operates separately from Harvard University Press.

As these examples all indicate, this management knowledge production system mixes national with strong international elements, and influences from elite American sources in particular have been very apparent in the UK. Additionally, an increasing number of think tanks—including, for example, those located in central London so as to be close to government departments—offer policy analyses and 'thought leadership' for practising public policymakers and managers, while still being 'semi outside' the traditional Civil Service, and so can be seen as an additional component of this knowledge production system.

In terms of overall positioning, we need to consider the implications of this expanding management knowledge production system for the reshaping of what we term 'management knowledges' in one key sector chosen for empirical investigation: English health care. We will explore management knowledges through the device of examining the content of management-orientated written texts (e.g. a Harvard Business School Press text) which have had sustained influence in some of the health care organizations we studied. While we include the publicly funded National Health Service (NHS) as a key component of our empirical analyses, we also consider alternative organizations, such as an independent-sector organization and a think tank, reflecting the increasing diversity of the English health care sector. We found that at least some of these health care organizations appeared highly receptive to more generic/private-sector management texts and associated knowledges, rather than solely absorbing sector-specific health management knowledge. We suggest that this is an important and interesting empirical finding that signifies an important change and which needs to be explored further analytically.

Our positioning also involves taking a political-economy and institutionally orientated perspective on the processes of the production and consumption of management knowledge in the English health care sector. This relatively macro-level perspective differs in important respects from other well-established prisms so far found in established management knowledge literature (e.g. the more micro practice-based perspective, the more rationalist and positivist evidence-based management (EBMgt) school; and also the more organizationally focused or meso-level resource-based view (RBV) of the firm). It also differs from much health care management literature on knowledge mobilization, particularly the growing 'implementation science' stream, which is in our view largely sectorally embedded, apolitical, and often not well theorized.

We will also consider the role of micro-level agency in knowledge mobilization in our sites, alongside the operation of macro forces, looking in particular at the behaviour of a set of local 'knowledge leaders' found to be active in our study. Our account of agency examines how these leaders sense and cope with changes in the wider political environment, so that our micro analysis still looks back up to the macro level.

# Why is the theme of the production and consumption of management knowledges in health care organizations both interesting and important?

Our interest in the broad theme of the production and consumption of management knowledges in the English health care sector was initially stimulated by the early idea that while implementation of evidence-based medicine (EBM) had been well studied at the clinical level, the extent to which a parallel evidence-based management (EBMgt) had proved influential in health care management had not attracted the same degree of scholarly interest.

This original idea was investigated in an empirical study funded by the UK National Institute of Health Research. The study contained six organizational-level case studies of management knowledge production and consumption processes in UK health care as revealed within associated tracer issues, some of which are drawn upon here and reanalysed in a more theoretical manner than was possible in our initial report (Dopson et al. 2013).

Additional foci of interest became apparent later and were explored further in personal and unfunded work.. For example, the initial study explored six local sites but had little to say on the role and behaviour of relevant national agencies such as the NHS Modernisation Agency, which we will explore later in more detail through the analysis of documents. We are especially interested in exploring and explaining what appears to be the failure of successive agencies in this field to build any stable policy niche. We also took an increasing interest in the impact of the macro-level and changing UK political economy—in particular the arrival of a new centre-right government and the age of austerity after 2010—on the NHS's agenda, with a consequent shift of interest towards managerial tools and methods which might promote large-scale productivity improvements. We will argue that these macro shifts have local implications for the micro-level sites in terms of preferred management knowledges, notably apparent in the rise of Lean-orientated texts and thinking.

# Outline of later chapters

The early chapters of the book will introduce and review some relevant academic literature, which will then inform the presentation of our case-study material in the later chapters.

Chapter 2 starts by reviewing various academic literature which have different implications for how we might usefully conceive of 'management knowledge'. This lively and contested terrain links to broader debates across the social sciences about the nature of 'knowledge', and more fundamentally of 'knowing' as a social practice. This review will go beyond traditional cognitive perspectives to consider the influential 'knowledge as practice' school (Gherardi 2001; Nicolini et al. 2003) within the discipline of organization studies which typically operates at a micro level in the local work setting. It will also review other work on knowledge management strategies and their limits (Swan et al. 1999, 2016). This literature stream goes beyond a narrow technology push or information and communications technology (ICT)-led perspective to consider wider organizational and sociological factors in shaping openness to new knowledge, including meso-level work on organizational competences in knowledge mobilization, associated with the RBV school of strategic management writing.

We also review more substantive 'knowledge' traditions within the English health care sector. There is here, of course, a strong influence from biomedicine, science, and more recently health services research. We explore the rise since the 1990s of the EBM movement within the biomedical and health services research domains, tracing its specific implications for its preferred knowledge types (such as meta analyses, systematic or Cochrane reviews, and randomized controlled trials). EBM was later taken by some writers as a positive role model for the development of an analogous EBMgt movement (Walshe and Rundall 2001; Tranfield et al. 2003; Rousseau 2006; Rousseau and McCarthy 2007), including in health care settings. Other management-orientated scholars (e.g. Learmonth and Harding 2006; Learmonth 2008) have, however, critiqued this position which is seen by them as academically imperialist and as inappropriately moving natural science knowledges into social science-orientated arenas and disciplines. We review this lively debate (Briner et al. 2009). Health managers, by contrast, have been seen to prefer tacit and experiential forms of knowledge (Macfarlane et al. 2011) to formal or randomized control trial-based knowledge, the former knowledge type being built up within strongly networked managerial 'communities of practice'.

Our analysis will be more aligned with EBMgt's critics, specifically as we highlight the role of the macro-level political economy, associated institutional forms, and its ideological manifestations in reshaping preferred management knowledges in local health care settings. This chapter will, finally, introduce more macro-level institutionalist perspectives on the diffusion of management knowledge (see Thrift, 2005, on geographical patterns of diffusion; also Sahlin Andersson and Engwall 2002c, and Engwall 2010, on inter-sectoral diffusion) including the intriguing and attractive notion of the 'business school/management consulting knowledge nexus'. So our analysis of dominant management knowledges in UK public-service organizations is informed by an awareness of macro-level effects in the domain of the political economy, which can usefully complement more micro-level (practice-led models) or meso-level (resource-based view or RBV) schools.

Chapter 3 starts by suggesting there may be a macro-level shift away from traditional public administration-style knowledge to the greater use of knowledge produced by a range of external and more private sector-orientated actors that are now evident in health care fields (see Scott et al. 2001, on the USA case). These actors include business school faculty, gurus, think tanks, and management consultants working within health care organizations. This management knowledge perspective is an additive contribution to what is by now a well-established public/health management reform literature.

There appears to be an embedded pattern of 'hyper reforming' in the UK state which has been evident since the 1980s, including in the health care sector. Chapter 3 applies this political-economy perspective of public management reforming to an analysis of major organizational changes in the UK health care field. Our core purpose here is to access and adapt comparativist public management literature (especially Pollitt and Bouckaert's 2011 five-dimension model of the structure of the state when considered in relation to trajectories of public management reforming) to help benchmark the case of the UK state and pick out specific implications for the health sector. We argue that major New Public Management (NPM) reforms have made the sector less protected from outside private sector-orientated influences and (among other effects) increased its openness to generic rather than public sector-specific managerial texts, techniques, and models.

Chapter 4 brings the public and health policy story up to date. Following the 2008 global financial crisis and the introduction of a government-wide austerity programme, severe funding and productivity pressures have continued to affect the UK health care sector (e.g. large-scale productivity programmes, such as Quality, Innovation, Productivity and Prevention (QIPP), discussed in more depth in Chapter 5). Specifically in this fourth chapter we explore debates concerning the future sustainability of the NHS and the wider health and social care system in the UK and also how post-2008 policies may now be reshaping the management knowledge preferred by management staff in English health care organizations. We consider the implications of major post-2008 austerity-related national policy pressures for the English health care system.

In Chapter 5, we discuss the importance of the QIPP productivity programme in the NHS and investigate the tools and techniques used to support its implementation, such as an increased role for management consultants in supporting the commissioning function and greater outsourcing. QIPP implementation has been severely—indeed disgracefully—understudied, given its major importance and the buoyant research funding which has been available for more micro and also less interesting/threatening research questions. We hope in this chapter, to kick-start a debate in what should be a developing and also a critically informed and social science-informed literature on QIPP's effects.

After these review chapters, the middle part of the book presents a group of descriptive/analytic case studies. We start at the national level, looking at bodies of change management knowledge (a current example being Lean) influential within what has proved to be a succession of national specialist agencies operating in the broad field of service improvement (Chapter 6) since the early 2000s. We also map and examine the troubled career of these public agencies and reflect on their constant reorganization, arguing they have so far failed to construct an enduring institutional power base when compared to comparator specialist agencies (e.g. NICE). We also detect a recurrent pattern of the importing of texts and models from American (rather than European) knowledge producers, although we find that there is rather more variety in the nature of the texts being imported than originally proposed.

The next chapters present case material on different management texts and knowledges found in the local health care organizations studied. The knowledge production processes found in a think tank specializing in advice to support health policy and management is explored in Chapter 7. We start with a review of the role of think tanks generally in public policy (see Weaver 2002) and then particularly in UK health policy development (Shaw et al. 2014). We examine what appears to be their recent expansion and also any evidence of the contraction of the traditional policy advice role from the Department of Health, reflecting moves to a more contestable market in UK policymaking (as advocated in HM Government 2011) alongside staffing downsizing in central government. In terms of the concrete setting studied, we found considerable 'epistemic boundaries' internally between the different subdivisions of the organization. We undertook further web-based research to examine current health management-related activity in major London-based think tanks, both health care specific, such as King's Fund, Nuffield Trust, and Health Foundation, and more overtly party-political ones such as Centre Forum. This chapter therefore contains new material as well as reflections on one of the original cases.

Chapter 8 looks at the influence of the management consulting sector in English health care. In particular, it considers how knowledge produced by a management consulting firm was applied within a local health care organization under top-down pressure to develop an ambitious strategy for productivity enhancement (reflecting the earlier chapter on QIPP at a national level), along with the (sometimes negative) reaction from the local clinical and managerial field. This negative reaction, in turn, reflected a fundamental mismatch of frames between the different actors. The chapter extends a related paper (McGivern et al. 2017) based on the same case study. We have also undertaken some additional desk and website-based research to examine current consulting 'products' orientated towards UK health care organizations and present some new material.

In Chapter 9, we consider the high impact of a well-known generic management text, *The Balanced Scorecard* (Kaplan and Norton 1996), adopted by an independent health sector provider as part of a corporate performance management framework. In particular the chapter highlights the importance of a particular type of knowledge leadership which was capable of blending management, clinical, and commercial knowledges on a number of levels. We note the importance of opportunities for knowledge transposition in an environment where financial issues were under control.

Chapter 10 shifts the focus away from the field and institutional levels previously considered and instead looks at questions of individual agency. In particular, it examines the activities of a small set of local 'knowledge leaders' (Fischer et al. 2016) found to be active and committed to particular knowledge texts and ideas in some case study sites. We found that agency and knowledge leadership, as well as macro-level structure or organizational routines, was important in these cases. Such leaders were able to mobilize collective organizational activity around key knowledge texts to help drive wider organizational change. We here examine the careers, motivations, activities, and skills of this small group that acted as local knowledge champions. They often showed sustained commitment to a particular management text (including through difficult periods) and were well embedded in complex social and organizational settings. They sometimes had to defend these ideas against apathy or even opposition. This chapter draws on and extends some of our earlier work (Fischer et al. 2016).

The concluding Chapter 11 restates our overall contribution to the existing literature on management knowledge in public-service and health care organizations. In particular, we add a macro-level concern for the effects of the wider political economy on reshaping preferred management knowledges within public agencies. We highlight the ongoing diffusion of management texts from elite American business schools, think tanks, and management consultancies into English settings (Ferlie et al. 2016) which have become more receptive to these ideas and less wedded to old-style public administration knowledge. We provide an additional focus on a macro-level and even internationally extended management knowledge production and consumption system within the health services field which now produces a 'mixed economy' of knowledge production. This contribution extends existing literature both on management knowledge and on public management reforming. We also develop a more explicit account of micro-level agency in our work on knowledge leaders than is apparent in much current literature. In addition, our conclusion considers implications for public and health policy and advances a future research agenda. The two appendices give an account of our methods and, for ease of reference, contain summaries of the (anonymized) descriptive case studies.

# 2 A review of literature and perspectives on management knowledge

## Introduction

To situate the empirically grounded discussions which will follow in later chapters, we now present an overview of relevant academic literature and debates that informed our original study and also some subsequent theoretical reflections on our original empirical data. The chapter draws on diverse literature from management and organization studies, but also health care research and political science. We organize this disparate literature around four traditionally separate streams which operate at different levels of analysis and discuss each in turn.

1. A practice-orientated and health services research literature on the use of evidence in health care and management practice.
2. A social science literature on the mobilization of knowledge in organizations and across boundaries, drawing on more micro, practice-based approaches as applied to health care.
3. A meso-level literature from the resource-based view (RBV) of the firm within the strategic management literature which examines the core competences that may enable.
4. A novel prism which looks at the role of political institutions and power relations, and how they relate to systems of management knowledge production and consumption. This provides an alternative political-economy perspective of knowledge use in organizations, which is more macro in focus than the previous literature streams.

We draw out some implications from each of the perspectives for the analysis of our empirical cases, and conclude with brief broader observations.

# Stream 1. From evidence-based medicine to evidence-based management: envisioning a new 'gold standard' for health care delivery

## EBM PRINCIPLES

In seeking to understand and explore the role of research evidence in health care organizations and service delivery, it is helpful to consider the wider 'epistemic' context (Knorr-Cetina 1999; McGivern et al. 2016) in which knowledge is traditionally produced and applied in this sector.

Since the 1990s, health care delivery has been strongly influenced by the rise and spread of the evidence-based medicine (EBM) movement which gained standing in North America and then the UK during the early 1990s (Traynor 2003, 266; Barends et al. 2012). The movement, which is now global in reach, is founded upon a biomedical science model (Dopson et al. 2003, 312) and grounded in scientific research principles, including the critical and rigorous appraisal of existing research evidence. 'Bench' science is, however, not seen as the sole source of legitimate knowledge; early EBM advocates interpreted evidence-based decisions as those which involve 'the integration of research evidence with clinical expertise and patient values' (Sackett et al. 2000, quoted in Haynes et al. 2002).

An early assumption therefore was that current research evidence when combined with professional expertise and client views would lead to better clinical decisions and health outcomes. A professional's tacit knowledge and diagnostic skills were to be central for health care decision-making, but the movement was clear that experiential knowledge alone was insufficient for optimal patient care. In this way, the movement shifted focus away from the traditional practice of 'eminence-based medicine' founded upon prestige, reputation, and the excessive professional influence of doctors (Timmermans and Berg 2003; Timmermans 2008; Ioannidis 2016, 83) and towards the more rational and scientific footing upon which contemporary medicine is based. Several writers observe that this was nothing short of a paradigm shift (Haynes et al. 2002; Darlenski et al. 2010). As Barends et al. (2012) note:

Whereas the old paradigm had valued pathophysiologic first principles, teacher authority, experience, and unsystematic clinical observation, the new paradigm stressed their fallibility. Clinicians should henceforth rely on evidence, and they should be able to decide what constitutes reliable evidence and what does not. To do so, they should be able to search, evaluate, and apply original medical literature.

EBM as a knowledge-based movement has worked hard to ensure that the latest biomedical research evidence is translated into health care practice, partly by ensuring that new modern professional education and learning is grounded in the latest scientific research. The General Medical Council in the UK, for example, sets standards for medical education and training which emphasize that doctors must 'provide effective treatments based on the best available evidence' (GMC 2013). The attention to EBM within medical curricula reasserts the scientific foundations of clinical practice and draws attention to the rapid evolution of health care professionals' knowledge base which must now be updated through continuous professional learning and stronger engagement with research production. More rational, up-to-date decision-making, it is hoped, will then reduce variations in clinical care (Barends et al. 2012).

A prime area of interest for EBM advocates is therefore the changing of micro-level clinical practice to ensure that that it aligns more with the developing evidence base. This focus, then, leads to a wider interest in models of behaviour change, and to designing and facilitating an institutional context (such as the National Institute of Health and Care Excellence, NICE) that influences micro-level clinical behaviour through the production of guidelines.

## THE PRODUCTION AND CONSUMPTION OF SCIENTIFIC KNOWLEDGE

As a paradigm, EBM is driven largely by experimental science, meta-analyses, and randomized control trials—forms of evidence originating predominantly from within universities and research centres but increasingly from industry as well (Sackett and Rosenberg 1995; Feinstein and Horwitz 1997; Ioannidis 2016). Evidence production derived from the university sector is consistent with a traditional 'science push' model (Landry et al. 2001) in which new knowledge is created by researchers to address specific questions and problems, and later disseminated using conventional academic routes such as journal publications, textbooks, and expert conferences. This process has been characterized as 'Mode 1' knowledge production (Gibbons 2000; Nowotny et al. 2003; Greenhalgh and Wieringa 2011), whereby universities and academics are the major players in circulating and promoting new concepts, research evidence, and ideas which have been subjected to peer review to ensure quality, independence, and rigour.

However, EBM also necessitated timely access by the field to high-quality research evidence and guidance if decision-making was to become evidence-based in daily practice. This need encouraged the development of approaches for the better organization and management of health care research evidence internationally by intermediary bodies such as NICE and the Cochrane Collaboration, both based in the UK. The creation of novel knowledge systems—such as searchable electronic databases of previously reviewed research studies—is especially noteworthy and the Cochrane Collaboration remains pivotal to the successful institutionalization of EBM globally. This organization, which brings together expert reviewers to sift through scientific evidence, acts as an online library for evidence-based health care practice and produces summaries of clinical trials and health care interventions/treatments that have been filtered through the methodological prism of systematic reviews and meta-analyses.

In addition, the Cochrane Collaboration supplies online training in EBM skills and practical workshops (such as on conducting meta-analyses). The organization works to ascertain the efficacy and impact of specific interventions across populations (e.g. the use of specific antibiotics, or vitamin supplementation during pregnancy) and informs the production of clinical guidelines to improve patient care and disease management. A longer-term objective of the Collaboration is to provide universal open access to its regularly updated systematic reviews so that health care professionals can more easily access evidence for decision-making (Cochrane 2016). Importantly, this strategy would negate the need for costly journal subscriptions to access the latest research evidence.

## LONGER-TERM IMPACT AND CRITICISMS

Many authors observe that the EBM movement has not only led to the production of best practice guidelines in health care, but it has enabled stronger publication standards in research and teaching to bring about improvements in patient care (Mykhalovskiy and Weir 2004; Greenhalgh et al. 2014). It has generated an international community of interest and passionate advocates (but also some critics) both within and beyond medicine. It is worth reviewing some of these criticisms, given that EBM is now taken as an exemplar for evidence-based practice in other fields of professional practice, such as management (Tranfield et al. 2003), education, and public policy (Hammersley 2005; Barends et al. 2012).

First, the primary focus of EBM has been on 'pushing' knowledge and disseminating research to clinicians to improve decision-making, with less concern about *how* decision-making is performed locally and during patient–clinician interactions. This has led to a number of criticisms and challenges from *within* the medical profession, given that at times EBM has been perceived as a threat to traditional medical autonomy and tacit control over work practice (Ioannidis 2016). EBM has also been critiqued by non-medical authors and social scientists who remain suspicious of EBM's homogeneous and positivist approach to knowledge in which the gold standard of randomized control trial-based evidence is conceived of as more legitimate than other forms of professional understanding (Greenhalgh 1999; Learmonth 2006; Learmonth and Harding 2006).

Concerns have also been expressed about the quality of the research underpinning EBM (randomized control trials), with some observers suggesting that research has been progressively 'hijacked' by industry interests, especially where industry-sponsored clinical trials are conducted in ways that make certain health care products appear favourable—such as by overestimating treatment effects (Kravitz et al. 2004; Greenhalgh et al. 2014; Ioannidis 2016). Within day-to-day clinical practice, EBM may also overlook the need for an individualized approach to patient care due to its dependency on findings related to patient populations as opposed to those with complex needs, psycho-social health problems or co-morbidities (Darlenski et al. 2010; Greenhalgh et al. 2014).

We add the observation that the EBM movement has instigated an expanding and somewhat self-perpetuating field of knowledge production aimed at reducing variation in practice, but that significant variation in health care still persists. The movement has resulted in a deluge of information for busy health professionals to review, but guidelines and knowledge frequently fail to be mobilized into practice. We argue this is partly because, historically, inadequate attention is paid by 'Mode 1' scientific institutions to the implementation processes by which new knowledge enters organizations and is applied, selectively, by health care professionals to problem solve *in situ* and within specific contexts (Dopson et al. 2001, 2002; Swan et al. 2016).

NICE, for example, has developed significantly over the last fifteen or so years as a major public agency in the health care sector and produces a large number of evidence-based guidelines for the field which have been seen as that institution's core 'product' (Ferlie and McGivern 2014). However, in practice, health professionals may be more predisposed to acquire new knowledge via peers and social learning mechanisms, especially if they are overwhelmed by new knowledge, information, and normative rules dictated by policy. Thus, on a day-to-day basis, and when making decisions under pressure, health care professionals may rely on internalized tacit knowledge and 'collective mindlines' drawn from their community of practice rather than referring explicitly to formal guidelines derived from external sources (Gabbay and Le May 2004, 2011).

It has already been suggested elsewhere (Dopson and Fitzgerald 2005) that social scientific approaches therefore have a great deal to offer the debates surrounding EBM and the process of mobilizing new knowledge into health care practice. In particular, the argument is that there is often a failure in the EBM and health services literature to adequately deal with how pluralist evidence and knowledge may be reconciled (or be irreconcilable) in practice. Decision-making in organizations is frequently an outcome of the negotiation of contextual power dynamics, debates among experts, and even direct conflict, rather than simply the conscientious application of logical and consensual processes, or the systematic analysis of research evidence. Even where the best available scientific evidence is drawn upon to reach a decision, it may have greatest saliency because it accords with (political) agendas or is backed by influential decision makers (Harrison 1998; Milewa and Barry 2005; Hodgkinson 2012). Organizational contexts and professional identities, it is argued, exert a profound mediating influence on the utilization of scientific evidence and the adoption of innovations in health care (Dopson and Fitzgerald 2005; Ferlie et al. 2005). This necessitates paying critical attention to the limitations of evidence-based approaches and how evidence is selected (or ignored) by decision makers, and why.

For these multifaceted reasons, we suggest that a broader understanding of how and why evidence-based knowledge is used in practice by individuals and organizations is helpful, and why research knowledge may—or indeed may not—readily spread across health care systems, networks, and different professional groups. This argument has in more recent years been acknowledged by NICE who have set up an Implementation Collaborative to investigate why it is that some of its technology appraisals take a long time to be implemented into the field of health care delivery. Organizational and system-level effects may be important to investigate in this respect, operating at a higher level than the individual clinician or clinical team.

Despite these criticisms and reservations, the EBM paradigm has clearly made an important contribution to contemporary health care practice and policy. By widening access to best practice clinical guidelines and research evidence, the movement has acted as a counterweight to some of the prevailing professional norms, intuitive leaps, and 'judgmental heuristics' that can misguide even the most experienced professionals and decision makers (Tversky and Kahneman 1974; Kahneman 2003, 2011). The selection and utilization of research by practitioners alone does not preclude the possibility that judgemental biases and politics may have an influence on decision-making locally; however, EBM does address the interests of patients in setting a standard for quality health care practice.

We now look at similar approaches to EBM which have emerged in the rather different field of management and organization studies (MOS), which is an applied social scientific discipline rather than one originating within the natural and biomedical sciences.

## THE (CONTESTED) RISE OF EVIDENCE-BASED MANAGEMENT

A lively debate emerged from the late 1990s onwards about whether lessons from EBM might be transferred to other fields of practice. EBM has, for example, been applied to areas as diverse as social work, public policy, criminal justice, and education (Black 2001; Barends et al. 2012; Hammersley 2005; Rousseau 2006, 2012; Cartwright and Hardie 2012). Over the last decade several leading scholars have sought to apply EBM principles to the practice of management; therefore, in this section, we look at how the EBM zeitgeist gained some (albeit strongly contested) traction in management and business research and education and how it has developed over time.

The idea of evidence-based management (EBMgt) emerged in the early 2000s on both sides of the Atlantic (Walshe and Rundall 2001; Tranfield et al. 2003). The notion was most strongly promoted in the *Academy of Management Journal* by a group of leading American management academics (Pfeffer and Sutton 2006a, 2006b, 2006c, 2007; Rousseau 2006) who argued that management and business decisions were too often driven by dogma, individual preference, intuition, gut feeling, mimicry, hype, and erroneous assumptions (Pfeffer and Sutton 2006a; Rousseau 2006). Rather than consult the latest scientific, management evidence, managers were more likely to approach external consultants or business 'gurus', and rely on previous practice, with the effect that research evidence was being 'left at the table' (Olivas-Lujan 2008). Managers were therefore at risk of basing decisions and company strategies on poor information or simply what they—or their contemporaries—had done before.

In books targeting an executive/managerial audience, EBMgt is presented as an approach to stymie some of these tendencies. Pfeffer and Sutton (2006c) suggest, for example, that EBMgt involves adopting a non-defensive confrontation with 'the real truth' and 'hard facts', with company executives interrogating their business intelligence to bring about better decision-making. The suggestion is that managers and executives should adopt a more critical perspective towards the knowledge and information sources that inform their thinking, especially in challenging management solutions which are purported to be 'best practice' by the populist business press or business advisers who may not be relying on research evidence, but rather purporting the most recent management technique or 'fashion' (Abrahamson 1996; Abrahamson and Eisenman 2001)—in an entirely non-evidence-based way.

Early on EBMgt enthusiasts appeared to suggest, somewhat uncritically, that a correlation existed between the rational application of scientific management research and more rational decision-making within organizations. EBMgt would serve to improve managers' decision-making and, at the same time, stimulate demand among practitioners for the production of better research evidence and information. For example, Rousseau (2006, 260) stated that: 'an evidence orientation shows that decision quality is a direct function of available facts, creating a demand for reliable and valid information when making managerial and organizational decisions'.

The view that an 'evidence orientation' could improve organizational performance and management decisions directed attention at the managerial workforce and their education and training; specifically, whether or not they were research literate in a similar way to clinicians (Walshe and Rundall 2001; Fine 2006). As Rousseau and McCarthy (2007) pointedly observe, 'we typically don't teach management students, from undergraduates to executives, to understand or use evidence'. Therefore, EBMgt became increasingly focused on management curricula and teaching professionals in universities, and the systematic appraisal and synthesis of existing management research in ways similar to the EBM movement (Rousseau and McCarthy 2007; Briner et al. 2009; Jelley et al. 2012).

A notable development has been the creation of the Centre for Evidence-Based Management, a not-for-profit member organization providing access to a range of resources such as teaching materials, evidence summaries, and evidence-based articles on management, perhaps drawing inspiration from the Cochrane Collaboration. The possibility of the production of EBMgt guidelines—replicating EBM's core product which has been produced at high volume in the UK health care system by NICE—now becomes an open one. In addition, a handbook has been produced clearly articulating EBMgt tenets and exploring some more nuanced perspectives (Rousseau 2012) on how EBMgt might evolve and influence the field of management practice.

Over time, there has been growing recognition by EBMgt advocates that various types of knowledge might feed into management decision-making. For example, Briner, Denyer, and Rousseau—academics who have done much to promote EBMgt—often emphasize that formal research evidence is only one form of evidence. They write: 'Evidence-based management is about making decisions though the conscientious, explicit, and judicious use of four sources of information: practitioner expertise and judgement, evidence from the local context, a critical evaluation of the best available research evidence, and the perspectives of those people who might be affected by the decision' (Briner et al. 2009, 19).

The Centre for Evidence-Based Management website also presents an inclusive model of decision-making, declaring that:

The starting point for evidence-based management is that management decisions should be based on a combination of critical thinking and the best available evidence. And by 'evidence', we mean information, facts or data supporting (or contradicting) a claim, assumption, or hypothesis. Evidence may come from scientific research, but internal business information and even professional experience can count as 'evidence'. In principle, then, all managers base their decisions on 'evidence'.   (Cebma)

Finally, in the recent handbook on the topic, Rousseau (2012) describes EBMgt as a management practice which entails:

(1) use of scientific principles in decisions and management processes;
(2) systematic attention to organizational facts;
(3) advancements in practitioner judgement through critical thinking and decision aids that reduce bias and enable fuller use of information; and
(4) ethical considerations including effects on stakeholders.

Hence, we see a loosening over time of the underlying precepts of EBMgt, which now incorporates a multitude of knowledge sources beyond management research.

## APPLICATIONS TO HEALTH CARE SETTINGS

Prior to the wider 'evidence-based management' movement, several academics had already noted that evidence-based medicine principles had potential implications for health care management (Axelsson 1998; Kovner et al. 2000). Walshe and Rundall's influential (2001) paper refers to the 'overuse', 'underuse', and 'misuse' of health care interventions as examples of poor management practice (e.g. the overuse of non-evidence-based hospital mergers). They comment that the professional worlds and training backgrounds of clinicians and health care managers are vastly different, with managers likely to have divergent qualifications and training, which contrasts with the standardized learning of the medical profession. So managers are unlikely to be predisposed to use formal research in the same manner as clinicians, given that 'there is no specified formal body of knowledge' about effective management that health care managers can access to improve their practice, even if they wanted to exploit new research evidence.

Kovner et al. (2000) also noted the tendency for large health care organizations to rely on external management consultants for 'riskier strategic interventions' and a concomitant failure by managers to 'rigorously challenge the information upon which such recommendations are based' (as we discuss later, using our empirical work on a management consultancy firm's intervention in a health care system).

## CRITICISMS AND LIMITATIONS

There is a valid argument that management as a function and profession has not developed strong research capacity. Managers have been found to rely on stories told within tight communities of practice (Macfarlane et al. 2011) and business gurus that redefine organizational problems and may serve to reinforce executives' status and legitimacy (Clark and Salaman 1998, 153).

However, critics of the EBMgt movement question the preoccupation with 'the higher prestige of medical science' (Learmonth and Harding 2006; Learmonth 2008; Morrell 2008) and point out that evidence is both socially produced and contestable. The social science departments that produce research are not the same as natural science settings which test treatment effects, and any simple read across is falsely grounded. Specifically, it is argued that EBMgt encourages a 'positivist' notion of knowledge and overlooks 'the role of situated judgment and ethics' in managerial and business decision making (Morrell 2008, 615). Learmonth strongly criticized early notions of EBMgt (as promulgated by Rousseau, Sutton, and Pfeffer) for focusing largely on business CEOs and therefore demonstrating a 'top management bias' (Learmonth 2008, 285) and for neglecting the 'ideological and methodological pluralism' found in MOS (Learmonth 2008, 284)—this was viewed as engaging in a project of ill-founded methodological imperialism.

Indeed, there has been a softening in position of EBMgt over time by these writers and a more pluralist vision of the forms of evidence that inform management decision-making has evolved; nonetheless, a narrow interpretation of science is at times promoted, suggesting a hierarchical view of knowledge. For example, Rousseau (2012, 5) writes: 'Scientific knowledge is distinct from other forms of knowledge. It is based on controlled observations, large samples sizes (N), validated measures, statistical controls, and systematically tested and accumulated understandings of how the world works (i.e., theory).'

The sheer plurality of disparate knowledge found in MOS renders the exercise of knowledge synthesis more challenging than in medicine (Learmonth 2006; Rousseau 2006). Management and organizational knowledge is moreover frequently ambiguous (Olivas-Lujan 2008, 16) and draws upon different theoretical and methodological paradigms that are not always commensurable (Scherer 1998; Scherer and Steinmann 1999). EBMgt proponents contend that systematic reviews of research evidence are nevertheless necessary to identify where 'stable effects' and 'replicable findings' exist (Rousseau et al. 2009). However, it is not clear how an equivalent methodology to that used in EBM (i.e. systematic reviews and meta-analyses of randomized control trials or observational studies) can be easily applied to management and business research, given that so few randomized control trial-type studies exist in that domain (Reay et al. 2009).

Indeed, as an epistemological point, it has been observed that 'there is no gold standard; no universally best method' and that even randomized control trials are typically 'narrow in scope' and limited for making inferences to individual patients (Feinstein and Horwitz 1997; Greenhalgh 1999; Cartwright 2007, 11–12; Keane and Berg 2016). Ultimately, then, this returns us to argumentation about the validity and quality of research knowledge, as has manifested in the EBM movement, where systematic reviews and randomized control trials commonly reside at the apex of a knowledge pyramid and descriptive case studies are ranked far lower alongside expert opinion (Evans 2003).

Over time the limitations of randomized control trials have been acknowledged by key supporters of EBMgt, especially in their later adoption of a realist perspective to produce systematic reviews in MOS—a positioning distinctive to the social sciences (Rousseau et al. 2008; Briner et al. 2009; Briner and Denyer 2012). Nonetheless, it is remains unclear what 'best' evidence for management practice should look like, or if it could ever realistically appear in ways similar to EBM's levels of evidence pyramid. As Tranfield et al. (2003, 212) explain, 'It is unlikely that aggregative approaches to research synthesis, such as meta-analysis will be appropriate in management research as the heterogeneity of studies prevents the pooling of results and the measurement of the net effectiveness of interventions'.

Moving away from the production of management evidence, to the context of its use, Arndt and Bigelow (2009) also critique the assumption that decisions based on research evidence will necessarily generate better results that are replicable across organizations. They note that decision-making in organizations is rarely that straightforward and outcomes vary substantially, even where the same management technique or research evidence is applied. Like Learmonth, they observe that EBMgt proponents tend to treat scientific evidence as objective and context free when knowledge is socially constructed.

In the *Handbook of Evidence-Based Management* (Rousseau 2012) a number of these valid criticisms have been addressed by various contributors, and there is an overall softening of tone of the movement's major followers. It will however take time and further empirical studies to ascertain whether better decision-making in business and organizations follows directly from the launch of EBMgt, as is often claimed. EBM has taken time to embed internationally and its limitations in the field of applied health care have only become more openly discussed with the hindsight of experience. Now there is generally more awareness of just how effortful it is to incorporate new evidence in practice, despite a plethora of evidence-based guidelines existing and being made readily accessible to clinicians.

Information alone is insufficient to drive individual behaviour change or organizational transformation (this is a point we revisit later in the book when discussing the effortful implementation of new management knowledge by local 'knowledge leaders'). That access to research evidence and decision support tools will automatically improve highly complex business decisions, or even organizational performance, is (only) superficially a persuasive suggestion, especially when considering the business scandals of the 2000s, the breakdown of the financial sector in 2008, and the legitimacy crisis said to be facing management and business schools (Learmonth 2006). There is no shortage of information or experts willing to generate new organizational solutions and 'facts'; it is the environmental constraints and conditions influencing the context of decision-making that are often overlooked (an argument we return to in the final section of this chapter and throughout the book).

In summary, while management scholars have advocated for the development of an evidence-based approach which takes EBM as a role model, others have critiqued this project as intellectual imperialism coming from the world of natural science and as a limited 'rational', linear, and diffusionist model of knowledge mobilization (Swan et al. 2016). Clearly, health care is an emblematic sector for assessing the progress of EBMgt, given the long shadow cast by EBM there. Therefore, concretely, the extent to which any EBMgt guidelines for managerial practice diffuse and are influential in the health care management field can be taken as an important indicator of influence of the movement which we can investigate empirically in our sites.

More broadly, if EBMgt guidelines are only weakly present in the field, the important question then arises: Have other 'knowledge products' colonized this vacant space? If so, what is their core content and what form of evidence is presented? How are they written and diffused into the field, and why are they taken up by professionals? Do they have seemingly authoritative characteristics as legitimate texts? Some of the later chapters in this book will, for example, discuss the high profile of specific management books in our sites and also a body of management knowledge around Lean promoted by a national service modernization agency.

## Stream 2. Practice-based theories of knowing and learning in organizations

'Practice-based' perspectives on organizations, learning, and knowledge (Brown and Duguid 1991; Schatzki et al. 2001; Schatzki 2006; Miettinen et al. 2009; Nicolini 2009) offer an interesting and indeed radical contrast to the evidence-orientated approaches to knowledge use, or the so-called 'science push' angle (Weiss 1979) already reviewed. Practice-based studies attempt to understand socially situated phenomena and meaningful human behaviours within specific cultural-historical contexts. The emphasis is on tacit, experiential, and relational forms of knowledge contra to the rather disembodied, abstract, cognitive, and rationalistic accounts of knowledge use frequently found in the EBM and EBMgt movements. Practice-based studies have expanded markedly in the organizational and managerial academic literature recently, including in key areas such as strategic management (Jarzabkowski 2004; Whittington 2006; Johnson et al. 2007), and now represent a significant disciplinary tradition and body of work.

Practice-based writers draw upon sociological and anthropological understandings to explore how individuals participate in organizational activities, actions, and communities of practice, frequently in work-based settings where social organization arises around specified problems or tasks (Wenger 1998; Nicolini 2009). A shared 'logic of practice' (Bourdieu 1990; Schatzki et al. 2001) is understood as influencing any social activity, including in the specific field of health care. As Wenger states (1998, 47), 'The concept of practice connotes doing, but not just doing in and of itself. It is doing in a historical and social context that gives structure and meaning to what we do. In this sense, practice is always social practice.'

Engagement in any form of interaction—for example, organizing an event or selecting the kinds of evidence to use in organizational decision-making—requires the skilful accomplishment of a range of activities that are socially recognized. This in turn implies agency—the ability of individuals to act and influence their social worlds and surroundings by engaging in, and interpreting, a range of behaviours and social practices. Inter alia, individuals monitor their behaviour (and that of others), produce written and verbal accounts of their performance and actions, and offer up interpretations of the world around them. These 'doing' activities, denoted by verbs, can be framed using a 'practice lens' (Corradi et al. 2010) which appreciates that such micro-level activity produces the daily reality of organizations as experienced by their members. Furthermore, it is through engagement in social practices that humans demonstrate their skills, competency, and knowledge, or in practice terms, their 'knowing' (Blackler 1995).

On a day-to-day basis, social practices will inevitably have a taken-for-granted, tacit quality unless they are disrupted (Gherardi 2004; Sandberg and Tsoukas 2011). For this reason, research in this subfield of management and organizational research concerns what people actually *do* in organizations and work settings, not simply what they say they do, since individuals cannot always articulate the rationale or logic cognitively informing their actions. The locus of analysis thus becomes situated practices and the inter-relational sphere: that of human-to-human interaction, but also 'humans and objects' and socio-material practices (Nicolini 2009; Sandberg and Tsoukas 2011). Research attention is thus directed at how people engage in workplace activities and routines, such as with computer programmes, new technology, knowledge, or innovations and processes that guide human decision-making.

There is no single agreed practice theory, and how the concept of practice is used in the organizational and management literature varies significantly (Nicolini et al. 2003; Gherardi 2004; Blackler and Regan 2009; Geiger 2009). However, the overall thrust of much practice literature is to move attention downwards to local, experiential, and embodied forms of knowledge. From this theoretical perspective, it is these very local, micro practices which taken together constitute the 'macro', as Nicolini explains: 'Macro phenomena boil down to a complex texture of doings and sayings (meetings, conversations, debates, disputes), places (labs, offices) and objects (buildings, documents) which can all be observed proximally' (Nicolini 2009, 1411). The process of 'knowing' as understood locally in organizations therefore becomes at least as important as studying formal 'knowledge' acquisition supported by the top-down dissemination of evidence-based guidelines and infrastructure such as the Cochrane Collaboration or NICE.

This practice school stands therefore in direct contrast to the EBM/EBMgt traditions reviewed earlier and also to purely cognitivist approaches to the individual accumulation of knowledge as an isolated enterprise. Thus, Brown and Duguid (1991, 40) comment that 'In a society that attaches particular value to "abstract knowledge," the details of practice have come to be seen as nonessential, unimportant, and easily developed once the relevant abstractions have been grasped. Thus education, training, and technology design generally focus on abstract representations to the detriment, if not exclusion of actual practice.'

This approach has strong implications for how particular forms of knowledge are seen as shaping decision-making in organizations. Geiger (2009, 134) argues that 'Knowledge as knowing is not the outcome of rational decisions resulting from scientific methods but instead describes a process of continuous enactment, refinement, reproduction, and change based on tacitly shared understandings within a practicing community'.

Ethnographic studies of the workplace, for example, suggest that people do not prescriptively follow a set of codified instructions or rules but engage in work in very adaptable ways (Orr 1996, 1998; Fischer 2012; Fischer and Ferlie 2013). Experiential knowledge is important here, as is the capacity to intuitively respond to the evolving social dynamics of changing situations and to problems that arise *in situ*. In this way, the application of knowledge is seen as specific to emergent problems and may vary across different settings and contexts (Orr 1998).

The latter is an important point (and one which we go on to explore later in this book): knowledge—and, we would also add, innovative management practices—may not simply be a 'rational fit' to particular organizational settings and problems; solutions and knowledge may need to have a 'cultural fit', 'political fit' (Ansari et al. 2010), or 'epistemic fit' (McGivern et al. 2016) to really influence action and decisions locally. The 'fit' between a specific type of knowledge or novel management solution, for example, depends partly on the specifics of the local context (Ansari et al. 2010; McGivern et al. 2016) and the shared, interdependent practices existent in that context. Therefore, what might be taken as a valid form of knowledge or evidence in one social setting, or even as best practice, may not be socially recognized as such in another. For this reason, and other factors, such as professional differences in how knowledge is received, new innovations in health care may fail to spread (Ferlie et al. 2005).

The corollary of this argument is that decision-making should not be viewed in isolation since any practice is inherently social (e.g. EBM depends upon a web of social activities, technologies, and practices that produce, disseminate, and share among health care professionals systematically reviewed evidence summaries). This perspective is demonstrated by Wenger's (1998) concept of 'communities of practice' which are informal, fluid units that situate experience and learning in specific contexts, and which are in turn connected to identity formation and personal development. Wenger emphasizes that practice is about the 'negotiation of meaning' and identity, and that communities of practice demonstrate coherence when they are mutually engaged in 'a joint enterprise' and have a 'shared repertoire' and language (Wenger 1998, 2000).

Nevertheless, they are not necessarily to be read as supportive groupings since they may feature underlying power dynamics and hold individuals hostage to their particular understandings, control who is eligible to participate in certain practices and which practices can be challenged (for a more detailed critique, see Contu and Willmott 2003; Handley et al. 2006). Accordingly, Miettinen et al. (2009) suggests that practice also needs to be considered in its macro context, involving what Nicolini (2009) describes as 'zooming in and out'.

## PRACTICE-BASED STUDIES IN HEALTH CARE SETTINGS

Practice-based thinking has had growing influence in the recent health care organizational and management literature (e.g. Nicolini 2006, 2011; McGivern and Dopson 2010; Greenhalgh and Wieringa 2011; Gkeredakis et al. 2011; Gabbay and Le May 2011; Dopson et al. 2013; Swan et al. 2016), as the limitations of evidence-based and linear and knowledge push-based models have become better understood. We now reflect on some recent empirical studies and commentaries drawn from the health care field that adopt this uniquely social science-based approach to knowledge use and learning in health organizations and networks.

Greenhalgh and Wieringa (2011) draw upon social practice literature to critique the concepts of 'knowledge translation' and 'translational medicine' for their failure to deal with tacit and experiential modes of knowledge in clinical decision-making. They remark on the complexity involved in making situated professional judgements in face-to-face consultation with a patient: 'The skilled practice of medicine is not merely about knowing a set of abstracted rules and recommendations but about deciding which of many competing rules is most relevant' (Greenhalgh and Wieringa 2011, 505).

Greenhalgh (2002, 396) previously described the intuitive process involved when a clinician selectively judges which rules (here we could also add knowledge or decision tools) to apply to a patient in specific circumstances. She suggests that it is in more 'unfamiliar situations' that clinicians are likely to use a 'more formal and rational approach' based upon explicit knowledge forms—when there is greater uncertainty.

This point is developed by Gabbay and Le May (2011) who discuss the prospects for generating 'practice-based evidence'. Their research revealed that even highly performing primary care clinicians do not usually directly access research evidence ('formal knowledge') and implement guidelines in the manner assumed by the EBM movement; rather they used formal knowledge as coping mechanisms and rules of thumb. This finding echoes an observation made by Schön (1983) that professional work depends upon 'tacit recognitions, judgments, and skillful performances', even when 'research-based theories and techniques' are explicitly important in these settings. Gabbay and Le May (2011) describe how clinicians' internalized *tacit* guidelines (what they term 'mindlines') were more influential in day-to-day practice than the explicit use of evidence-based guidelines because clinicians were drawing on various types of knowledge 'to deal with everyday practice' and less so on 'research evidence while practising' (p. 192). This behaviour is interpreted as part of negotiating the situated contingencies of clinical work:

Clinicians, especially in primary care, constantly needed to resolve many competing roles and goals, balancing, for example, the therapeutic, preventive, managerial and wider professional aspects of their work. The resultant tensions continually shaped much of what they did, but were rarely address by the formal knowledge promulgated by advocates of EBP [evidence-based practice].   Gabbay and Le May (2011)

Dopson et al. (2002) also show that where evidence is contestable, local 'inter-active processes' such as 'debate' and 'negotiation' between individuals and groups become an important part of collective and sensemaking processes. The study of social interactions and the production of shared meanings through sensemaking (Weick 1995) helps us understand how new knowledge may be successfully embedded in particular contexts, adapted, or even rejected.

To discuss one specific example, Nicolini (2006, 2011) has studied longitu-dinally processes around organizational knowledge by examining the intro-duction of telemedicine within health care settings in Italy. He begins by reviewing three types of practice-based approach to conceptualizing organiza-tional knowledge: (1) viewing knowledge as residing in social relationships, social networks, and communities (such as communities of practice); (2) viewing knowledge as 'a tool' with the emphasis being on 'knowing' how to do certain things; and (3) a 'more radical stance' where knowing is 'associated with the pursuit of specific interests and takes place within identifiable power relations' (Nicolini 2011, 603–4).

Advancing the latter approach, Nicolini analyses the introduction of tele-medicine by highlighting its tentative nature and the fact that telemedicine is not a singular type of new organizational knowledge put into practice; rather, it is an innovation approached in multiple ways through the enactment of historically situated practices which are interconnected in specific sites (2011, 615–17). Telemedicine depends not only on a health professional's skilful practice of enacting care for patients remotely, but on patients responding and giving the health professional discursive cues and information as requested, and possessing health knowledge themselves: 'From a practice-based perspec-tive it makes no sense to argue that knowledge, like a substance, is something that participants have, use, employ, or consume. Rather, the image here is that of tuning in and contributing to an existing regime of sayings and doings that as a regime is neither on the side of the knower or the known' (2011, 610).

In a recent text (Swan et al. 2016) on knowledge mobilization in health care, drawing on UK and international empirical findings from a range of researchers (and to which we contributed a chapter—see McGivern et al. 2016), different authors examine how knowledge and information are applied in practice in health care settings, and for what reasons. Echoing earlier criticisms of EBMgt and EBM, Swan et al. (2016, 20) describe a wider 'ecology of practices' around knowledge use in health care, observing that 'what counts as "evidence" is locally produced, rather than simply defined by a set of universal facts, and that, moreover, given that practitioners are invested in their practices, even a clear "proving" that something works will be insufficient to ensure that it is adopted'.

In a chapter in this text, Newell and Marabelli (2016) explore how knowledge about children's health care was mobilized across Canadian health care networks, applying practice theory to attend to issues of coordination and power. Rather than conceptualize power as chiefly concerning access to material resources or elite authority, as found in a Marxist perspective and much organizational theory, they view power as located within everyday practices, drawing on theorists such as Foucault, Bourdieu, and Latour who emphasize the distributed and embodied nature of power in social life, and how it is constantly being negotiated. This perspective is seen as especially helpful for comprehending health care networks where network members are usually dispersed across multiple organizations and no one person has the ultimate authority to direct change across the network.

The chief problem in this case study was poor communication about a child's health across professional boundaries and services, leading parents to act as the information retainers and coordinators of their child's care. A pilot project set in motion a series of organizational practices to make improvements in care coordination and interagency information sharing, with new practices being initially being pushed by families with the support of concerned professionals. In this case study, powerful practices included: the use of family stories to drive change, drawing on parents' expert knowledge and emotive narratives about their experiences; appeals to 'the power of reputation' of senior figures to lend support to change efforts; an emphasis on face-to-face talk and interactions; and the use of local texts, official documents, and objects to provide legitimacy and 'symbolic power' in the form of research evidence, PowerPoint presentations, and an information-sharing tool—all of which could be circulated and direct the process of change in a consistent form over time (for a further exploration of the use of PowerPoint as an epistemic object in a management consultancy initiative, see Chapter 8). This example demonstrates how a concern to remedy inadequate knowledge sharing across health and social care services set in motion an array of new interconnected practices; this shift in turn exposing how different work practices managed to shape change, particularly through the powerful practice of communicating emotional stories.

Discursive practices may further support the spread of specific management solutions across geographical boundaries and internationally. Nicolini et al. (2016) describe how Root Cause Analysis as a popular management technique (originating in the US Navy) was mobilized globally over time by the employment of discursive practices around patient safety by health agencies: 'first, by raising public and professional anxiety about the performance of pre-existing practices around patient safety, and second, by creating reassurance through proposing a new management solution to solve the crisis it had artfully created'. Key insights from this example include awareness of how a particular management technique is modified as it travels, through a process of interpretation and translation, and the role of linguistic, textual, discursive, and network practices in supporting the mobilization of a new type of management knowledge.

## PROS AND CONS OF PRACTICE-BASED APPROACHES

We observe that *some* social practice theorists—in their attention to social processes and collective activity—may overlook individual agency and the role played by prominent persons in influencing local contexts of knowledge use: 'One critique of social learning theory is that it focuses too much on the organizational context, and thus cannot, for example, encompass the mobile, knowledgeable, and potentially influential individual. This may be the transformational leader or the ordinary professional who imports new ideas to the work and who perhaps gets changed by outside encounters' (Elkjaer 2003, 50).

We have reviewed these leadership and agency dynamics elsewhere (Fischer et al. 2016) and return to this point later in the book. We suggest that socialcultural perspectives in the organization and management literature are extremely valuable for conceptualizing how knowledge is socially mediated and transformed through action (Dopson and Fitzgerald 2005) and especially as tangible forms of evidence, knowledge, and innovation travel across space and time. However, practice-based theories may risk marginalizing the individual when practices become the main unit of analysis (for a more considered view of agency and knowledge mobilization processes, see Swan et al. 2016).

In addition, the effects of wider, contextual power relations (Contu and Willmott 2000) and socio-economic and political forces may not readily be discerned through micro-level practice-based accounts, and even more notably so in the UK health care sector. Although work practices are negotiated at a local level (e.g. in clinical teams) through frequent interactions and professional communities of practice, countervailing professional institutions, economic and structural influences will nevertheless shape daily interactions. The NHS, for example, has been subjected to repeated top-down restructuring attempts by successive governments and has experienced imposed reforms since the 1980s which arguably set limits on the opportunities to develop innovative and high-quality services available to health care professionals at the micro level (Ferlie et al. 1996).

We can ask therefore: have top-down reforms really disturbed locally nego-tiated and professionally dominated orders, or helped to maintain them? One interesting case in point is the Health and Social Care Act (2012) which radically altered existing relations between managers and clinicians in primary care settings by creating new organizational forms—clinical commis-sioning groups led by GPs (Ledger 2014). This reform process may indeed have brought about novel organizational and working practices around the country and the (re)negotiation of clinical-managerial power relations at the micro level, but without a top-down reform drive providing the overarch-ing impetus, would such new practices have been brought into existence in this manner?

Health policy and administrative reforms shape public-sector organiza-tions' degree of autonomy and set specific mandates for organizational activity (Rosenberg Hansen and Ferlie 2016, 4). Therefore, studying the wider policy and economic context remains important for contextualizing practices at the micro level in health care and can be especially helpful for explaining drivers for new management knowledge processes in health care organizations (Ledger 2014). We return to this theme when we consider the active role of the political economy of health care in more depth and the reasons why strategic management knowledge may begin to enter the health care field.

Nevertheless, a clear advantage of taking a practice perspective is the sheer strength of these often rich empirical studies for understanding issues such as collective agency, context, social relations, and materiality—and how such factors shape knowledge use and innovations in specific contexts. Practice studies can also provide 'thick descriptions' of processes of knowledge use and learning in an array of historic sites—such as within single organizations, interconnected networks, or even across international agencies.

Another major advantage is the intellectual challenge posed by practice theorizing to overtly rational, atheoretical, or normative assumptions about knowledge use that presume that evidence will diffuse into practice in a linear manner; that providing evidence is of high quality and made readily accessible, professionals will seek to access it. Numerous empirical studies in the practice-orientated literature instead reveal how this assumption is decontextualized (e.g. Gabbay and Le May 2011; Swan et al. 2016) and remind those interested in organizational knowledge processes that evidence invokes a variety of different practices and interpretations—including variable, contested dis-courses around useful evidence which require social sensemaking and collective interpretations.

# Stream 3. The meso level: the resource-based view and the health care organization

This third section of the chapter moves up from the micro level addressed by the two previous literature streams to briefly consider the meso-level question of how knowledge moves into and within organizations, and to explore implications for the health care sector.

## THE RESOURCE-BASED VIEW OF THE FIRM

Another way to conceptualize knowledge use within organizations is to adopt a resource-based view (RBV) which stems from the field of strategic management and came to prominence in the early 1990s. This approach examines the internal assets and capabilities of firms and organizations—the 'special characteristics' that proffer strategic advantage, growth, and competitiveness (Penrose 1959; Wernerfelt 1984; Barney 1991; Galbreath 2005, 979; Barney et al. 2011).

The RBV school developed within the strategic management field by taking a more inclusive look at a firm's resources beyond traditional economic categories such as labour, products, and capital, instead examining firm resources more broadly, especially those that might lead to higher profits (Wernerfelt 1984). Importantly, resources that may be critical to a firm's success can be both tangible and intangible. For example, employees' tacit knowledge, managerial and leadership skills, and non-codified organizational routines (intangible assets), or, alternatively, patented technologies, organizational infrastructure and processes, or learning resources (tangible assets) (Galbreath 2005; Barney et al. 2011).

Assets in resource-based theory (RBT) are viewed as conferring distinctive advantages on firms in highly competitive markets depending on how they are acquired, developed, and deployed. They are likely to hold particular value where they are not easily replicated or are highly innovative. It is a well-established argument of RBV that it is crucial for firms to continuously develop their internal resources and to grow new capabilities in order to stay ahead of the competition. As Wernerfelt points out, 'A good analogy is a high tree in a low forest; since it will get more sun, it will grow faster and stay taller' (1984, 174).

There have been a number of offshoots of RBV theorizing, including the development of important concepts such as 'absorptive capacity' (Cohen and Levinthal 1990) and 'dynamic capabilities' to study in detail firm strategies, processes, routines, and innovative practices—especially those focused on the acquisition of new knowledge and organizational learning (Teece et al. 1997). We will briefly look at these concepts since they have relevance for understanding knowledge mobilization and creation processes within organizations, including in the health care sector (Ferlie 2016).

## ABSORPTIVE CAPACITY

First, we consider the concept of 'absorptive capacity', which focuses on a 'firm's ability to acquire and exploit external knowledge' from the environment for competitive advantage (Cohen and Levinthal 1990; Bierly et al. 2009, 418). It is chiefly concerned with how businesses search for and use new knowledge in order to innovate and stimulate organizational learning and be commercially successful. It is frequently studied in relation to R&D investment and research-intensive industries, such as manufacturing and technology firms. Cohen and Levinthal, who originated the idea, view a firm's ability to search for new knowledge (its absorptive capacity) as related to its existing prior knowledge base. To effectively exploit new knowledge and learn from it, a firm requires existing, relevant knowledge to be able to value relevant knowledge from the outside environment (Cohen and Levinthal 1990, 129). 'The ability to evaluate and utilize outside knowledge is largely a function of the level of prior related knowledge. At the most elemental level, this prior knowledge includes basic skills or even a shared language but may also include knowledge of the most recent scientific or technological developments in a given field' (Cohen and Levinthal 1990, 12).

Cohen and Levinthal's (1990) observations are founded in literature on cognitive science, decision-making, and learning that consider how prior learning and memory shape subsequent learning about specific tasks at the individual level. At a more general level, there are clear implications for firms such as building strong internal communication processes, an organizational culture open to using and sharing knowledge, and ensuring horizon-scanning and brokering capabilities that support the active search and exploitation of knowledge and innovations from the external environment and across social networks (Tortoriello 2015). Indeed, a firm with a high level of absorptive capacity may exhibit an overall knowledge strategy as well as a variety of 'meta-routines', such as cross-working teams, incentive structures, and ability to learn from external partners and collaborators (Lewin et al. 2011).

The corollary of these arguments is that without investment in effectively sourcing and assimilating knowledge (such as process innovations, management expertise, or scientific evidence), knowledge can become trapped within silos and teams, hence it is strategically important that new knowledge is exploited across subdivisions within the firm. As we have seen, the concept of absorptive capacity emphasizes that firms and organizations understand the strategic value of knowledge before extracting it from the environment because it is insufficient for firms to acquire knowledge without also grasping how that knowledge has value for learning and performance (Todorova and Durisin 2007).

## ABSORPTIVE CAPACITY AS A 'DYNAMIC CAPABILITY'

Other writers have gone on to conceptualize an absorptive capacity as a 'dynamic capability' to facilitate further theorizing and research on this topic, providing a more 'evolutionary perspective' on a firm's development over time in response to environmental pressures and shifts (Zahra and George 2002; Bierly et al. 2009, 185; Ferlie 2016, 174). The dynamic capabilities framework focuses on firm routines and resources and is viewed as helpful for identifying 'the dimensions of firm-specific capabilities that can be sources of advantage, and to explain how combinations of competences and resources can be developed, deployed, and protected' (Teece et al. 1997, 510). As with absorptive capacity, the dynamic capabilities approach provides a lens to study the strategies by which firms seek to strengthen internal knowledge and learning processes to boost performance and respond to changing circumstances. We now explore applications of these concepts in non-commercial settings.

## THE RESOURCE-BASED VIEW IN THE PUBLIC SECTOR AND HEALTH CARE SETTINGS

Although 'knowledge-based value creation' is a central tenet of RBT (Barney et al. 2011, 1308), and the health and education sectors are both highly knowledge-intensive fields (Ferlie 2016), this approach has been more often applied to private industry where staying ahead of fast-paced technological change—and developing niche capabilities—is deemed necessary for survival. Public management applications of RBV and RBT have been less apparent in the literature, especially the detailed study of organizational dynamic capabilities within health care (but there has been some exploration—see Casebeer et al. 2010; Harvey et al. 2010; Piening, 2013; Ferlie 2014).

In recent years there has been a steady shift of attention towards public-sector settings, especially as the knowledge mobilization literature on health care has expanded and drawn upon the management literature to theorize beyond conventional approaches—most notably from academics based in the UK and Canada (e.g. Crilly et al. 2010; Ferlie et al. 2012, 2015; Burton and Rycroft-Malone 2014; Ferlie 2014, 2016; Swan et al. 2016; see also Knudsen and Roman 2004; Elwyn et al. 2007; Kothari et al. 2009; Berta et al. 2010; Casebeer et al. 2010; Harvey et al. 2010; Kash et al. 2013; Croft and Currie 2016).

In one example, Casebeer et al. (2010) persuasively argue that RBV is helpful for understanding public-sector organizations because these are required to use limited internal resources strategically to improve performance—rather than merely pushing for higher profits. They observe how health care managers are increasingly expected to enact strategic roles to achieve organizational performance objectives. In their qualitative study of a Canadian health care setting and its attempt to take forwards innovative projects, they identified 'the dynamic capability of learning through experimenting as a route to continually improving the organisation's abilities to perform' (2010, 262). A distinctive capability was therefore fostering a culture that was supportive of staff learning through flexible leadership and management, thus helping staff to leverage existing (and limited) resources in the organization to make improvements. As learning through experimenting was both identified and enabled as well as aligned to organizational strategy and cultural norms, this 'knowing through doing' approach has led to innovations in performance through the ability to try out and develop new ways of working within essentially existing and constrained resource contexts. (Casebeer et al. 2010, 271).

In the UK, Croft and Currie (2016) have applied absorptive capacity to study health care commissioners—the professionals (both clinical and non-clinical) responsible for purchasing health and community services for local populations, in a manner that is financially accountable and based on health needs. They were interested to see what 'combinative capabilities' influence commissioning organizations' use of knowledge, and how absorptive capacity might be improved in the highly regulated health care environment in which these organizations operate (p. 77). To do this, the researchers focused on 'four processes of knowledge mobilisation that constitute an organization's absorptive capacity: acquisition, assimilation, transformation, and exploitation' (p. 69).

Croft and Currie (2016, 78) found that 'socialization capabilities' and 'coordination capabilities' were particularly influential on knowledge mobilization in these settings, largely because of the highly professionalized and regulated context. Public and patient involvement knowledge, for example, were emphasized in processes of knowledge acquisition and assimilation, but much less so in the transformation and exploitation of new knowledge. The authors suggest that further work could be done by health care organizations and managers to develop internal absorptive capacity, such as by ensuring that public and patient involvement is fully integrated across these four distinct knowledge mobilization processes—so that public and patient involvement knowledge really informs decision-making. This may however be limited where 'power differentials' (p. 80) exist between professionals, managers, and patients, and if coordination capability is thwarted by prevailing social and cultural norms.

There are also indications that poorly performing health care organizations may have low absorptive capacity and exhibit poor organizational learning

(Harvey et al. 2010). So an important point is raised in the literature about the limited capacity of health care organizations to fully exploit and assimilate quality improvement (QI) knowledge, innovations, and clinical evidence that could significantly benefit patient care and service delivery (Berta et al. 2010; Burton and Rycroft-Malone 2014).

Drawing on RBV and public management theories, Harvey et al. (2010, 97) connect poor knowledge processes with organizational performance and put forward three propositions:

(1) That 'the performance of a public organization is positive related to its investment in absorptive capacity' (p. 87);
(2) That 'the effectiveness of strategies for building absorptive capacity, and hence achieving performance improvement, is contingent on the nature of the tasks the organization undertakes and the dynamism in the environment within which it operates' (p. 89);
(3) That 'the relationship between prior organizational knowledge and absorptive capacity will be determined by the learning-related attributes of the corporate paradigm, in particular the extent to which the corporate paradigm values new knowledge and is reflexive' (p. 91).

## PROS AND CONS OF THE RBV APPROACH

The RBV lens provides a fresh way of looking at the 'knowledge translation' problem or 'bench to bedside' flow of knowledge in health care which, as we have noted, is too linear a view of knowledge utilization. Indeed, it is now widely appreciated in empirical research on knowledge mobilization that the 'knowledge application process' is more complex than is commonly understood (Berta et al. 2010, 1332). The RBV of the firm has the advantage of addressing, empirically, the specific internal capabilities, resources, and combinations of capabilities that health care organizations need to truly assimilate new knowledge for improvement and performance.

Nevertheless, Burton and Rycroft-Malone (2014) remind us that evaluating the performance of health care organizations is more complex than in private settings given the complex financial and collaborative arrangements found there and the sheer number of stakeholders involved. They further observe that, while RBV holds potential for understanding the types of resources and capabilities necessary for successful quality improvement, its application to the study of health care organizations has nonetheless to date been fairly limited and 'untested' empirically (p. 114).

There is also the question of how knowledge processes occur in mandated health care networks which have grown in number, as well as single vertically integrated organizations, notably in 'wicked problem' areas as this may be difficult in practice (see Ferlie et al. 2011, 2013; Oborn et al. 2016).

Another potential concern is that adopting an RBV/RBT perspective assumes that there should be more strategic or 'business' thinking occurring in the public sector and that if stronger market forces are present, public agencies should aim to be competitive (Casebeer et al. 2010; Ferlie 2016). However, this normative argument is not assumed in the literature. The conditions under which public agencies operate are invariably shaped by wider political-economic conditions (see also Stream 4) and shaped by the nuances of administrative regimes which are found to vary across countries (Pollitt and Bouckaert 2011).

Nevertheless, like other authors, we maintain that given the existence of high numbers of public–private partnerships now found internationally, pressures on not-for-profit organizations to market their services to 'consumers' and the seismic fallout from financial recession and growing resource pressures affecting much of the public sector, researching the dynamic capabilities of public organizations to respond to these environmental shifts and continuous policy 'turbulence' has purchase (Casebeer et al. 2010; Ledger 2014; Croft and Currie 2016; Ferlie et al. 2016).

Seen in this light, administrative reforms such as the New Public Management, which emphasize market-based principles and contractualism (Hood 1991; Lane 2000), can be interpreted as rendering the public sector more receptive to strategic management and performance-related knowledge over time. This is especially salient when political reforms edge the public sector, including health care, towards privatization and stronger competition between autonomous agencies (Piening 2013; Croft and Currie 2016; Ferlie et al. 2016; Rosenberg Hansen and Ferlie, 2016, 2–3)—a point to which we will return.

Nevertheless, to date the literature on RBV has been skewed towards competitive markets and not quasi-markets or highly policy-mandated public services, hence the empirical research on this topic is limited. Theoretically, then, RBV requires further tailoring to non-competitive environments, as already attempted by Harvey and colleagues (2010). Otherwise RBV may not define what specific capabilities are important across different sectors (and why) and the contextual contingencies that shape what good performance looks like in the public sector (e.g. strong patient focus, transparency, organizational learning, commitment to evidence-based practice, and ongoing professional development).

Finally, key authors of the RBV have observed methodological issues that should be taken into account, such as measuring and tracking intangible assets and resources (Barney et al. 2011) and this is especially complex in highly regulated and professionalized contexts like the health care sector. As Rosenberg Hansen and Ferlie observe, 'the possibilities for using strategic management models in public organizations depend on their core features' (2016, 3); therefore these features, and their distinctiveness, need to be outlined carefully. The task of applying RBV empirically is therefore not as straightforward as might be assumed.

In conclusion, we concur that the health care sector is an especially appropriate 'epistemic fit' (McGivern et al. 2016) for RBV literature given requirements for organizations and professionals to use research and innovation to drive the implementation of new treatments and service transformations, and in light of financial and performance pressures. We further contend that since health care organizations in the UK, and in England especially, have been subject to a series of New Public Management market-orientated reforms, effective performance management in these domains can be argued to be critically important for organizational survival in today's health care sector.

# Stream 4. The political economy of public management knowledge production

We now move up to the macro level of analysis to explore the political and economic factors that shape preferred management knowledge stocks in health care, building on earlier reviews of the literature and themes identified through empirical work in the health sector (Ledger 2014; Ferlie et al. 2016). The focus is here at the national level of analysis and over an extended period of time.

The point has been made that countries' dominant narratives of public management reform (Pollitt and Bouckaert 2011) tend to reflect their underlying political, economic, cultural, and institutional contexts. Such narratives should be seen as exerting both broad (across various public services) and long (over an extended period of time) effects and once embedded, they are both resilient and difficult to dislodge, at least under normal conditions.

In the UK case, it has been further argued that the political crisis of the 1980s which resulted in a dramatic turn to neo-liberalism (Hood 1991; Ferlie et al. 1996; Hood and Dixon 2015) also witnessed a rare but substantial reorientation away from traditional public administration models and towards NPM reform doctrines within what was now diagnosed as an over-extended and wasteful public sector. Such a reorientation was further facilitated by the centralized set of political institutions available to the UK government in implementing its public services reform programme. The NHS was a large, expensive, and visible public service that went early into the NPM reform process (starting with the Griffiths Report: Department of Health and Social Security 1983).

NPM doctrines clearly moved public services organizations closer to the preferred model of the private firm. There were, however, further macro-level institutional effects: ministers were less likely to rely on the advice of civil servants (seen as too establishment-minded and over-cautious) and be more open to alternative sources of advice, such as think tanks and management consultants. The policy process was opened up (Pollitt and Bouckaert 2011), at least to preferred new actors. It is therefore not surprising that the management consultancy sector grew rapidly in the UK from the 1960s onwards and that it also appears to have secured a stronger influence in government when benchmarked against some international comparator countries (Saint-Martin 2004).

Finally, business schools were established early and grew rapidly in the UK from the 1960s, later than the better known case of the USA (Khurana 2007) but earlier than in many other countries. The MBA emerged as a qualification of choice for many managers. NPM reforms opened up government to more influence from these expanding business schools, including the importing of texts from senior faculty in some elite American business schools (such as Harvard). Indeed, the supranational and even global circulation of some management texts and ideas—including into UK government—became evident (Sahlin-Andersson and Engwall 2002a, 2002b).

We now move on to explore some of these aspects of the underlying political economy of public management production in greater detail.

## KNOWLEDGE SYSTEMS AND THE KNOWLEDGE ECONOMY

It has been argued that 'knowledge workers' are an elite occupational group in today's society since they convert knowledge into profitable products and innovations used to drive economic growth and profitability (Beck 2000, 40; Drucker 2007). As we have already seen, the RBV perspective builds on this as a starting point, maintaining that if businesses harness new knowledge and develop organizational and individual learning capabilities as a strategy, they are more likely to perform well. As economies grow they are therefore increasingly dependent on service industries and the 'knowledge-intensive' sector which produces new technologies, innovations, and knowledge-based solutions to market (Starbuck 1992; Blackler 1995; Alvesson 2001). In the sociological and management literature this knowledge-based economy is a transformational shift that took place in the late twentieth century, resulting in a greater focus on capitalist produced 'knowledge-based products' and services (Harris 2001).

Within a dynamic knowledge economy perspective, various organizations supply knowledge (knowledge producers) and themselves respond to economic, political, policy, social, and technological developments. According to writers on knowledge working from a macro perspective, there are important consequences resulting from the transformation of modern economies, including a rapid rise in knowledge-intensive firms (KIFs); for example, management consultancies, IT and software specialists, new forms of knowledge production (e.g. digital solutions), greater commodification of knowledge (e.g. in the form of patents), increasing competition for skilled knowledge workers, and more emphasis on communication technologies (Lundvall and Johnson 1994; Stehr 1994; Houghton and Sheehan 2000; Harris 2001; Powell and Snellman 2004; Foss 2005; Armbrüster 2006).

However, these social, economic, and technological developments generate new problems for organizations, such as how to manage the plethora of knowledge (and data) now available and how to respond to greater uncertainties around knowledge. This gap generates new responses, such as the desire for the effective management of knowledge and data through knowledge management systems (the Cochrane Collaboration can be seen as one such example supporting the practice of EBM in health care).

An issue with this perspective, as with RBV, is the temptation to treat knowledge as a commodity and solely as a source of competitive advantage—for both individuals and organizations—due to its inherent economic value. It becomes a normative, taken-for-granted assumption that knowledge exploitation necessarily leads to economic growth and innovation (Stehr 1994), and as we have already noted, this view is often contested, particularly by practice-based approaches that seek to capture local knowledge complexities (e.g. Swan et al. 2016). However, we observe that little is understood theoretically and empirically about how these macro-level knowledge dynamics may be playing out in the public sector and specialist sectors such as health care, which are both highly regulated and dependent on new knowledge and skilled knowledge workers.

## FROM EBM TO MANAGEMENT CONSULTANCY AND GURUS: EXPLORING SUBSYSTEMS OF KNOWLEDGE PRODUCTION FROM A POLITICAL-ECONOMY PERSPECTIVE

One useful approach which we adopt here is to take a 'political economy of knowledge' perspective which explores how knowledge flows are linked to macro societal factors, such as culture, capital, politics, power, and hegemony (Stehr 1994, 107; Thrift 2005, 5). From this position, the circulation of knowledge is analysed in connection to broader political, economic, institutional, and societal shifts. We maintain that this holistic perspective is useful for understanding the vast 'expansion of management knowledge' in the late twentieth and twenty-first centuries which can be seen as a distinctive form of knowledge production (Sahlin-Andersson and Engwall 2002c, 278; Thrift 2005; Engwall 2010). For example, Thrift describes the existence of a 'business school/consulting nexus' in which close relations between business school academics, management 'gurus', and consultancy firms emerge as a distinctive 'cultural circuit' of knowledge in late capitalism (Thrift 2005, 6, 37). So, we ask: Does this influence management knowledge flows into the health care sector and what might be the link with contemporary political, economic, and policy conditions?

In the health sector, and as already covered, the EBM movement is a dominant knowledge paradigm and may be interpreted as a hegemonic knowledge system influencing practice. Academics, government policy, and evidence-focused institutions such as NICE and the National Institute for Health Research (NIHR) have each encouraged clinicians and health care managers to be more orientated towards undertaking research and evidence-based practice to improve patient care and service delivery (e.g. see Walshe and Davies 2010, 2013). However, although evidence-based practice is widely supported rhetorically, there have been criticisms that health care managers are often lacking in evidence-based training and research awareness—unlike clinicians (Walshe and Rundall 2001). We observe that there is still little exploration of stocks of health care management knowledge in use currently. We argue that health care managers are more orientated to non-EBM/EBMgt knowledge systems that operate in the wider 'knowledge economy', such as management consulting firms, business school gurus, and think tanks. This observation in turn renders these organizations worthy of greater exploration, thus going beyond a narrow focus on the implementation of EBM principles which has already been much commented on and researched empirically.

Armbrüster (2006, 205–6), for example, observes that processes of privatization and the rise of modern communication technologies in knowledge economies generate new opportunities for management consulting firms to sell a panoply of services to clients. Consultancy firms become experts in creating and applying sector-specific knowledge and can begin to occupy niche institutional spaces, such as when working for local authorities, governments, or public health organizations (Fincham et al. 2008; McGivern et al. 2017). For example, populist management ideas that such firms have historically promoted to improve performance include Total Quality Management, Business Process Re-Engineering, and Lean Production Techniques, and these have been studied empirically in the field of management and organization studies and found to have been promoted internationally, both in public- and private-sector settings (Clark and Salaman 1998; Sturdy et al. 2009; Mueller and Whittle 2011; Wright et al. 2012). There can be a particular emphasis by these firms on spreading standardized management innovations and practices (like Total Quality Management). Hence Wright et al. 2012 (p. 654) suggest that:

Management consultants are often central figures in not only the promotion and diffusion of new organizational practices, but also their implementation. As management 'fashion setters', consultancies are important agents in identifying, popularizing, selling and then measuring and comparing ('benchmarking') new standards of organizational practice.

In addition, business schools play a significant role in promulgating management 'fads and fashions' (Abrahamson 1991) and key management ideas promoted by leading academics, such as the work of Porter and Teisberg (2006) on value-based health care, or Peters and Waterman's (1982) classic management performance text. As we explore later in this book, management ideas and knowledge (which may or may not be evidence-based) can travel internationally from academic centres and into distant public, private, and also health care settings; indeed, in later chapters we demonstrate how Kaplan and Norton's *Balanced Scorecard* (1996) text was adopted locally to drive change and how new management solutions were derived from employing external consulting firms as experts (see Chapter 8; McGivern et al. 2017).

As institutionalist writers observe, 'Ideas do not diffuse in a vacuum but are actively transferred and translated in a context of other ideas, actors, traditions and institutions' (Sahlin and Wedlin 2008, 219). We thus view it as necessary to recognize that not only do fashionable management solutions and innovations spread nationally and internationally from a 'business/consulting nexus', but that only *some* ideas appear to gain traction in health care settings with managers and clinicians, suggesting that certain types of management knowledge may become more 'powerful as they circulate' (Sahlin and Wedlin 2008, 221).

However, empirical research on consultancy–client relationships nevertheless indicates that the picture may be far more complex than more traditional diffusionist accounts of knowledge spread suggest. Sturdy et al. have examined a number of consultancy projects longitudinally and conclude that new knowledge may be created and co-produced between consultants and clients, therefore *both* consultants and clients are embedded within complex social, institutional, and historical relations (Sturdy et al. 2009, 172–93). There are also 'client experts' working in parallel with external firm experts (Sturdy et al. 2009, 174), thus suggesting that the knowledge circuit suggested by Thrift is more nuanced and complex.

## THE POLITICAL-ECONOMIC LINKAGE: MANAGEMENT KNOWLEDGE AND HEALTH CARE SETTINGS

Why might some management solutions, innovations, or texts become more popular in health care settings than others? We argue that this question has been under-explored theoretically to date in the health services literature. We see a connection between management knowledge and prevailing public administration models and this is an important macro-level factor in analysing management knowledge flows into public-sector organizations. For example, UK NPM reforms have encouraged 'business-like' practices to be adopted from the private sector; however, it is not clear whether or not this results in lasting changes in practices, or even in the types of knowledge(s) favoured by public-sector managers (Ferlie et al. 2016, 187).

The context for our study reveals major policy shifts affecting the health sector and the NHS specifically, and arguably continual upheaval in a series of structural reforms which generated ongoing policy 'turbulence' (Ledger 2014). In addition, English health policy has since 2010 taken place in a political-economic context of enduring financial recession and austerity politics. This has had a major impact on the NHS given a combination of rising public demand for health services and an economic and fiscal downturn from 2008 onwards.

As a strategic response, a raft of efficiency measures has been brought in by successive governments to make national-level savings, notably including the QIPP (Quality, Innovation, Productivity, Prevention) programme. This initiative was introduced by the New Labour government as a means of securing efficiency savings and quality improvement in the NHS and was continued under the Liberal–Conservative Coalition from 2010. QIPP had a projected a savings target for the NHS in the region of £20–£22 billion—to be met by local and regional projects by 2020. This funding shortfall still looms over the service many years later (Gainsbury 2016) and as we explore in the book and elsewhere, this can be seen to have influenced the types of management knowledge and solutions selected by health care organizations, resulting in local 'knowledge effects' (Ledger 2014; Ferlie et al. 2016).

As we have argued elsewhere (Ferlie et al. 2016), the wider political economy in which management knowledge, evidence, and public service organizations are situated creates a context which is receptive to certain types of knowledge and not others. In a political economy dominated by austerity, 'harder' forms of management knowledge, promising quick, measurable financial saving and performance improvements are more likely to be taken up than 'softer' forms proffering slower but perhaps more sustainable change. Hence, here we may see the take-up in public health care organizations of 'knowledge products' produced by the management consultancy/business school nexus (also see McGivern et al. 2017), rather than texts more grounded in the EBMgt approach. Furthermore, this development has the double effect of further articulating NPM-based reforms, practices, and thinking (Ferlie et al. 2016).

In the UK context, the combination of the legacy of earlier policy and public administrative reforms, prolonged economic austerity, and changing societal demands for health services, all have the potential to shape the management knowledge deemed important for the performance of health care organizations. These wider macro influences can also be studied at the meso level of health care organizations, especially as we seek to understand how managers come to use knowledge strategically to meet policy, productive, and performance pressures within their own organizations.

# Concluding remarks

This chapter has reviewed and discussed four different streams of literature which all construe the nature of public and health management 'knowledge' in very different ways and at different levels of analysis.

The EBM paradigm has been described as a particularly successful and dominant knowledge production system that has not only produced major institutional shifts, but has also matured, with internal critiques about the very idea of EBM now entering the health care literature. However, the rather rationalistic notion of knowledge use commonly associated with EBM was somewhat unproblematically adopted in the discipline of management with the idea becoming influential that EBM could improve organizational and individual decision-making.

This contested debate has revealed a lack of consensus around what constitutes quality evidence in non-health care-orientated subjects such as management, and how it should be adopted. This debate forms an important backdrop to exploring through empirical research whether or not health care managers are as 'research illiterate' as commonly claimed, or whether they are perhaps orientated to management knowledge in ways previously overlooked.

The practice perspective on knowledge use further unpicks rationalist assumptions about how knowledge has local influence. It is a powerful and critical lens for understanding how and why one piece of management knowledge or research may be a 'rational' fit for one setting, but not enough—on account of collective norms, practices, and processes that shape knowledge use *in situ*.

The strategic management literature, specifically the RBV school, emphasizes greater attention to organizational learning processes, to how firms actively seek knowledge from the external environment, and to how they develop new knowledge and innovative capabilities to perform competitively. Arguably, with increasing performance pressures on public-sector organizations, this literature which derives from studies of the private sector can offer a novel perspective on not-for-profit institutions such as those found in the health sector.

Finally, we contend that a political-economy perspective has not been adequately explored in public management settings, particularly in the health care field, and as it relates to professionals' access and use of management research and knowledge. Theoretically speaking, the management knowledge effects of NPM reforms, for example, are a notable gap in the literature stemming from the study of public administration. A number of organizations function as knowledge producers proffering management solutions to health care organizations and these dynamics can be explored empirically, but in recognition of prevailing political-economic conditions. Hence, 'harder' knowledge, promising quick, measurable financial savings and performance improvements, may be taken up most readily in a political economy dominated by austerity, furthering NPM reforms, practices, and thinking.

# 3 The political economy of English public services reform and implications for management knowledges in health care organizations

## Introduction and purpose

As Scott et al. (2001, 20–1) argue, 'an institutional change is signalled in the health care field, for example, when hospital managers once trained in schools of hospital administration are replaced by health care executives trained in business schools'. Scott et al.'s (2001) remark raises some important issues. There appears prima facie to be some evidence of a similar shift towards accessing business-orientated management knowledge by the UK health care field: for example, Lean-based techniques developed in Japanese manufacturing settings are now being widely accessed in UK health care settings in the search for major productivity improvements, albeit not without problems (Radnor et al. 2012). Our later empirical chapters will provide further evidence of significant absorption of generic management texts and knowledges.

This shift in our view reflects rising influence from a diverse set of often more business-orientated knowledge producers located outside the traditional health care sector. These new actors and influences include management consultants, perhaps implementing 'off the shelf' corporate change programmes such as business process re-engineering (McNulty and Ferlie 2002, 2004), business school-based authors, pro-market think tanks, and the authors of best-selling generic management texts (as later case-study-based chapters explore in more detail).

If this long-run change is evident within the English health care field, we need to ask: How and why has it occurred? We will argue that the fundamental process involved is that many English public agencies—including those in the NHS—have over an extended period of time (i.e. since the 1980s) become more porous and open to 'business-like' thinking. They have moved away from behaving like traditional Weberian public agencies, with their basis in sectorally specific and public administration-based knowledge. We also argue that major national top-down 'reforms' sponsored by UK national government have been influential in this basic remodelling of public agencies, including those in the health care sector, to make them more 'firm like'. There is then an active political economy of public management reforming operating at a macro level which should be considered.

Broadly speaking, these reforms suggest a rising New Public Management (NPM) logic (Hood 1991; Ferlie et al. 1996; Hood and Dixon 2015) apparent in the UK public services (including in the health care sector) from the early 1980s onwards, based on the three core principles of marketization, managerialization, and the measurement of performance (Ferlie 2016).

Within the health care sector specifically, a cluster of key reforms to the organization and management of health care appear especially important in expressing these NPM ideas and have been apparent across governments of various political complexions. The first major change highlighted was the introduction of a more assertive form of general management in the mid-1980s (as recommended in a review by Griffiths 1983) to replace the historically more consensual and facilitative style of 'administration' prevalent in the NHS since its foundation in 1948.

A second major reform was enacted through new legislation, namely the 1990 Health and Community Care Act. This Act brought in significant and enduring organizational changes. The first such change was the introduction of a purchaser/provider split and the quasi-market to replace a previously line-managed and vertically integrated system where resources had been allocated through planning. New organizational forms emerged both on the purchaser side (so District Health Authorities became macro purchasers and local General Practitioner Fund Holders micro purchasers) and on the provider side. Previously directly managed NHS hospitals were now converted into NHS trusts with enhanced operational autonomy. The purchasers were in theory able to contract with non-NHS providers to deliver services, although in practice the market remained highly managed. In addition, private-sector-style corporate governance arrangements were brought in within the new NHS trusts with the creation of smaller and supposedly strategic boards of executive and non-executive directors, on the model of the Anglo-Saxon public limited company (Ferlie et al. 1996), which replaced the previous larger and more representative authorities. All these reforms were brought in by a succession of radical right Conservative governments (in power 1979–97) for which the reform of a large and expensive social democratic state was a strategic political priority.

These earlier reforms were followed by the creation of the new organizational form of autonomized and market-facing NHS foundation trusts (2004 onwards) by New Labour governments (in power 1997–2010), under the provisions of the 2003 Health and Social Care Act. They followed the same overall firm-like model, albeit with minor dilutions of the original governance structure to include a second-tier supervisory board, the Board of Governors, which involved more stakeholders (although the governors often found it difficult to enact a clear role vis-à-vis the more powerful main board in practice—see Allen et al. 2012).

The approach of New Labour to health care reform has been seen as complex and ambiguous (Powell 1999), both seeking to move beyond earlier NPM reforms, yet also to maintain and even accelerate them. On the one hand, there was a growth of network and collaborative approaches in health care management (Ferlie et al. 2013), informed by so-called network governance ideas (Rhodes 1997, 2007; Newman 2001; Osborne 2010) which represented a possible post-NPM narrative of public management reform. Collaboration was now to be preferred to competition as a governance mode, especially in the case of complex or 'wicked' problems (e.g. health inequalities, whole-area working) which required different public agencies and indeed sectors to work together in concerted action (Ferlie et al. 2011, 2013). Some of these managed networks in the health care sector also endured beyond the lifetime of New Labour governments. On the other hand, pro-marketization policies continued, especially in what might be seen as the later New Labour period (around 2005–10—see Mays et al. 2011), perhaps as the time-consuming and more emergent nature of earlier network governance reforms became more apparent.

Further marketization (under the doctrine of 'any willing provider') and greater externalization of service provision to alternative non-NHS providers—especially in the domain of community health services—was further encouraged by the 2012 Health and Social Care Act, introduced by the Conservative and Liberal Democrat Coalition (in power 2010–15). Many of these contracts were externalized to large outsourcing-orientated private firms (such as Virgin Care, the website of which reports it now operates over 400 health care and local authority services across the UK), rather than to alternative not-for-profit forms such as non-governmental organizations or staff-owned mutuals.

This brief review indicates that many of these reforms have been introduced by Acts of Parliament (1990, 2003, and 2012), and under governments of three political colours. Passing these Acts not only requires parliamentary time and debate but also depends on clear and sustained high-level support and leadership. Reform through a parliamentary Act is not to be undertaken lightly, especially in the health care domain which is often fraught and attracts the attention of lobbies and media. Sustained political leadership would be needed to get an Act through Parliament from the health ministers (along with securing broader Cabinet and Prime Ministerial assent) and civil servants in the Department of Health would also be required to give substantial policy and administrative support.

So the mid/late 1980s are here construed as a fundamental and enduring break point in the organization and management of UK public and health care services, where a major shift took place (for better or worse) in the logics underpinning health services delivery (Griffiths 1983; the 1990 Health and Community Care Act). This NPM logic can best be seen as a mix of market- and management-based principles. This is not to say that NPM reforms always achieved the results intended and indeed there could be unintended or even perverse consequences: Hood and Dixon's (2015) recent overview of the long-term impact of NPM reforms taken as a whole suggested that as a result UK government 'cost a bit more and worked a bit worse' (p. 183). In particular, government's loss of control of large outsourcing contracts (e.g. in IT programmes) led to a loss of cost control, as did the long-term effects of private-sector capital investment (the private finance initiative) used to modernize the hospital estate rapidly in the New Labour period.

Despite this controversy over their long-term impact, these NPM reforms fundamentally reflect the arrival of a new political and policy discourse within the domain of UK public management. These rising NPM-orientated values included efficiency, value for money, agency performance, more choice by users, and enhanced operational management capability or assured 'delivery' of policy objectives. Critics (Dunleavy 1995) suggest that this excessive focus on operational management eroded the traditional policymaking capacity of the upper civil service which was alert to systems-level effects, leading to various 'policy disasters' (such as the introduction of the poll tax as a new form of local government finance, which was later abandoned).

As previously suggested, there was some move towards softer and counter-balancing 'network governance' reforms in the New Labour period (1997–2010) designed to unpick some fragmenting effects of earlier NPM reforms—such as 'joined-up government', whole-area working, and managed networks (Newman 2001; Rhodes 2007; Ferlie et al. 2013). However, other aspects of the NPM—such as performance management, target setting, and private capital investment in the public-sector estate—continued and even intensified.

So we argue there is an active and continuing top-down political economy of UK public services reform, including in the health care sector, which should be taken as a leading and politically visible sector for NPM reforming. Indeed, the Department of Health has been held up by some as a model 'delivery orientated' department (Greer and Jarman 2007) within wider central government. We further argue that such shifts at the macro level go on to shape behaviours at the meso organizational level of the health care organization, including through the creation of NPM-compatible organizational processes and forms such as quasi-markets and NHS trusts.

Comparativist scholars of public management reform (Painter and Peters 2010; Pollitt and Bouckaert 2011) argue that nation states vary both in their underlying model of government and in their long-term trajectories of public management reform. We will apply and adapt their basic model of the structure of national government to the UK case and then tease out implications for likely approaches to public management reform.

# Characterizing the political economy of UK public management reform

First, then, we seek to characterize key parameters in the UK's political economy of public management reforming and then trace some more specific implications for the health care sector. The analysis covers an extended period of time, going back to the 1980s, as that decade can in our view be seen as a major break point historically.

Some comparativist scholars of public management argue that nation states can be clustered into family groups in terms of their common orientation to underlying models of government. For example, Painter and Peters (2010) offer a classification of nine family groups globally, of which the first is labelled the Anglo-American group. This group is seen as having a relatively restricted concept of the role of government, when compared to alternative Napoleonic or Germanic clusters. Even within the Anglo-American group, however, there is some internal variation, with the UK being traditionally seen as a more unitary state with weaker local government than the more federalist USA. The civil service within the Anglo-American cluster is seen as more open to management doctrines as opposed to the highly legalistic character of the Germanic civil service.

Pollitt and Bouckaert's (2011, ch. 3) analysis of different politico-administrative regimes usefully highlights five basic dimensions of the state to inform their more specific analysis of national-level public management reform trajectories. We will now outline the key features of their model which we see as a useful heuristic device and apply it to public management reform in the UK case, and then more specifically to the NHS.

Their first dimension refers to the basic structure of the state and specifically the extent of centralization, including both the vertical dispersion of authority (or the sharing of authority between different levels of government) and the strength of horizontal coordination at the centre of government: 'all other things being equal, reforms in highly decentralised states (whether they are unitary or federal) are likely to be less broad in scope and less uniform in practice than in centralised states' (Pollitt and Bouckaert 2011, 51). In terms of the focus of public management reform efforts, centralized states (Pollitt and Bouckaert 2011, 52) are more likely to be in the service delivery business—including directly delivering key and politically sensitive services such as health and education—rather than such service delivery being undertaken by the strong regions apparent elsewhere.

Their second dimension (pp. 54–5) concerns the taken-for-granted national conventions surrounding executive government, including whether governments tend to be majoritarian (where normally only one political party forms the government), take an intermediate form, or are more consensual in tone, perhaps as a result of coalitions between political parties. The style may in turn be related to the electoral system which affects the ease with which smaller parties can win seats in Parliament and then the extent to which coalitions are seen as normal. So, governments may normally either be single party-based or two- or even multi-party coalitions. Coalitions may in turn either take the form of a coalition between a large and a small party to achieve just over 50 per cent of seats or a 'grand coalition' of the two main parties (as is currently the case in Germany). It might be thought that majoritarian governments (normally the case in the UK) might well have more radical and top-down strategies for public management reform than those that are coalition-based.

Their third dimension explores the pattern of minister and mandarin (or senior civil servant) relations as together these two groupings often form the elite that makes policy decisions about public management reform. A key question is whether the two career paths of these occupational groups are more integrated or separated. In the USA, for example, more senior civil service positions are temporary and directly politically appointed than in the UK, where the civil service is expected to be neutral and also permanent. Indeed, the senior civil servant in a UK ministry is officially termed the Permanent Under-Secretary of State, as opposed to the temporary appointments of elected politicians as ministers or Secretaries of State. Such senior civil service appointments would normally proceed over successive governments, providing a high security of tenure and also continuity in sources of policy advice. Some NPM-orientated governments (e.g. New Zealand) have tried to reduce the strength of mandarins' traditional tenure by restyling them as chief executives, to reassert stronger political control and provide for more active performance management (Halligan 2013). One might expect the 'ownership' of politically controversial reforms to public services to be lower in systems where civil servants' careers take a separate path from those of politicians and where they have high tenure.

Fourth, Pollitt and Bouckaert (2011, 61–6) consider the nature of the underlying administrative culture and philosophy and how it might affect administrative reform trajectories. A basic distinction is drawn between the Anglo-Saxon public interest model, which has a relatively restricted role for government, and the *Rechtsstaat* (or state of law) models found in continental Europe (e.g. Germany), which have a more positive role for the state. Within *Rechtsstaat* states, there is often a well-developed body of special administrative law and civil servants become a special cadre with an engrained mission to protect the constitutional state. The implication is that *Rechtsstaat* systems may well be 'stickier' and slower to reform than public interest settings. In addition, legal and rule-bound norms and knowledge in these settings increase resistance to non-juridical managerialist and performance-based thinking and provide some legal and constitutional protection against radical managerial action.

Fifth and finally, there is a question raised about the extent of the diversity of the policy advice offered to ministers in relation to public management reform with the implication that 'the wider the range of customary sources of advice, the more likely it is that new ideas—especially from those outside the public sector—will reach ministers' ears in persuasive and influential forms' (Pollitt and Bouckaert 2011, 66). This fifth dimension is the one which relates most directly to our core theme of the management knowledge production system so is especially interesting to explore further.

Does the civil service have a virtual monopoly on advice or is the policy system more open to alternative advice providers? There are various other sources which might in principle provide external advice to ministers. Major international bodies (such as the Organization for Economic Cooperation and Development, the International Monetary Fund, or the World Bank), for example, appear to have been influential in diffusing public management reform ideas globally. Public-sector downsizing proposals and NPM-based reforms (such as transparency and measures designed to promote good governance) may often be imposed on developing countries in financial need as part of structural adjustment packages agreed by international donor bodies, as in the case of Greece currently. The European Union is another supranational body active in state-building efforts in post-Soviet bloc accession states in Central and Eastern Europe. Its baseline assessment system for the government systems of candidate states is softer than NPM reforms, more concerned with values of quality and social inclusion as well as attached to traditional notions of Weberian good governance (Verheijen 2010).

A further traditional source of advice in Anglo-Saxon counties has been policy-facing academics who are seen as expert in particular policy fields and who may be brought in as temporary advisers or sit on committees of enquiry. More recently, there has been increasing use by some governments of businessmen as supposed efficiency experts (e.g. by President Reagan in the USA of the 1980s), also of management consultants (Saint-Martin 1998, 2004) and a growing number of think tanks (Weaver 1989) which bridge the worlds of ideas and public policy. Such think tanks may either be sectorally expert (e.g. health policy) or rather more politically and ideologically aligned in nature. Finally, the politicization of advice to ministers with the growth of special political advisers outside the conventional civil service is another trend evident in some countries (Pollitt and Bouckaert 2011, 66).

These are all helpful structural dimensions which enable comparative analysis of public management reforming across states to proceed. We add to their list a sixth and more subjective dimension, namely the status of public management reform as a high-level political issue. What, in other words, is the political salience of public management reforming at the highest reaches of government? Is the reform of the state seen as a strategic political priority for the prime minster/president, who would then set up special advisory teams or units within their own offices to provide direct advice to the political centre? Or is it seen as a second-level and more technical matter which can be safely left to the ministry of public administration (or the Cabinet Office in the UK) as a coordinating department? Or is it devolved still further to the individual ministries (such as the Department of Health), with the risk that no coherent cross-government strategy emerges?

# Applying Pollitt and Bouckaert's adapted framework

We now apply this adapted analytic framework to the UK government and then more specifically to the English health care sector. We note also where some underlying conditions appear to have changed since the Thatcher governments of the 1980s, which is taken as the period when our analysis starts.

## STRUCTURE OF THE STATE

The UK has traditionally been portrayed within much traditional political science literature as a unitary rather than a federal state, unlike (say) the USA. In this conventional account, political power is concentrated in the centre of London, notably in the Houses of Parliament and the central government departments (the so-called 'Westminster and Whitehall' model), including the Department of Health within the health policy domain. The competences of local and regional government have historically been weakly developed when compared to other more federalist European countries, such as Germany or Spain, and UK health services have historically been delivered nationally through the *National* Health Service rather than regionally.

However, there were major changes to the British constitution and in the distribution of health policymaking competences in the New Labour period (1997–2010), given a significant programme of devolution. Health policy competences were devolved to new assemblies in Scotland, Wales, and Northern Ireland around 2000. Major variation in the content of health policy quickly became evident between what were now the four UK nations, with England being more pro-market than the other three (Greer 2004). There are at the time of writing four elected ministers of health within the UK, drawn from four different political parties.

These devolutionary changes initially had only weak effects on the governance of the health care sector within England (where all our study sites are located) as there were no devolved regional assemblies set up there in the early 2000s (although this pattern has been recently changing as devolution has been extended to some English regions, as we explore in the next chapter). The operational NHS system in England remains firmly guided from above. It is currently regulated by NHS Improvement (following a 2016 reorganization and merger of various predecessor agencies) and the Care Quality Commission (CQC), which can be seen as the two national sector regulators which lead on finance/governance and care quality issues, respectively. NHS Improvement (as the name suggests) also claims on its website to take a stronger interest in service improvement activity than its predecessor bodies, which included the strongly financially orientated Monitor.

The English NHS field also has to take strong account of operational guidance from NHS England (created in 2013). In technical administrative terms, it is constituted as an executive non-departmental body of the Department of Health. While NHS England was originally concerned with developing the new post-2012 clinical commissioning groups (CCGs) in the primary care sector, it has more recently acquired more system-wide functions, for example, overseeing development of the so-called Sustainability and Transformation Plans (set up in 2016) across health and social care regional economies and also progressing the urgent task of restoring financial balance after big deficits emerged in various health care systems and localities from 2014 onwards.

There is also the question of the extent of horizontal coordination across Whitehall and implications for the status of the Department of Health. Horizontal coordination could in principle come from three different central departments. The first is the Cabinet Office which specializes in public management reform strategies across the various central departments, but which is often seen as a relatively low-profile department with few power resources. It does, however, have a standard methodology for reviewing the capabilities of individual central departments. Its capability review of the Department of Health (Cabinet Office 2007), for example, assessed it as well placed in the management of performance and reasserting financial control but weak on articulating a coherent strategy for the future of health and social care. It was also seen as poor at change management and as failing to promote a coherent or positive culture, as the 'high proportion of staff drawn from the NHS and other non-civil service backgrounds, combined with a number of restructuring exercises, have contributed to the sense that the department lacks its own culture distinct from that of the NHS or a set of behavioural values that are common to all Department of Health staff and which drive a positive culture' (Cabinet Office 2007, 17).

The second central department of interest in terms of horizontal coordination is the Treasury or the finance ministry (so it is armed with the strong power of the purse) which has a keen interest in stimulating departmental productivity and performance across Whitehall. A core tool in the New Labour period was the Public Service Agreement method whereby the Treasury bilaterally made agreements with spending departments, which set them objectives in exchange for resources. For example, the Department of Health was set eight Public Service Agreement targets in the 2004 spending review, including 'by 2010, increase life expectancy at birth in England to 78.6 years for men and 82.5 years for women' (Cabinet Office 2007). However, these Public Service Agreements were abolished by the Coalition government in 2010 in an attempt to lighten the performance management systems inherited from New Labour (Panchamia and Thomas 2010).

The third central department of interest is the Prime Minister's Office which may take a top-level and strategic political overview. The question is whether public management reform reaches the top of the Prime Minister's ever busy agenda. If so, what institutional arrangements are put in place (to be considered later) to encourage departmental 'delivery' lower down the system? Prime ministers may also vary personally in their style and preferred balance between direction and devolution to the departments. The administrations of Margaret Thatcher and Tony Blair, for instance, appeared to have constructed public management reform as a strategic issue for them personally, whereas that of David Cameron (2010–16) appeared in this field, as in others, to be more collegial and devolutionary.

These three different central departments may or may not be aligned in their cross-departmental efforts depending, for example, on the nature and warmth of the political relationship between the Prime Minister and the Chancellor of the Exchequer, which indeed appeared to be difficult at times in the New Labour period.

There is also an academic controversy within some political science literature about whether these core central departments in UK government should be seen as hegemonic or whether, in a cabinet system, the 'departmental barons' in the big spending departments (including the Department of Health) retain a strong power base. Some authors detect a long-term growth of an executive centre in the Prime Minister's Office (Holliday 2000) and argue that the central core of government remains well resourced (Marinetto 2003). Certainly, both the Thatcher and Blair administrations were marked by strong advisory units set up within 10 Downing Street to advise the Prime Minister directly (later largely unwound under David Cameron) on public management reform, including an attempt to construct a semi-scientific knowledge base around 'delivery'. On the other hand, Rhodes (2007; also Bevir and Rhodes 2006) argues that the core centre has only hyperactive 'rubber levers' to pull which appear highly visible but have little real or long-term effect. In this view, power remains dispersed within the departments in a more 'decentred' mode.

There is the specific question of how these core central departments have related to the Department of Health within the health policy domain. Greer and Jarman's (2007) interesting study of the transformation of the Department of Health from a conventional Whitehall department to what they see as a politically and ministerially desired 'Department of Delivery' in the New Labour period (1997–2010) is instructive. Civil service numbers were reduced and in addition (and this was a distinctive development within this department) it was 'hollowed out' by NHS managers from below who replaced traditional civil servants: at the time of their study, only one of the thirty-two most senior posts in the department was occupied by a career civil servant.

Greer and Jarman concluded (2007, 31): 'the Department of Health is NHS dominated with a strong managerial ethos and very little civil service representation at the top. This is the outcome of a long process in which managerial skills came to be valued more than those of the civil service and the management of the NHS more than the broader remit of health'. They suggested that possible disadvantages of such managerialization included the weakening of the old cross-Whitehall civil service networks which might be especially useful for tackling many 'cross-cutting' issues, which might involve other social policy departments such as education or work and pensions. Over-managerialization also presented a danger of a loss of organizational memory and a poorer capacity for independent civil service advice into ministerially driven health policymaking. Greer and Jarman (2007, 15) also note: 'Number 10 has been deeply involved in the Department of Health and the Treasury has cited it as a model department. It is clear enough that it is doing much of what the government wanted.' It is not clear from this statement to what extent the Prime Minister's units and the Treasury exerted a direct influence on the department or whether they less directly supported and commended what was in any case a strong internally driven process of managerialization. This managerialization was already evident in an earlier study (Day and Klein 1997), which also detected the emergence of distinct civil service and managerialist cultures (and this theme is later repeated in the report by the Cabinet Office 2007).

The Department of Health, in essence, constitutes a small policy centre but also connects with a vast and politically visible operational field. The managers in this operational field have to a considerable extent 'hollowed out' the department from below. The NHS field retains strong reporting lines up to the ever-monitoring national operational centre, especially in times of financial pressure and ballooning deficits.

Up to the mid-1980s, national management capacity in the health care sector was poorly developed. Initially, an NHS Management Board was set up in 1985 (Day and Klein 1997) in an attempt to separate policy and operations, duly reflecting key NPM doctrines. The Board later morphed into the NHS Executive (1995) with a stronger management presence and as part of an attempt to construct a line management system across the whole NHS (Day and Klein 1997) for the first time. The NHS Executive also had its own headquarters in Leeds, leading to a boost in business for the rail network as civil servants now had to travel frequently on trains between London and Leeds (Day and Klein 1997, 14) to attend meetings.

Overall, therefore, we suggest there appears to be strong vertical concentration of power in England (and the NHS field) but the extent of horizontal coordination across Whitehall, specifically the extent to which core coordinating departments influence the Department of Health, is contested. Greer and Jarman (2007) argue that the Treasury has held up a delivery-focused and heavily managerialized Department of Health as a model department for Whitehall more widely. On the other hand, the lack of a strong career civil service presence in the department's core team suggests only weak representation in core Whitehall networks. Its policymaking capacity may also have been eroded by waves of downsizing. Greer and Jarman (2007) suggest strong 'hollowing out' of the department from below by the NHS managerial field which brought with it an intense focus on operational delivery. The frequent use of the word 'delivery' in English health management discourse is a strong NPM signifier linguistically.

## THE CONVENTIONS OF EXECUTIVE GOVERNMENT

The UK parliamentary system is normally majoritarian in nature as the first-past-the-post electoral system makes it difficult for smaller political parties to win seats and favours the formation of one-party governments which seek to enact the manifesto on which they were elected. The 2010–15 coalition between a larger and a smaller party (Conservatives and Liberal Democrats) was an important exception to this pattern but was followed by a reversion to single-party government (Conservative) after the 2015 election. There has not been a grand coalition between the two main political parties in the UK since the 1940s (unlike Germany). The two-party system is more confrontational than consensual in tone, with incoming governments often demonizing the inherited public management reforms of the last government (as in 2010 with the Coalition's denouncing of New Labour's 'tick box' culture in the NHS as in other public services). The non-elected revising chamber (House of Lords) lacks democratic legitimacy and plays a much more minor role than the House of Commons. Executive government is led by a cabinet of senior ministers (including the Secretary of State for Health) who take collective responsibility for all major policy decisions.

Broadly speaking, therefore, our analysis suggests English conventions of government favour nationally based, top-down, and synoptic approaches to public management reform, including in health care. The content of such reforms may however be quickly reversed with a change of national party-political control, with yesterday's reforms quickly becoming demonized in their turn.

## THE PATTERN OF MINISTER AND MANDARIN RELATIONS

Pollitt and Bouckaert (2011, 61) see the UK government as characterized by a neutral and permanent civil service where personnel have a reasonable expectation of a high degree of tenure. They also comment on the long-term rise of the number of so-called 'special advisers' who provide more directly political advice to ministers. We further note more permeability between traditional career pathways with more personnel originally from local government back-grounds now being placed in senior Whitehall posts than was evident historically, perhaps as a result of a greater premium being placed on their extensive service delivery experience at a local level—perhaps in a big city authority—within the 'delivery'-based central departments. As we will explore, there also appears to be greater diversity in sources of policy advice. Nevertheless, the core civil service remains in place, even if it has been recently downsized (Cabinet Office 2012b). Repeated references, once again, to the need for a 'pacier' and change-orientated civil service in this recent policy text (Cabinet Office 2012b) suggest that many previous attempts to change the underlying and cautious culture of the civil service may not have been entirely successful.

As already noted, the Department of Health appears to have become an NPM model department and has even been seen as an outlier within Whitehall with its strong managerialism and 'delivery' focus. Greer and Jarman argue:

The Department of Health comes closest to being the department many politicians want when they seek to make the bureaucracy more responsive—small, working through agencies, almost free of civil servants at the top (and maybe middle) ranks, less committed to job security, relatively focussed on the delivery of political objectives rather than policy or risk analysis, weak in policy research capacity but willing to respond to central direction and filled with subject specialists rather than generalists.    (2007, 15)

We argue such a configuration potentially opens a receptive space within the department for the high-impact diffusion of managerialist thinking and texts.

## Underlying culture and philosophy of government

The UK remains an Anglo-Saxon public interest state without the special codes of administrative law found in European *Rechtsstaat* states. Nor do UK civil servants—still less NHS managers—have the legal protections accorded to German upper civil servants. There is a body of UK public law, however. The UK Administrative Court can intervene when asked to undertake a judicial review of administrative decisions, although the costs borne by complainants in such cases can be heavy and can even discourage them from taking such drastic action. The process of judicial review in the UK is closely concerned with whether the present law has been well applied and the correct procedures followed. If found against, it is open to ministers to go back to Parliament to seek to change the law.

Despite this narrow construction, Hood and Dixon (2015, 123) argue that, over the last thirty years, the scope of judicial review has increased to bring more public bodies into its remit and the criterion of 'unreasonableness' has been relaxed. Hood and Dixon's (2015) longitudinal study of the impact of UK NPM-style reforms over three decades took some 'due process' indicators to explore whether these reforms led to an erosion of traditional Weberian virtues in public agencies, for example, in such areas as fair and consistent decision-making. One indicator taken was the number of requests for judicial review, seen as a possible marker of citizen discontent with the process of administrative decision-making. They concluded (p. 124) that non-immigration-related requests for review tripled over the period (with an even greater increase in immigration-related requests, which can however be seen as a special case). While the proportion of such cases which were given leave to proceed further at the first hearing also fell, some of this could be accounted for by an increase in cases with informal settlements which led them to be classified as 'withdrawn'. There was in sum some (admittedly contestable) evidence of increased recourse by groups and citizens to judicial review to contest administrative decisions.

There are some specialist areas in health care with a well-developed body of administrative law, such as mental health tribunals which rule on individuals' detention within mental hospitals. Management decisions in the NHS—especially around the rationing of services and the closure of hospitals—might potentially also be seen as territory ripe for judicial review, given their importance for local populations and their frequently controversial and contested nature.

Some interesting recent judicial review cases included a successful request from an AIDS charity against NHS England's decision not to fund a new drug that could prevent infection with HIV on the grounds that it did not have the power: a phased implementation is now being rolled out (NHS England 2016b). A group of junior doctors (eventually unsuccessfully) challenged the Secretary of State for Health over a new national jobs contract (where the Secretary of State also asked the court for a £150,000 cost protection order: Crowdjustice 2016). Local community groups were also successful in securing judicial review in 2013 to stop the Secretary of State's proposal to close key services in the popular Lewisham hospital in South London (Courts and Tribunals Judiciary 2013) as part of a wider restructuring of services locally. The grounds given were narrow in that the view was that the trust special administrator appointed by the Secretary of State had exceeded his powers in intervening beyond the trust directly concerned. The Secretary of State appealed in this case but lost.

Despite these interesting cases, the extent of judicial review in health care remains rare and narrowly constructed in terms of whether the Secretary of State or his agents have exceeded their existing powers. The NHS has set up extensive internally facing advisory machinery to help reduce the number of cases going forward to judicial review. For instance, NICE issues guidance on the clinical and cost effectiveness of new drugs and treatments for the NHS. Its standardized decision-making processes include both expert technical appraisal and also sophisticated stakeholder consultation and consensus-building processes (Ferlie and McGivern 2014) which build scientific and interest group legitimacy and which are difficult to challenge. Proposals for hospital closures now go an Independent Reconfiguration Panel with a mix of lay, clinical, and managerial members at an early stage to receive informal advice. The panel tries to develop consensus before the parties have recourse to expensive and time-consuming judicial review.

We conclude, on balance, that the juridification of English health policy and management arenas remains narrowly constructed and that therefore politicians and managers retain considerable scope for decisions and action.


## The pluralization of policy advice

While there remains a strong and independent civil service in the UK, central departments have recently been downsized (Cabinet Office 2012b) with an average planned 23 per cent headcount reduction between 2010 and 2015. The Department of Health historically had a small headcount, estimated as only 4,280 in 2004 (Greer and Jarman 2007) as it had already at that stage been subjected to several restructuring and downsizing exercises.

Page et al. (2014) note that many central departments have been successful in managing these ambitious headcount reduction targets. They estimate there was a 16 per cent reduction in Department of Health headcount between 2010 and 2013. By 2016, recent workforce data suggest the central Department of Health now had an estimated civil service headcount of 1,900 full-time equivalent staff (FTE), of which only 168 were in the senior civil service grades. However, some departmental staff may have been exported to large non-departmental public bodies, including NHS England, which might distort the figures. The newly appointed Permanent Secretary (2016) is once again a career civil servant and an ex-Permanent Secretary at the Department of Education. There is a double-headed leadership in practice, with the Permanent Secretary working alongside the high-profile Chief Executive of NHS England who heads up the large managerial function.

The traditional Westminster and Whitehall model sees the civil service as the core source of advice to ministers. Yet some political science authors argue the civil service has recently been increasingly complemented by other sources, reflecting 'the pluralization of policy advice in Whitehall' (Gains and Stoker 2011). There have always been short-term and task-focused committees of enquiry led by eminent outside experts and this pattern continues (a good recent example in health care is the 2013 Berwick Report on events in Mid Staffs NHS Foundation Trust hospitals).

In the New Labour period, some senior experts were brought in from outside as so-called 'policy tsars' to coordinate policy in particular fields nationally. The health care sector housed various policy 'tsars', known more formally as

National Service Directors, who often advised the Department of Health on how to ramp up quality standards across the NHS in important and visible conditions (e.g. 'the cancer tsar'). These health care tsars were often clinical academics and professors from major universities with well-established personal research reputations which gave them the scientific legitimacy so important in the health care field, although the time period they lasted in the very different world of Whitehall was variable. They can be seen as representing a novel and senior-level hybrid role between civil servant and outside expert.

A third development has been the expansion of the number of special advisers. Pollitt and Bouckaert (2011, 61) suggest that from the mid-1990s (i.e. the early New Labour period) there was an increasing use of special advisers within Whitehall. They are used to enhance the level of political advice given both to the Prime Minister (who is supported by a large number of special advisers) and to departmental ministers. Special advisers tend to be younger and more politically orientated than the 'tsars' and often have an applied public-policy or think-tank background and, indeed, in some cases future, once their spell in Whitehall comes to an end.

Gains and Stoker (2011) argue that many special advisers combine the three functions of policy development, political support, and media ('spin') work. It is their ideas development work that is of special interest here as potentially they can broker links and move ideas between the civil service, political parties, pressure groups, and academics. Clearly special advisers' close links with think tanks are of great interest and potentially importance, although one special adviser interviewed by Gains and Stoker (2011) was also keen to identify key academic experts in a particular policy field directly as influential sources of advice. Occasionally, senior social science academics are seconded to act as special advisers for a period but then go back to their university chairs.

Recent data (HM Government 2017) suggest there are currently three special advisers in the Department of Health, while the Prime Minister's office now has just over thirty special advisers, with some of the more senior advisers appearing to have a roving brief across departments. Greer and Jarman (2007, 26) suggest that the downsizing of civil service posts in the department may have led to more of the continuing policy work being undertaken by special advisers and management consultants instead.

Think tanks are another source of advice from outside the civil service. The organization and evolution of the field of policy research institutes or 'think tanks' in both the USA and UK has been explored by Stone (1996). Think tanks were historically founded as quasi-academic and non-profit organizations (such as the Brookings Institute in Washington, DC), undertaking applied and policy-orientated research on a public interest basis and employing highly technically trained and more applied social scientists to work on policy-related questions. Compared to university academic departments, however, think tanks placed more emphasis on network building and their outputs were broader, stressing the use of a greater variety of communication modes beyond the peer-reviewed article or monograph (Stone 1996, 16): 'the primary products of think tanks are research analysis and advice. Policy advice comes in a variety of formats, ranging from the multiple messages of books, journals, newsletters, magazine stories and op ed pieces, to tapes, videos, radio and television programming'.

Since the 1970s, newer think tanks have sought to differentiate themselves in what has become a crowded market: an expanding number of think tanks with an interest in health policy is also evident in the narrower London context. Stone (1996) suggests that there are four different subgroups to be discerned: (i) ideological think tanks; (ii) specialist or sectoral think tanks; (iii) locally based think tanks (found more in the USA than the UK); and (iv) 'think and do' tanks which combine advice with advocacy and social action.

Politically aligned think tanks are clustered in central London, often housed close to the Houses of Parliament and providing ready access to ideas, advice, and seminars to parliamentarians. One of the oldest London think tanks is the centre-left Fabian Society, close to the intellectual wing of the Labour Party (founded as long ago as 1884). There has been a presence of New Right think tanks in London since the 1950s. The Institute of Economic Affairs was founded as early as 1955 and supplied basic free-market ideas which helped fuel the Thatcher revolution of the 1980s. The Institute of Economic Affairs was highly influential under Margaret Thatcher's administrations and its advice enabled her to supplement or even bypass traditional civil servants. This trend to the New Right was partially offset by the influence of the centre-left Institute of Public Policy Research (IPPR), founded in 1988 (also informally known as 'a pink tank'—Stone 1996, 23), which helped develop New Labour thinking for its period in government. These think tanks may also provide a flow of special advisers to ministers. Unusually, IPPR has a separate presence in Edinburgh, Manchester, and Newcastle, as well as London. Stone (1996, 23) detects a less rationalist and more ideological tone in some of the newer think tanks: 'a common theme among the new institutes is an emphasis on marketing and promotion. Their advocacy in policy debates combines a strong ideological policy or partisan position with aggressive salesmanship'.

Other think tanks are sectorally based and party-politically neutral (e.g. Chatham House specializes in international affairs). Within the health care sector, well-known London-based think tanks include the King's Fund (with an interest in health policy and leadership); the Nuffield Trust (the economics of health), and the relatively newly founded Health Foundation, a major charitable endowment with a special interest in service and quality improvement. The Wellcome Trust not only acts as a large research grant funder for medical research but also takes a special interest in science policy where it has strong influence as a major funder. English health policymakers have also been interested in the broader but sectorally relevant work of two more recently founded think tanks: the Young Foundation's work on social enterprises and social innovation and that of NESTA on the digital economy. More politically aligned think tanks which are active in the health policy area include Reform (centre right) and IPPR (centre left).

Finally, management consultants have emerged as highly significant players in providing advice in the arena of UK public services reform, including in health care. Many large consultancies have set up major offices in central London so are geographically close to government, helping the interchange of key personnel.

We have little academic work on the role of management consultants in the UK health care sector, despite their importance. Kirkpatrick et al.'s (2016) chapter is a rare exception. They suggest that while management consultants were not involved in writing some of the key reform texts of the 1980s (Griffiths 1983 was a seconded businessman, Enthoven 1985 an American academic), the new quasi-market (1990–7) provided them with major business opportunities in developing the new billing and ICT systems required.

Kirkpatrick et al. (2016) further suggested that these consultancies display strong adaptability to changing political conditions. While the New Labour period was marked (at least initially) by a swing away from the quasi-market, New Labour governments also outsourced policy and implementation advice. So consultancies (Kirkpatrick et al. 2016, 533) now (re)represented themselves as partners in 'modernization', supporting e-government and also giving advice on service changes. Kirkpatrick et al.'s (2016, 525) review of considerable post-2010 consulting activity (e.g. in offering analysis to the new commissioning support units set up to improve capability in the underpowered purchasing side) led them to conclude 'how management consultants have become deeply involved in most aspects of the business of managing and organizing health care in the NHS'. They were also developing broader think tank-like activities and partnering with major universities (such as a joint venture between McKinsey and Company and the London School of Economics). Finally, they were supporting large-scale organizational change programmes within the NHS such as Lean, big data, and culture change (where there is a partnership between KPMG and the NHS Leadership Academy). We will present our case-study data on the role of management consultants in health care reform in a later chapter.

## Is public management reforming constructed as a top-level political issue?

One final consideration to add to Pollitt and Bouckaert's (2011) list of dimensions is more subjective than institutional in nature. It is the question of whether public management reform is constructed as a top-level issue which remains high on the always crowded agenda of the Prime Minister. Alternatively, is it a theme largely delegated to the Cabinet Office (which may lack the clout of the PM's units) or even the individual departments (with the implication that cross-Whitehall reform strategies are then likely to be weak)?

Public management reform might be thought to be a largely politically invisible and highly technical subject, of interest to voters only when government's costs are excessive (leading to strong resentment of high taxation), and/or the quality of key services is exceptionally poor and easily detectable as such by consumers and voters (as in the case of schools where pupils leave unable to read or write). Under which political circumstances, therefore, might public management reform rise up to the top of prime ministerial agendas? For Margaret Thatcher, restoring governability to the public sector was an overriding political aim after the wave of public-sector strikes of 1978–9 which helped bring her to power. As well as introducing legal changes to the industrial relations framework to reduce the power of the unions, staff in public agencies were now subjected to the fierce NPM-style discipline of markets and management. In addition, the government's strategic aim of reducing the size of the public sector and associated high taxation levels and making the private sector more competitive required active cost controls and efficiency-increasing measures across the whole of the public services, including in the large and expensive health care domain. The Treasury had the key power of the purse over all the spending departments and could use it to provoke cost control and downsizing.

The political pressures facing Tony Blair in the early 2000s were very different. New Labour had promised to end a long period of Conservative 'neglect' in public services investment and started to redeem this pledge in the early 2000s with big increases in NHS funding now coming through. Its core political coalition included the public-sector unions and much of urban local government, alongside groups of voters/consumers who wanted high-profile improvements in core services (e.g. better educational outcomes in schools, lower waiting times in the NHS, refurbishment of shoddy estates). Blair set up and used his own Prime Minister's Delivery Unit (created in 2001 under the direction of Michael Barber in the Cabinet Office) to monitor and stimulate departmental progress on top-priority Public Service Agreement objectives (Panchamia and Thomas 2010). The Prime Minister's Delivery Unit kept pressure on by, for example, producing league tables of departments on an evidential basis. They tried to ensure that large increases in public spending (as in the NHS from 2000 onwards) were quickly translated into visible service improvements that would reap electoral rewards.

After 2010, however, David Cameron dismantled the special units inherited from Blair (though he retained a large group of special advisers) and the leadership of public management reform passed down to the Cabinet Office.

Austerity pressures became increasingly dominant, again increasing the power of the Treasury. Coalition government (2010–15) may also have made the public management reform strategy less ideologically coherent. We consider the story of public and health policy reform in the 2010–15 period more fully in the next chapter. We do not go beyond 2015 to the premiership of Theresa May as our data belong to an earlier period and in any case, it is far too early to come to any informed assessment.

Overall, we suggest that for both Margaret Thatcher and Tony Blair public management reform became a key political priority, albeit for very different reasons, but that its importance as a top-level issue declined after 2010 under David Cameron. A possible implication may be that the Thatcher and Blair periods may have a greater long-term legacy in the domain of public management reform than that of Cameron.

## Concluding remarks and overall assessment

Using Pollitt and Bouckaert's (2011) framing as a heuristic device, we therefore suggest the political and institutional conditions found within the English political economy broadly facilitate top-down, controversial, and politically driven public management reforming strategies (Pollitt and Bouckaert 2011). Reflecting basic institutional conditions, such reforms can also be expected to seek to open the public sector to outside and more 'business-like' forms of thinking, as indeed seen in the NPM reforms strongly apparent throughout the period reviewed.

Scotland and Wales present a different picture after the devolution reforms of the early 2000s and appear less market-like in their approaches to public management reforming. However, the core of English government remains both centralized and market orientated. The political system remains broadly majoritarian and non-consensual, although the 2010–15 coalition was an important exception to this rule. While there is still an independent civil service with a high expectation of tenure, its position appears to have been weakened by repeated restructuring and downsizing exercises, and the growth of special advisers offering more political sources of advice. The juridification of government remains narrow and contained, leaving the door open to a broad scope for political and managerial action. It is possible that there has been considerable pluralization in terms of sources of policy advice to ministers which now go well beyond the traditional civil service to include such providers as think tanks and management consultants, strongly clustered in central London.

We adapted the Pollitt and Bouckaert (2011) model by adding a sixth dimension: the extent to which public management reform was constructed as a strategic and top-level political issue. Our review of the administrative history of UK central government suggested that there were significant periods (under Margaret Thatcher and Tony Blair) in which public management reform was a top-level prime ministerial issue. We still know too little about the extent to which the departments of the core central executive have been able to influence the Department of Health, although all three (Cabinet Office, Treasury, and PM's office) have been active in the health field. However, we noted that the high-level importance of the public management reform issue appears to have declined at the prime ministerial level after 2010.

The health care sector in England—where there is no elected regional tier of government and a weak local government presence—strongly reflects these broader conditions and should not be seen as an exception to them. The NHS Executive still takes overall responsibility for ensuring and monitoring operational delivery at field level. The Department of Health appears to have been 'hollowed out' from below by the NHS managerial field and to have developed a strongly managerialist focus on 'delivery' more than policy development.

We finally argue that these basic conditions potentially create an opening to alternative knowledge producers, texts, and knowledges coming from outside the traditional public sector, alongside the wider rise of novel actors (special advisers, think tanks, management consultants, expert advisers) and evidence of their movement into Whitehall settings.

Despite Scott et al.'s (2001) interesting observation cited at the start of this chapter, possible long-term changes in preferred public management *knowledge(s)* remain a generally under-studied topic within the conventional public management literature. Hill and Hupe (2009, 89) do briefly suggest that NPM reforms have created a significant knowledge shift from traditional political science/public administration knowledge within government towards the greater use of organizational economics and public-choice models. However, their high-level observation requires further study of these shifts in practice and the processes by which they occur.

Well-known private sector-orientated management texts appear to have been readily diffused into UK health care organizations. The earliest well-known example explored general organizational themes such as change management and excellence (Peters and Waterman 1982). Hughes' (1996) analysis of this text's ready diffusion into the Welsh NHS in the late 1980s—despite its attachment to a 'soft' cultural school of strategy which might be thought to sit badly with the emergent and delivery-focused NPM work cultures—is interesting as an empirically well-grounded case study of an early diffusion process. This text seems to represent the first example of what was to become a repeated diffusion cycle as it is followed by a number of other high-profile management texts, again suggesting the mid-1980s should be seen as an important break point in the political economy of UK public management reform.

So, there has been strong interest in models of performance management and measurement (Kaplan and Norton 1996; see also the case study in

Chapter 7 presented later), business process re-engineering change programmes (Hammer and Champy 1993; McNulty and Ferlie 2002, 2004), and value-based approaches to health care (Porter and Teisberg 2006), all now being picked up by major NHS hospitals in London (Trenholm et al. 2016), despite the American origins of these texts. Additionally, alternative and softer 'organizational learning' ideas were strongly endorsed by Berwick (2013) as a preferred direction for health policy. These generic management themes, of course, make more sense in the new 'firm-like' settings created by waves of top-down and NPM-orientated reforms, notably so in the NHS foundation trusts and also in the growing number of independent health care providers.

In the next chapter, we bring the English public management reform story more up to date by considering the main policies in relation to strategies of public management reform and then more specifically health care management introduced by the Coalition government of 2010–15. This chapter will also explore the increasing impact of policies designed to ramp up productivity levels in English health care in the new era of austerity after the global financial crash of 2008, notably in the large-scale QIPP change programme. We argue that these pressures further facilitated the importing of operations management-orientated Lean-based texts and knowledges from the private sector, which held out the promise that health services could become simultaneously more cost-effective and quality assured.

# 4 English public management reform after 2010

## From Big Society to austerity

## Introduction

This chapter characterizes the main approaches to public management reform in England apparent during the 2010–15 period of government which was (unusually) formed by a coalition between the Conservative and Liberal Democrat parties. It then picks out more specific implications from wider public sector-wide reform narratives for the study and conceptualization of organizational changes within the English health care sector. This chapter thus updates the previous chapter's presentation of two earlier macro-level narratives of UK public services reform, notably the New Public Management (NPM) narrative ascendant in the long period of Conservative governments (1979–97) and a later network governance (NG) model associated with New Labour governments (1997–2010). It concentrates on the English case because network governance reforms around 2000 devolved competences in health policy to the three other UK nations and also because all our case studies are based in England.

We draw on a small but developing narrative-based stream in public administration scholarship (Borins 2011) which examines the 'stories' found in public policy and management texts. UK public management reforms are often rhetorically justified in official texts, notably so in successive government documents which produce officially sanctioned proposals (known as white papers) for renewing the machinery of government (see Pollitt's 2013 helpful overview). There appears to have been a recurrent pattern of policy-driven and top-down reforming in the UK public services for over forty years (Moran 2003; Pollitt 2013). These successive white papers seek to produce persuasive narratives which mix values, facts, positive case studies, and doctrines to promise readers a better future (Ferlie et al. 2016). We ask: What narrative—if any—of public management reforming was dominant in the period of the Coalition (2010–15)?

We start with some basic but important contextual points. First, the 2010–15 Coalition government (Conservative and Liberal Democrat) was an unusual period in terms of the party-political composition of government. The Coalition was a rare experiment for the normally majoritarian UK political system, as it included two different political parties working in a formal coalition. Their agreed programme in the key domain of fiscal policy was to pursue a strong deficit-reduction policy and to restrain public expenditure. The Coalition replaced a long period of New Labour governments (1997–2010) and lasted a full parliamentary term, contrary to the predictions of sceptics. It was followed in the 2015 general election by the election of a Conservative-only government and the minority party (Liberal Democrats) lost many of its parliamentary seats. Leading representatives of these two different political parties were in the 2010–15 period jointly writing public policy texts, so there might well be thought to be a loss of ideological coherence, as brokering and negotiation over different words, ideas, and pledges would necessarily take place between the two governing parties.

Second, the 2010–15 period was both distinctive and challenging economically and fiscally. The global economic crisis apparent from 2008 onwards had strong effects in the UK, reflecting its vulnerable basic conditions of a highly open economy, an inflated property market, a large and exposed financial services sector, high levels of personal, corporate, and government borrowing, and a large fiscal deficit for government. The period of buoyant public expenditure growth apparent in the 2000–8 period under New Labour (see Chapter 3) now suddenly ended. These deteriorating fiscal conditions potentially opened up an important policy role for the Treasury with its typical emphasis on fiscal consolidation and pursuing substantial public expenditure reductions across different government departments. The political choice taken was to pursue a strong programme of deficit reduction (not in the end realized) and to load this deficit-reduction strategy on public expenditure reductions rather than tax increases.

The chapter will examine several important public and health management-related policy texts produced by Conservative-leaning think tanks and then the government from this period. However, we conclude that it appears difficult to establish a strong overall or sustained narrative of public management reforming (see also Pollitt 2013). The chapter explores what we see as an early 'Big Society' proto-reform narrative which was being proposed around 2010 but then argues that it failed to become institutionalized. We trace some basic communitarian ideas within currents of social science which lay behind this Big Society drive and then explore how they diffused into the world of Conservative politics and public policymaking through key writers and associated think tanks. This thinking led to some attempts to restimulate professional engagement and leadership, most notably in the creation of clinical commissioning groups (CCGs), in 2013, as a new form of membership organization in the primary care sector. However, we will present a vignette of the changing fortunes of CCGs which illustrates the limits to this clinical leadership strand of policy. We suggest that principles of clinical engagement and downwards modes of accountability had little staying power in the CCG settings as financial restrictions—policed from above—started to bite here too.

In the end, however, we argue that wider post-2008 austerity pressures ended up driving the wider public and health management reform agenda, closely associated with a tight overall fiscal policy set by the Treasury. So, austerity replaced Big Society. Another reason highlighted for the failure of the Big Society project to take off was the loss of interest in public management reform at the political heart of government (i.e. the Prime Minister's Office), so that reform leadership was delegated to what might be seen as the less powerful Cabinet Office which acted as a coordinator across Whitehall.

Within the English health care sector, just as in other public services, the chapter argues that there was a marked revival in this post-2008 age of austerity of NPM-style doctrines of marketization, strong financial control, and productivity enhancement. While the health care sector was relatively protected financially when compared to other public services (e.g. local government), it still faced major productivity pressures.

The chapter will start by reviewing communitarian ideas that lay behind the initial Big Society project and then explore how they crossed into the political and public policy worlds through the medium of London think tanks and associated key authors. It will then argue that the 'proto'-reform narrative around Big Society was eventually overwhelmed by a rival and more powerful austerity discourse.

## Communitarianism and the Big Society project

An initial vision of what was called the 'Big Society' was central to the strategy for public management reform outlined in the 2010 Conservative election manifesto and then brought into the Coalition government (2010–15). It was personally supported and championed by the newly elected Prime Minister, David Cameron (House of Commons PAC 2011). Norman (2010, 2) recalls that Cameron first called for a Big Society approach to public services reform in the Hugo Young annual lecture of 2009. His then Director of Strategy (Steve Hilton) was also closely associated with the development and advocacy of these ideas. However, in this and the next two sections we argue that, in retrospect, Big Society achieved intense but also short-lived pre-eminence.

Norman (2010, 199) was relatively optimistic at an admittedly early stage that the project would be implemented and would achieve high long-term impact: 'the Big Society's political programme is being vigorously implemented. It is likely to amount to the most thoroughgoing attempt for a century to redefine the relationship between the individual, the state and public and private institutions'.

Writing in 2011, Scott concluded:

At the current time, Big Society, or BS as some Tory backbenchers have termed it, has nonetheless achieved a remarkable ideological ascendancy. Regardless of how it fares in the coming years, and the prognosis for revivified social action amidst austerity cannot be good since empirically people volunteer less at times of recession, BS is a triumph in articulating and updating the neoliberal settlement.   (Scott 2011, 132)

Scott (2011) also suggested that exaggerated rhetoric of Big Society ideas could soon be followed by their collapse, given what already appeared to be internal contradictions. We will return to the theme of exaggerated rhetoric and BS in our concluding chapter, when we consider our findings in the context of recent global changes since our empirical research.

Big Society thinking was less market-based than the old Thatcherite recipes of the 1980s, as it implied extensive use of the third sector on the service delivery side, as opposed to simple privatization. Unlike 1980s-style neo-liberal doctrines which came intellectually from public choice theory and organizational economics, Big Society built on communitarian ideas emerging in the 1990s within currents of thought in sociology, as advocated by major American social scientists such as Etzioni (1994, 1998) and Putnam (2000).

Etzioni (1994, 1998) outlined key ideas of this American communitarian move-ment which reacted against what was seen as a period of high liberalism. Their slogan could well be summarized as: 'too many rights; too few responsibilities'. Communitarianism represented in his view a radical 'third way' between trad-itional liberals and conservatives. There was a need in this analysis to set a better balance between individual rights (on which there had been too much stress) and wider social responsibilities. Building the good society lay beyond relying just on the market (or the state) as a governance mechanism and recognized the import-ance of informal social bonds and the development of a collective moral sense.

Etzioni (1994) traced through possible public policy implications of this high-level positioning. Communitarians were likely to defend the idea of the 'public interest' and be sceptical of the role of moneyed or special interests in the public policy process. They would be concerned to protect civilizing 'public goods' (such as urban parks) against private appropriation. They would also be likely to defend the importance of strong family structures (including two-rather than one-parent families) and high-quality schools as basic socialization mechanisms. They would be interested in fostering community building ini-tiatives in deprived social settings, often being undertaken by grassroots pro-jects and community groups working at the neighbourhood level. Social movements and associated social-movement organizations were of particular interest as they were often non-profit organizations which had a strong culture and ideology which was effective in raising collective energy and commitment levels among their supporters. We comment that social-movement organiza-tions could be important in certain areas of health care service provision where identity politics helped shape a user voice, as in the strong influence of user-orientated social movements in such varied settings as mental health, child-birth, and HIV/AIDS.

In an influential book, Putnam (2000) empirically and quantitatively traced what he saw as a major sociological trend, namely the long-run decline since the 1960s of 'social capital' (as expressed in participation in social networks) and associated levels of civic engagement within American society. He was most concerned about the atomization of American society and its serious negative implications for citizens' well-being.

There were various factors involved in his view in such atomization, including the growth of television, suburbanization, the decline of church-going, and generational succession, with the dying out of the 'civic generation' of the 1940s and 1950s. Normatively, Putnam (2000, ch. 24) called for a wider project to rebuild social capital. In what remained a relatively brief discussion of concrete implications for re-tilting public policy (pp. 412–14), Putnam calls for a revival of grassroots political participation and restrictions on big donations to political campaigns. Organizations that can produce 'bridging social capital' (i.e. bring previously unconnected people together), such as team sports clubs and also arts organizations, should be favoured in policy. Decentralization of responsibility for service provision to neighbourhood councils should be encouraged, although national government should still play an important agenda-setting role and help in sponsoring promising social innovations (as it had on occasion in the past).

The Big Society project had domestic political purposes as well as intellec-tual roots in communitarian social science. It was specifically associated with a so-called Red Tory movement which was politically and ideologically trying to outflank what had politically been a successful New Labour modernization project. Red Tory thinking tried to move the Conservative Party back into the centre ground, in part by signalling a more active and less neo-liberal social policy. Just as New Labour had 'triangulated' between the Old Left and the New Right, so the Big Society project tried to reclaim some social bases more associated historically with the Labour Party.

Blond's (2010) important and influential text *Red Tory* moved communitar-ian ideas further into the UK party-political and public policy domain, closely linked to a sympathetic London-based think tank, Res Publica, which was directed by Blond. His core diagnosis of the British political malaise (p. 2) was as follows: 'this gap between the politics of the elite and general mass disaffec-tion reflects, and is caused by, a wholescale collapse of British culture, virtue and belief'. The supposed disappearance of previously well-developed UK civil society was seen as a major negative development with profound social effects:

by civil society, I connote everything that ordinary citizens do that is not reducible to the imposed activities of the central state or the compulsion and determination of the marketplace. So defined, it appears we are a flat society. By this I mean that there are only two powers in our country: the state and the marketplace. All other sources of independent autonomous power have been crushed. (Blond 2010, 3)

The result was a dominant market/state where these two principles were now fused together rather than operating in opposition.

We note the attempt in this formulation to draw a divide between the concerns of the political elite and those of the disaffected masses. Interestingly, also, civil society groups (Blond 2010, 3) were deemed in the past to have enabled this non-elite to exercise some social and political power. They were here defined so as to include trade unions and co-operative societies, traditionally associated with the Labour Party, alongside other bodies such as local government and churches. Such historically evident organic working-class culture had in Blond's political analysis been eroded since the 1960s by a culture of conspicuous consumption and a cult of liberty which all too soon turned into licence, fuelled by the ideologies propagated by the New Left intelligentsia.

What then might be the solution? His chapter 10 (Blond 2010) addresses the question of how to build a reformed 'civil state' (p. 239) 'in which professional responsibility has been restored to individuals and professional groups'. There was a supposed need to harness the dedication and insights both of front-line workers who had been disengaged by over-controlling, top-down NPM reforms and also of public service users and citizens. The UK was indeed held up—and critiqued—as a radical proponent of the neo-liberal form of the state internationally. NPM reforms inspired by 1980s-style public choice theory had led in Blond's view to a harmful explosion of management, regulation, and audit systems which should now be rolled back, saving considerable costs: 'wasteful middle management and damaging accountability and audit structures can be reduced' (p. 240). There was also a plea for a revival of the old professional logic of self-regulation and peer-to-peer motivation within public services organizations that should be much flatter than they were at present.

The inheritance from earlier NPM reforms was assessed as clearly negative and leading to considerable operational problems:

its most practical legacy is two severe and structural problems in our public services. On the one hand, we have a demoralised public services workforce, sick of command and control and suspicious of anything described as reform. On the other, we have a track record of declining public-sector productivity that bodes ill for future attempts to restore the public finances.   (Blond 2010, 251)

The proclaimed remedy (chapter 10) was the greater use of social enterprises, employee ownership, and staff mutuals (p. 256) as new organizational forms to better harness the commitment of (often poorly paid) front-line public services workers. Here attention was paid to the motivation of producers as well as the wants of consumers. Mutuals would be likely to display less risk aversion and foster more innovation than public services organizations, yet they also had a greater sense of mission and a more equal culture than private firms (p. 258): 'where the governments of the 1980s and 1990s sought to outsource services to the private sector, this raises the question of "insourcing", devolving ownership and responsibility to the employees of services themselves, without some of the potentially disempowering and disincentivising effects sometimes associated with outsourcing and privatization'. Service quality improvements could be better assured through collegial and horizontal systems of peer review than the formalized external regulation typical of NPM systems. In addition, service users should be involved within a model of co-production. There had admittedly been some attempts to restimulate professional engagement in the public services in the New Labour period (such as in the Darzi Review 2008 in the health care sector which championed clinical leadership), but micro-management from above had broadly been the dominant mode of governance.

The large-scale and successful John Lewis Partnership in the UK retail sector (co-owned by its staff who are termed 'partners' and formally governed by a trust rather than shareholders) was held up by Blond (2010) as a role model for the public sector. We comment that John Lewis is unusual in its considerable scale and also commercial success and that many other co-operative ventures have remained small-scale and undercapitalized.

Norman (2010)'s exploration of Big Society, or what he termed 'compassionate conservatism', put the concept in a wider political and historical context. Writing from a Conservative perspective, he critiqued the individualist assumptions of conventional economics and called for the development of a more 'connected' society which could act as an alternative both to neoliberalism and also the extensive Fabian state favoured by the Labour Party (p. 2): 'our alternative to big government is not no government—some reheated version of ideological laissez-faire. Nor it is just smarter government. Our alternative to big government is the Big Society'. Norman (p. 29) conceded that there had been some examples of decentralizing reforms under New Labour (including the creation of NHS foundation trusts) but he argued (p. 29): 'the overall trend under Labour was towards centralization, however, with the state becoming hugely more pervasive after 1997'. There was a pattern in his view of micro management and ever-expanding regulation in public services management under New Labour that needed to be checked and reversed.

Norman has written widely on the Big Society theme, both previously when he was the director of the Westminster-based Policy Exchange think tank and then as Conservative MP for Hereford (from 2010 onwards). He suggested that a major concrete example of the Big Society programme in action was the rapid roll-out after 2010 of the free schools programme (led by Michael Gove, the then Secretary of State for Education), which brought in new actors and innovative school founders from outside the traditional public sector. Food co-ops would be another promising area that could develop the Big Society movement further in his view.

The implications for the redesign of public services organizations were considered rather sketchily by Norman (2010) in his chapter 12. They included 'empowering front line staff and allowing them to get on with the job' (p. 216) so as to reclaim autonomy and purpose from top-down micro-management and free staff up to pursue more important objectives of quality improvement within the public services. Although the professional mode of organizing was not mentioned, this analysis would be consistent with some recent attempts to restimulate professional control and reduce NPM-style managerial control in the health sector (Freidson 2001; for a recent application of these professional logic ideas to UK health care, see Martin et al. 2015). In addition, there was some expressed support for a revival of local government as a more independent power centre in its own right and for the localization of service provision.

So, the Big Society project, which developed around 2010, represented an attempt by some writers aligned to the 'modernizing' wing of the Conservative Party to construct a novel public services reform narrative which could move beyond the old state/market binary inherited from the 1980s. They also sought to critique what was seen as the negative inheritance from earlier New Labour reforms of the public services, despite the substantial increase in spending levels.

There was in these texts a distinctive encouragement of civil society, social enterprises, and especially the new idea of staff mutuals (Scott 2011) in public service provision. Such support for the third sector and social enterprises had in our view also been apparent in the earlier network governance narrative, as even then they were seen as representing non-capitalist alternatives to the problem of what to do about incumbent public-sector monopolies with sustained performance deficits which did not seem to respond to other improvement strategies. So there was perhaps more continuity with the now demonized New Labour period than was superficially apparent. Norman (2010) argued that any such experiments with social enterprises had remained small-scale and counter-cultural in the New Labour period (public services workers were technically given the right to form social enterprises in 2008, but few did so—Blond 2010, 271).Yet this pattern of failure to scale up continued to be apparent in the later 2010–15 period.

# Big Society ideas and health care reform

Klein (2013, ch. 10) suggests the so-called Lansley Reforms (Andrew Lansley was the Conservative Secretary of State for Health appointed in 2010 under the new Coalition government) repeated the content of many earlier New Labour health care reforms (such as competition, diversity, and choice), albeit on a bigger and bolder scale. In the specific area of developing clinically based leadership, we suggest they also built on the recommendations of the Darzi Report (2008), also published in the New Labour period.

There were many organizational changes introduced in the Coalition's initial health policy white paper (HM Government 2010a) and then the bill presented to Parliament by Lansley. They notably included the wholesale replacement in the primary care sector of 152 old primary care trusts (PCTs) by 211 new clinical commissioning groups (CCGs) which were intended to be more open to the exercise of leadership from grassroots health care professionals, especially family doctors. This reorganization could be seen as part of a declared (and in the end limited) policy shift from centralization back to localism. Targets were also set for the rapid reduction of management costs across the sector, with the abolition of the regional tier of Strategic Health Authorities as well as PCTs. There was also the review and then the closure of a number of other public advisory bodies in the sector to help produce very substantial administrative savings (the target was a 45 per cent reduction in management costs over four years) (HM Government 2010a, 5.3). This reorganization of the primary care sector was successfully brought into legislation in the 2012 Health and Social Care Act which took effect in 2013. We will explore some of the background to this organizational change further.

The new government had quickly produced a white paper (HM Government 2010a) which laid the foundations for the 2012 Act. The political foreword, signed by the Prime Minister, Deputy Prime Minister, and Secretary of State for Health alike, emphasized the decentralization of decision-making to health care professionals as one main theme:

We will empower health professionals. Doctors and nurses must be able to use their professional judgement about what is right for patients. We will support this by giving front line staff more control. Health care will be run from the bottom up, with ownership and decision making in the hands of professionals and patients.

The subtitle of the white paper was overtly libertarian in nature: *Liberating the NHS*. Moreover, the first paragraph of the main text (1.1) clearly referred to health policy in the wider context of the Big Society project: 'it is our privilege to be custodians of the NHS, its values and principles. We believe that the NHS is an integral part of a Big Society'.

While a few policy streams from the New Labour period were commended in the text (including Darzi's 2008 work on quality, 1.7), in general their legacy was seen as negative, over-managed, and over-controlling. Several organizational reforms were proposed which 'will liberate professionals and providers from top down control' (4.1). On the commissioning side, 'in order to shift decision-making as close as possible to individual patients, the Department will devolve power and responsibility for commissioning services to local consortia of GP practices' (4.6). These CCGs would still be accountable through an accounting officer up to the NHS Commissioning Board and would need to hold local practices to account too. But there would be local flexibility about how they might organize themselves and they should have substantial freedom over local commissioning decisions.

On the provider side, existing NHS providers were to be 'freed up', as all NHS trusts migrated to more decentralized foundation trust status (although this rolling out was not in the end achieved). This transition would increase the range of organizational forms that might be used within the health care sector, including experiments with social enterprises (especially in community services which were seen as more contained and promising settings):

Our ambition is to create the largest and most vibrant social enterprise sector in the world ... as all NHS Trusts become Foundation Trusts, staff will have the opportunity to transform their organizations into employee led social enterprises that they themselves control, freeing them to use their front line experience to structure services around what works for patients.   (4.21)

The implication was that there would be flexibility about local governance structures with the potential to move away from the standard two-tier governance model (i.e. a main board plus a second-tier of a Council of Governors) hitherto adopted by foundation trusts.

## Austerity overwhelms Big Society

We will now argue that this Big Society proto-narrative which implied a substantial shift to mutuals and social enterprises in providing public services was not later followed through effectively or on a large scale. As early as 2012, it was noted (House of Commons PAC 2012, 10) that there was no lead minister for driving Big Society reforms across government. This lack of high-level political leadership may well have added to incoherence and loss of focus. Big Society ideas were also found to be complex and difficult to communicate to the public at a political level. Moreover, key coordinating departments such as the Cabinet Office and Treasury were not taking on the clear cross-Whitehall leadership role needed if major cultural change within the big spending departments (including health) was to move towards new thinking: we add that Treasury texts from the period show a stronger interest in different issues of deficit and public expenditure reduction. Nor did the Open Services White Paper (HM Government 2011) (considered in the next section) provide in a clear plan for the implementation (House of Commons PAC 2012) of Big Society ideas.

The white paper Cm 8145 (HM Government 2011) set out early ideas for public management reform across government. However, Pollitt (2013) has suggested this text was characterized by only a weak meta-level public services reform narrative. There was, in his view, a 'pot pourri' (or mixed bag) of different elements apparent, when compared to the earlier and clearer NPM and network governance-based narratives. It was further weakened by being isolated from the austerity-orientated fiscal framework being developed by the Treasury at a higher level.

Important NPM-related ideas of a commissioning/providing split, user choice, and a pluralization of provision were evident in this text (HM Government 2011), although combined with a more localist approach than evident before. The New Labour inheritance was strongly critiqued (para. 1.7, p. 7): it was argued that public expenditure had increased from 38 to 48 per cent of gross domestic product (GDP) over the 1997–2010 period, yet inadequate performance persisted in service delivery areas which affected major life chances (such as health inequalities). One difference from standard NPM policies in this text was an increasing suspicion of powerful public-sector managers and a renewed defence of public services professionals, as it was argued that earlier approaches were 'damaging the public service ethos by continually second guessing highly trained professionals' (p. 7, para. 1.6).

There was the usual critique of bureaucratized and top-down approaches (Pollitt 2013) to public service provision. Cm 8145 instead sought (para. 1.3, p. 6) 'a decisive end to the old-fashioned top-down, take what you are given, model of public services. We are opening public services because we believe that giving people more control over the public services they receive and the opening up of delivery of these services to new providers will lead to better services for all'. Such providers could include the third sector as well as the private and public sectors. Chapter 6 considered the question of how to increase diversity of provision, reduce regulation and current barriers to market entry and exit. Cm 8145 (para. 6.14, p. 42) stated: 'We are doing much more than just sweeping away regulations. We are giving public sector staff new rights to form new mutuals and bid to take over the services they deliver, empowering millions of public sector staff to become their own bosses. This will free up the often untapped entrepreneurial and innovative drive of public sector professionals.'

Of special interest here were specific proposals (para. 6.17) to encourage more staff-owned mutuals. Public-sector staff, including in the NHS, were to be given the right to provide services. A Mutuals Task Force was set up, chaired by Professor Julian Le Grand from the London School of Economics. My Civil Services Pension was to become a pioneering pensions mutual company (the first mutual in central government), but it would have some private-sector involvement too.

An interim review by Le Grand and the Mutuals Task Force (2012) found some mutuals had quickly been spun out of public agency settings, with a pipeline of new mutuals coming through. Sectorally, the Department of Health had provided one of the strongest leads in Whitehall in giving staff the right to provide. By December 2011, forty new mutuals had been formed in the health care sector, but it appears from a reading of the text that they were often in small-scale community care rather than acute-sector settings as there were fewer barriers to entry and capital requirements in the community sector. At the same time, Le Grand and the Mutuals Task Force (2012, 3) argued there was a 'long way to go if the more ambitious aspirations of government for mutualisation across public services are to be met'. There were significant technical and cultural obstacles to large-scale exercises in mutualization. Bidding requirements associated with contracting out appeared skewed in favour of large corporate providers. There was also a lack of understanding in the field about these new models.

Overall, we suggest the Big Society policy bandwagon soon faded, as seen in the collapse of the national Big Society Network (set up in 2010) by 2014, amid unfortunate allegations. As early as January 2012, voluntary sector watchers Rochester and Zemmick (2012) sharply suggested the main lessons from 2011 were as follows:

For many parts of the voluntary sector 2011 was a year of brutal clarity, as the Coalition Government's spending cuts and restructuring of public services began to bite. It was also a year of irritating opacity, as David Cameron's vision of the Big Society, despite policy statements, seminars, conferences and copious punditry and speculation, came to be seen as pious flummery.

The liquidation in 2015 of the high-profile charity Kid's Company, which had been a poster child for the Big Society movement within the domain of services for troubled young people, was a further embarrassment. The short-term bubble of Big Society policy discourse seems to have left behind only minor long-term traces. It can best be seen as a brief but intense policy fashion (Abrahamson 1996) which soon evaporated and had less staying power than either the earlier NPM or network governance reform narratives that were both more successful in institutionalizing themselves.

But with the erosion of the Big Society 'proto-narrative' of public management reform, what—if anything—emerged to take its place? It appears that a narrower austerity discourse, associated with the drive for fiscal deficit reduction and sponsored by the powerful Treasury, moved into the vacuum. The *Budget 2010* (HM Treasury 2010) is a foundational text which set a basic fiscal framework for government as a whole, highlighting the supposed need for rapid and sustained deficit reduction. It started by asserting (p. 1): 'the most urgent task facing this country is to implement an accelerated plan to reduce the deficit. Reducing the deficit is a necessary precondition for sustained economic growth'. It noted that public expenditure had ballooned from 41 per cent of GDP in 2006/7 to 48 per cent in 2009/10 and argued that the plans now being put in place should reduce that figure back down to 40 per cent by 2015/16.

The text projected a 10 per cent structural budget deficit for the UK in 2010. Page et al. (2014) estimated the UK budget deficit indeed peaked at 11 per cent in 2009, and was one of the largest in any Organization for Economic Cooperation and Development country. The Treasury plan was that a cyclically adjusted current balance would be achieved by 2015 (which in the end was not the case). Aggressive deficit reduction would be pursued by achieving £32 billion in spending reductions (including welfare reform savings and a public-sector pay freeze which had major long-term repercussions for recruitment and retention of the NHS workforce but which provided an easy source of short-term savings) and £8 billion in tax increases. The political choice was to adopt a 4 to 1 ratio between spending reductions and tax increases. Clearly, the option of 'buying change' in the public services through large expenditure increases apparent in the New Labour period was no longer a possibility. A new Office of Budgetary Responsibility would be created to offer independent and expert advice on sustainable public finances.

This foundational macro-level document had important repercussions for departmental expenditure limits, which were to be agreed with all spending departments, including the Department of Health. Cm 7942 (HM Government 2010b) provided details of individual departmental settlements. Along with international development, the NHS was somewhat protected with a projected real-term growth of 1.3 per cent between 2010 and 2015. Page et al. (2014) suggest the average departmental change over this period, by contrast, was a cut of 19 per cent. By 2013, perhaps surprisingly, central departments were making stronger progress in expenditure reductions than initially required, with the Department of Health also showing a (small) underspend against target. However, the five-year view (NHS 2014) identified major long-term cost pressures already building up in the NHS, as will be explored in more detail.

So, we argue that the Big Society proto-reform narrative was in the end overwhelmed by a more powerful austerity policy. We now examine two important 'tracer issues' drawn from the health sector which illuminate how these two alternative public management discourses played out in the field over the 2010–15 period.

## Post-2010 health policy

The white paper (HM Government 2010a) on health care reform further introduced the doctrine of 'any willing provider' and argued for the extension of principles of patient choice to such additional areas as maternity services and mental health. Its attachment to the commissioner/provider split and to the pluralization of the supply side can be seen as NPM orthodox, as was its stress on performance measurement and management. On the other hand, it also reorganized primary care organizations (through the creation of CCGs) to bring in more professional representation and influence, notably from GPs, and to swing the balance of power away from NHS managers. These ideas can be seen as more compatible with the Red Tory discourse reviewed earlier.

There was also a strong anti-bureaucratic rhetoric apparent in this text (Pollitt 2013), with a commitment to cut NHS administrative costs by a substantial 45 per cent (2010–14). The Department of Health would radically reduce its own size and the old intermediate tier (Strategic Health Authorities) in the NHS would be abolished. Numerous health-related bodies would be included in a government-wide review of 'arm's-length' bodies (see Chapter 6 for the more specific repercussions for reorganizing service improvement agencies in the health care field), and those not needed would be abolished.

Sheaff and Allen (2016) examine the extent to which the supply side in health care delivery had indeed been 'liberated' in this period. Within the traditional public sector, NHS trusts were now allowed to obtain up to 49 per cent of income from private patients under the 2012 Act, which was potentially a major shift in the funding mix but one which was more likely to be realized in a relatively small number of specialist hospitals with an international reputation. Each CCG was also required to make at least three 'Any Qualified Provider' contracts in 2012, and more subsequently. While data were not easy to come by, it appears (Sheaff and Allen 2016, 218) that the mix of provision continued to shift towards non-NHS providers. Of the 195 major contracts let competitively in 2013/14, eighty went to corporations and forty-eight to social enterprises (although the latter's contracts were larger in cash terms at that stage, perhaps surprisingly).

Some for-profit corporations—notably Virgin Care—appear to have been successful in winning a large number of significant NHS contracts in the community health services sector (Sheaff and Allen 2016, 220), where it had been thought that it might be easier to establish social enterprises. NHS staff terms and conditions were guaranteed for existing staff on transfer but not for new staff, perhaps increasing staff resistance to conversion. The Virgin Care website states:

We operate over 230 NHS and social care services throughout the country across three broad service types:

- Primary care services—GP practices, urgent care centres, minor injury units and walk-in centres
- Intermediate care services—usually services that your GP refers you for such as audiology, dermatology, ophthalmology, rheumatology, back and joint pain, Ears Nose and Throat, ultrasound (to name a few)
- Community services—wheelchair services, prison healthcare, sexual health, community hospitals, neuro-rehabilitation, frail/elderly care, health visiting, district nursing, services for children with complex mental, physical and sensory learning difficulties, end of life care.   (Virgin Care 2016)

The broad picture in this period, therefore, was one of a continuing erosion of traditional public-sector forms of delivery, with the growth of private income flows within NHS trusts and a mandated outsourcing by CCGs of contracts to private and third-sector providers (potentially including social enterprises), but with some private-sector 'outsourcing' firms quickly emerging as large-scale providers.

## Whatever happened to CCGs: from professional empowerment (2013) and back to NPM-style control (2016)?

As already indicated, CCGs were set up in 2013 to replace the old primary care trusts (PCTs) as the basic unit of organization in the primary care sector. All general practices had to join a CCG which was a membership-based organization, a highly unusual organizational form in the NHS. A major remit of CCGs was to stimulate greater clinical (especially general practice) engagement in front-line commissioning, which was especially important as they had substantial commissioning budgets to allocate.

Some ideas which appear highly compatible with the Big Society vision of more localized and professionally driven organizations in the domain of public services provision were evident in early guidance. CCGs were given substantial autonomy in deciding how to operate locally and in devising their own governance structure within a locally agreed 'constitution':

CCGs will be different from any predecessor NHS organization. While statutory NHS bodies, they will be built on the GP practices that together make up the membership of a CCG. These member practices must decide, through developing their Constitution, and within the framework of legislation, how the CCG will operate.

(NHS CB 2012, quoted in Checkland et al. 2016, 154)

This non-prescriptive guidance led in turn to a proliferation of different subcommittees and governance structures at local level (Checkland et al. 2016), which indeed might be taken as a sign of genuine decentralization. Some of the CCGs set up smaller scale and geographically focused locality groups to increase local engagement further. While the original hope was that all CCGs' members would be engaged in commissioning, 'in practice, constitutions, strategic plans and commissioning plans were generally developed by an executive group of GPs (aided by managers) and then submitted to the wider membership for approval' (Checkland et al. 2016, 158–9). The possible impact of budgetary austerity in the NHS on reducing the autonomy level of CCGs was signalled as a future issue by Checkland et al. (2016, 164).

CCG governing bodies often have a high proportion of professional members (especially GPs) and a lower number of lay members or general managers than the boards of NHS foundation trusts. They were supposed to demonstrate downwards accountability to the members (local practices) as well as upwards accountability to NHS England. This distinctive composition and accountability line suggest they might in principle be able to restimulate professional engagement with commissioning and reduce levels of local managerialist oversight, while their composition also raises concerns about transparency, vested interests, and lack of independent challenge.

The early evolution of a sample of CCGs has been tracked in a longitudinal and mixed methods study (Holder et al. 2015; Robertson et al. 2016). One apparent success was that they appeared to generate higher engagement levels than in previous models of commissioning organizations: 'key to this is having local, well known and approachable GPs who are perceived as being more accessible than PCT managers had been in the past' (Robertson et al. 2016, 20). At the same time, Robertson et al. (2016, 23) found that 'efforts to involve GPs in commissioning decisions are being put at risk by a loss of autonomy among CCGs'. Thus, they were also facing top-down direction from NHS and demands for the return of documentation (such as strategic plans) within such tight timescales that it became difficult to consult the membership effectively. Robertson et al. (2016, 47) concluded:

The Health and Social Care Act was designed to reduce top down control in the NHS through the creation of NHS England and the transfer of commissioning powers and budgets to local GPs. During our research we have seen that, in practice, the reality of the last few years has been a tightening of central control.

In 2016, further central requirements were placed on CCGs, including further instructions on how to use resources.

Rapidly growing financial deficits at local level, apparent since 2014, also led to a reassertion of direct top-down financial control on trusts and some CCGs by the sectoral regulator, Monitor, and its successor, the merged super-regulator NHS Improvement, created in 2016. King's Fund (2016b) estimated that 47 per cent of trusts and 23 per cent of CCGs were projecting to end 2016/17 in deficit. The average annual cost improvement target for trusts was 4.2 per cent and the average annual QIPP saving target for CCGs was 3.3 per cent.

NHS Improvement and NHS England announced an extra £1 billion for NHS trusts in July 2016 to cut the combined projected provider deficit to £250m in 2016/17 (NHS England 2016a). However, there were also conditions imposed. A financial total would be agreed with all individual trusts and also CCGs as a minimum level of financial performance against which boards, CCG governing bodies, and CEOs 'must deliver'. The reassertion of top-down and NPM-style control over some recently created CCGs by the national commissioner/regulator is striking.

NHS England was now 'requiring' CCGs to deliver a balanced budget in aggregate. Further special measures regimes would be devised for deficit trusts and also CCGs. In addition, publicly available performance ratings for CCGs were published for the first time in 2015/16, and would be developed further in the future. On this basis, twenty-six CCGs were rated as inadequate and required to produce an improvement plan. NHS England (2016a, para 1.12) now firmly stated:

CCGs rated as inadequate will be required to develop and implement a performance improvement plan under legal Directions from NHS England. In addition, a range of other interventions are being applied under the new special measures regime. These include: adjusting a CCG's area and membership practices, disbanding the CCG, requiring that a CCG shares a joint management team or creating an Accountable Care Organisation. Nine CCGs are being newly placed in special measures.

To take one example, Coventry and Rugby CCG was placed in special measures and specifically instructed to strengthen its leadership, which led to new leadership being brought in from outside the area.

By way of comment, the language ('performance', 'delivery', 'special measures') and the policy tools used in this NHS England (2016a) text appear highly NPM orthodox and driven by the core aim of containing escalating financial deficits through reasserting central controls. The policy tools of league tables, special measures, and imposed leadership changes were now being strongly manifested within the domain of the recently created and supposedly autonomized CCGs, as well as on the provider side of NHS trusts, where there had been a much longer history.

## Concluding remarks: from Big Society to austerity

We conclude, first, that the 2010–15 history of public management reform in England included an early phase where there was a provisional floating of what we call a 'Big Society proto-reform narrative'. This narrative sought to move beyond the traditional state/market binary of the 1980s (i.e. between retaining nationalized industries or their privatization) by emphasizing the role of the third sector, especially in promoting social enterprises and the signature theme of promoting staff-owned mutuals within public service delivery.

However, we also suggest this proto-narrative failed to institutionalize itself or develop traction, and so did not in the end achieve the long-term impact of the NPM or network governance reform narratives previously reviewed. In part, this failure was because of the ideological incoherence in setting overall policy direction which had to be brokered within a coalition involving two different political parties with different ideologies. But such low impact could also be explained in part by the observation that public management reform moved down the new Prime Minister's agenda, with a culling of special advisory units in Number 10. David Cameron displayed a more devolved and collegial style of leadership than Margaret Thatcher or Tony Blair, with the implication that there was less direct challenge from the Prime Minister's Office to the big spending departments. As a result, the less powerful Cabinet Office became—by default—the leading department for public management reform but appeared to find it difficult to broker significant change across the whole of Whitehall or to have real impact within the big spending departments. The launch of the Big Society proto-narrative also coincided with the beginning of the period of the great economic crisis which had strong effects in the UK, soon marking a move back to austerity policies.

So, this brief Big Society excursion was in our view followed by a period dominated by austerity policies and an associated policy discourse, with a reversion to many (although not all) aspects of a strong NPM narrative. The powerful Treasury set a tight fiscal framework for the spending departments, along with targets for steep manpower reductions. Value for money and efficiency savings once again became key policy objectives, replacing the expansionist agenda of the 2000–8 period. However, and perhaps unexpectedly, a strong anti-managerialist tone also led to attempts to reduce civil service costs and posts markedly.

We conclude there was in this period relatively weak corporate leadership across Whitehall for strategies of public management reform, beyond the Treasury setting a tight financial framework. In this central vacuum, department-level reform strategies became more salient. The key health policy text (Cm 7881, HM Government 2010a) from the Department of Health suggests strong reliance on principles of marketization and performance measurement. It is true that there was also some anti-managerial rhetoric apparent there, including an attempt to re-engage professional engagement from general practices in the newly created CCGs. Nevertheless, market-led policies of outsourcing and contracting out continued and even intensified. The new CCGs rapidly came under surveillance from visible performance management systems and special measures regimes to deal with financial matters, largely replicating those control measures already seen in the hospital sector, were soon put in place.

The CCGs tracer noted both the new creation of a new form of membership organization in 2013 which did in some ways appear compatible with early Big Society ideas and also the re-elaboration of top-down control systems, notably to help retain financial balance.

Our analysis of these NHS-based policy and management reforms broadly tells against the view of Dunleavy et al. (2006) that 'NPM is dead' or that NPM has now reached only a 'zombie'-like state (Margetts and Dunleavy 2013), at least within the English health care sector studied here. Dunleavy et al. (2006) develop an alternative and intriguing account of post-NPM 'digital era governance' where (in their view) the negative and fragmenting effects of NPM reforms are reversed by the reassembling of a core state capacity. Such reintegration is often highly dependent on new and rapidly developing ICTs which can cross conventional boundaries.

Our view, by contrast, is that an NPM-style markets/management mix rather remains as largely (and curiously) embedded (Trenholm and Ferlie 2013) in the English health care sector, despite what are clearly notable and dysfunctional effects on capacity for systems-level working in dealing with important cross-cutting problems (e.g. an ageing society). While there were some important experiments with network governance reforms (Ferlie et al. 2013) in the New Labour period, many core NPM policy instruments remain in place and, if anything, have accelerated more recently. We have already commented on the strong concern displayed for increased productivity and ensuring financial control in the 2010–15 period. NHS England and Monitor played important central control roles. Moreover, pro-competition policies were successfully pushed through in the 2012 Act, despite widespread opposition, so that the degree of marketization may be increasing, notably in the community care sector where it is easier for new entrants to win contracts. NHS trusts were also permitted to expand their flow of private income considerably, making them more 'private firm like' (Rosenberg Hansen and Ferlie 2016). Taken as a whole, this raft of changes suggests a move back to the NPM principles of markets, value for money, and active performance management.

Of course, there may well be other important public services outside health care, such as the expanding post-9/11 'security state', which display an alternative pattern of reintegrated 'super-agencies' (such as the Department of Homeland Security in the USA) supported by strong ICT systems, where the post-NPM digital era governance model espoused by Dunleavy and Margetts may have more validity. Our broad interpretation, however, is that the English health care system has not moved on to a post-NPM mode of organizing and has indeed moved back towards some NPM core principles—notably marketization, clear values of efficiency and productivity, strong top-down financial control systems, and elaborated performance management regimes—in the 2010–15 period considered in this chapter.

# 5 The Quality, Improvement, Productivity, and Prevention (QIPP) programme in the English National Health Service

Building on the previous chapter we now explore the importance of the QIPP productivity programme and in particular look at the tools and techniques underpinning its implementation. We argued in the Introduction that QIPP implementation has been understudied, given its importance in the journey of NHS management, and merits a critically informed exploration. This is the focus of this chapter.

The broader austerity-related discourse was evident in an endorsement of the Quality Improvement Productivity and Prevention (QIPP) Programme (Cm 7881, HM Government 2010a, ch. 5). QIPP was a large-scale NHS-wide change programme designed to enhance the value of the existing NHS spend to enable it to cope with long-term cost pressures without, it was hoped, having negative effects on service quality.

In its first phase (2009–15), QIPP aimed to make some £15–20 billion of productivity improvements which could then be invested in more sustainable forms of health care. Its desire to protect service quality maintained the thrust of the earlier Darzi Report (2008), with its emphasis on assuring a high-quality health service. So QIPP sought to avoid a simple cost reduction strategy. The chronology indicates that QIPP was initially developed in 2009 under the Labour government as the prospect of tighter resource constraints after the 2008 global economic crisis rapidly moved into view. David Nicholson (2009)—the then NHS Chief Executive—used the phrase 'Quality, Innovation, and Productivity' ('Prevention' was added later) in his 2008/9 annual report, trying to avoid a simple cost/quality binary by optimistically asserting that more could really be done with less (p. 40): 'the evidence has convinced us that our best chance lies in linking quality and productivity using innovation to drive sustained improvements across the system...the evidence from the US, for instance, shows the best performing hospitals also have the lowest cost'. This call later became widely known as the 'Nicholson challenge', although the evidence base cited in support of the challenge should be seen as partial.

From an early date, external management consultants—notably McKinsey & Co.—were brought in to advise the Department of Health and the NHS on how best to respond to the QIPP challenge. McKinsey & Co.'s (2009) 123-slide PowerPoint presentation titled 'Achieving World Class Productivity in the NHS: Detailing the Size of the Opportunity' was an important early text in framing the challenge (hereafter referred to as 'World Class Productivity'). Taking a discursive perspective, Van Elk (2016) analysed 'World Class Productivity' in relation to the 'discursive practices' in the text, which include the casting of savings realization as both inevitable and desirable and as using economic and market-based logics as a primary mode of thinking. Some of these observations will be considered further in a later chapter.

While further growth was protected up to 2011, after that date NHS spending would become much more challenging (Nicholson 2009, 46):

We should also plan on the assumption that we will need to release unprecedented levels of efficiency savings between 2011 and 2014—between £15Bn and £20Bn across the service over the three years...that level of productivity gain can only be realised through the kind of quality improvements and advances in innovation described earlier in the report.

The 2010 NHS England budget in cash terms was about £100 billion (King's Fund 2016a) so this represents a highly ambitious 15 to 20 per cent productivity increase target over just four years (4 to 5 per cent savings annually and repeatedly).

QIPP was reaffirmed in 2010 by Cm 7881 (HM Government 2010a) as a key financial parameter. It was here stated that the new reforms would energize QIPP work further (5.16): 'work has begun to release £15/20B of efficiency savings for reinvestment over the system over the next four years while driving up quality. Achieving this ambition will be extremely challenging but will be essential'. The QIPP initiative (5.17) 'will continue with even greater urgency, but with a stronger focus on general practice leadership. The QIPP initiative is identifying how efficiencies can be driven and services redesigned to achieve the twin aims of improved quality and efficiency'. There were brief references to: the redesign of stroke services (we comment that this was a high-profile but pre-existing work-stream); the 'productive ward programme', which will be explored later; energy efficiency; and the use of new technologies in long-term conditions.

Given the abolition of the old regional tier of SHAs, QIPP implementation would now need to be supported by the new (and still emerging) general practice consortia and local authorities, with the help of Monitor, the sector regulator (para. 5.18). With the benefit of hindsight, this statement may have overestimated the capacity of what were still nascent CCGs to undertake such a demanding task.

Nicholson's foreword in the 2010 NHS operating guidance (Department of Health 2010b) somewhat didactically stated that 'the NHS must also maintain a relentless focus on achieving the £15/20 billion efficiency savings over the next four years by improving quality and productivity so that this can be reinvested back into the service'. There were references to national QIPP work-streams being set up and local QIPP plans now 'being in place'.

In practice, QIPP consisted of three major areas of activity (Charlesworth et al. 2016, 42–3): (i) pay restraint and reduced administration costs (making about 40 per cent of the savings initially); (ii) lower national tariffs and increased hospital productivity (again making about 40 per cent of savings initially); and (iii) system redesign, such as shifting services from hospital to primary or primary care settings (making about 20 per cent of savings, although this was recognized as the most uncertain and complex area—also see Appleby et al. 2014, 16).

The Department of Health (2010b) announced significant management cost savings which it stated should be reinvested in front-line clinical services. It abolished the intermediate tier of management, Strategic Health Authorities (although the picture of abolition is not that clear in practice, as NHS England then recreated regional teams to support its work, such as a London-wide team). There was a supposed clamp-down on management consulting spend, although some of our cases show a continuing presence from such consultants, some-times indeed brought in to advise on how to implement QIPP locally. The reorganization of the primary care sector presaged a period of organizational turbulence and loss of organizational memory in 2012–13, strongly evident in one case-study site.

A National Audit Office report (2012) found that so far the NHS had been finding the savings required by QIPP mainly through tariff cuts and pay freezes but that (p. 8): 'evidence indicates that the NHS has taken limited action to date to transform services'. In defence, such service changes would always be likely to be highly complex and time-consuming, given that productivity-enhancing innovations would often require services to move out of hospital settings and into primary or community-based settings, populated by different agencies and professions.

The House of Commons Public Accounts Committee (2013) also suggested that the savings from service transformation activity were slow to come through (p. 3), with only 7 per cent of the savings estimated to be so far generated in this manner, as opposed to the 20 per cent target. The committee was also concerned that the failure to build political and public legitimacy could slow down implementation (p. 3): 'the department has not yet convinced the public or politicians of the need for major service change or demonstrated that alternative services will be in place'. The operation of the electoral cycle could mean that major changes would become difficult in the run-up to a general election.

Quoting Department of Health data, Appleby et al. (2014) suggest that QIPP achieved £5.8 billion in savings in 2011/12 and an estimated £5 billion in 2012/13. Over these two years, the largest sources of savings were NHS tariff efficiencies/imposed cost reductions (£5.8 billion), followed by a staff pay freeze (£1.7 billion) and administrative savings (£0.9 billion). Service transformation was not identified as a separate heading but a general 'other' category accounted for only £1.26 billion in total. Charlesworth et al. (2016, 60) similarly suggest that, although headline savings were achieved, more fundamental changes to technical or allocative efficiency were not secured at the pace and scale desired.

QIPP has now been rolled forward to 2021/22 (Appleby et al. 2014) in an even more ambitious 'QIPP Phase 2' (Dunn et al. 2016). The NHS Five Year Forward View (NHS England 2014) suggests a financial gap of almost £30 billion might emerge up to 2021 on present assumptions, requiring further major productivity increases. Appleby et al. (2014) also predicted that, despite retaining financial control up to 2014, the NHS would move into financial crisis during 2015/16, as quality-related cost pressures (such as appointing more nursing staff to ensure patient safety) came through after the Francis, Keogh, and Berwick reports (all 2013) on systemic failures of care, and as the initial reliance on short-term 'salami slicing' of budgets no longer produced easy results.

Dunn et al. (2016) found a small financial deficit across the NHS in 2014/15 but also a major escalation in 2015/16. They estimated NHS providers would end the 2015/16 year with a record deficit of some £2.5 billion, and with an underlying deficit of £3 billion once one-off special measures were stripped out. Dunn et al. (2016) estimated that two-thirds of NHS providers were in deficit (concentrated in the acute sector) and that eleven providers would report a deficit of more than £50 million. Earlier approaches to cost saving appear to have run their course: 'however, the two key national strategies for improving productivity...freezing pay and reducing the prices paid to hospitals (by cutting tariff prices in real terms) now look unsustainable' (Dunn et al. 2016, 15).

In a more qualitative study, Appleby et al. (2014) investigated the organizational response to QIPP in six NHS trusts, concluding (p. 4) that 'the record of the six trusts involved in this qualitative study broadly reflects the national picture: savings have been made (and recycled) and targets set by providers to balance expenditure and income have largely been met over the years since 2010/2011 (and before)'. The trusts achieved an annual cost improvement rate of 4.5 per cent annually for the first couple of years of QIPP. Despite respondents' widely expressed desire (p. 42) to go beyond the traditional 'salami slicing' of existing budgets and move to more radical reconfiguring of service delivery, however, the short-term decision-making routines at trust level encouraged less creative responses, such as freezing vacant posts, to meet initial targets quickly.

The first task undertaken at local trust level (Appleby et al. 2014) was often to provide a detailed analysis of the local financial gap and then to populate a cost improvement plan, by looking at potential for income generation as well as cost savings. Trust-level thinking could—perhaps understandably—be focused on local deficit reduction, with wider demand management tasks associated with QIPP being recast as the responsibility of others, such as commissioners. So, there was the danger of poor integration across the local health and social care economy. We comment that the commissioning side was also going through a period of great turbulence at this time, as Appleby et al.'s (2014) respondents observed. NHS trusts had to cope with the abolition of both Strategic Health Authorities and PCTs, while the new CCGs, still forming, were small-scale and 'light' on specialist expertise, which may have made it difficult for them to exert credible system-level leadership.

However, Appleby et al. (2014, 47) commented that one trust studied sought to get beyond conventional 'salami slicing' towards a more transformational form of service redesign. It would be interesting to do a follow-up study on what happened in this potentially more ambitious site. There were also some wider attempts reported across the six trusts to achieve productivity-enhancing clinical innovations (such as medicines management), supplementing more conventional work on infrastructure and back-office costs. These innovations appeared to be relatively small-scale and confined to settings within the hospital, rather than across the health and social care system. Appleby et al. (2014, 6) raised the danger of clinical disengagement from QIPP as the narrow focus on cost compression evident in practice might demotivate and disengage clinicians and other NHS staff.

## National work-streams to support QIPP

Twelve national work-streams were set up to support QIPP implementation (HPERU 2010), for example, in the important field of safe care. From the knowledge mobilization perspective adopted here, the work-stream of greatest interest was 'Supporting Staff Productivity' which involved the then specialist national advisory agency, NHS Improving Quality (NHSIQ). Its 'Productive Series' texts are important within this prism; HPERU (2010, 3) notes: 'The series aims to support NHS teams to redesign the way they manage and work and consequently achieve significant improvements—predominantly in quality while reducing costs. It is expected that this work-stream will focus on the systematic adoption of the Productive Series and evidence based productivity improvements.' Lean and operations management-based thinking proved to be influential in these arenas. A later chapter will examine in more detail the career of national-level service improvement advisory agencies along with the texts and tools they produced.

The nature and effects of QIPP have so far been badly under-researched, despite its major potential importance. Think tank-based commentators have produced some macro-level and quantitative evidence which suggests QIPP relied on crude cost compression (e.g. reductions in the NHS tariff, restraint on pay, cost-reducing changes to labour market contracts) in practice, with little evidence of the major productivity-enhancing service transformation initially espoused. We will add to the very limited organizational-level and qualitative evidence (apart from Appleby et al. 2014) that is currently available by exploring the career of QIPP in some case-study sites in later chapters.

We finally make the observation that—despite the broader thinking reviewed at the start of the chapter—communitarian language seems remarkably absent from the texts analysed in the Lean work-stream, which is more orientated to the discovery and use of standardized tools and techniques to drive up productivity—while also protecting quality—in mass-volume health services under fiscal stress.

# 6 Case study 1

## Service improvement agencies in the English NHS: a disappointing impact

We start this chapter with an intriguing quote from a recent blog that urges UK health policymakers to recover a historical memory of the administrative history of successive NHS service improvement agencies, if only to prevent yet further cycles of reorganization and organizational forgetting:

> as we know from the oft Kafkaesque history of NHS architecture, national bodies that have been set up as improvement agencies—such as the Modernisation Agency and the NHS Institute—have had a short shelf life, abolished as lower priority than their more macho type1 counterparts using, shall we say, more traditional tools.

> Surely it will be worth the new 'NHS Improvement' familiarising itself with the Department of Health archives documenting the activities of the NHS Institute and the Modernisation Agency... (Dixon 2015)

Our original study explored the content and diffusion of management knowledge(s) in various local-level English health care organizations, but we did not at that stage consider the management knowledges apparent at this higher level of specialist, national, NHS service improvement agencies. We tackle this gap here, using as our sources a wide (and so far underexplored) range of documentary materials, texts, and visualizations available on agency websites. These archives are more virtual in nature than the conventional written archives.

This chapter examines two main themes. The first half outlines the history of successive agency reorganizations apparent in the NHS service improvement field (from 2000 to 2016) and explores possible reasons for what we see as these specialist agencies' failure to carve out a strong and stable jurisdiction. We propose a 'ladder of agency autonomy' model to inform this assessment.

The second half of the chapter examines the content of the service improvement-related knowledges promoted by these agencies. Our initial proposition that they would adopt and diffuse management technologies exported from elite American business schools and management consultancies (e.g. Lean) is supported, yet only partially. There is also some intriguing evidence of broader and self-generated thinking, including what might be seen as a counter-cultural move to social movement-based approaches to service improvement, involving the pursuit of energized and collective forms of 'owned' change from below and which have been primarily espoused by sociologists rather than management academics.

# Theme 1. The chequered administrative career of NHS service improvement agencies: few ladders but many snakes

The high-level New Public Management (NPM) narrative of public management reform influential across UK government from the 1980s onwards was reviewed in a previous chapter. This narrative suggested as one major doctrine that central ministries and departments should downsize into a smaller strategic core and strip out their operational functions which would be performed by external agencies working under a performance contract set by the ministry. Central ministries could then reorientate towards a 'steering and not rowing' (Osborne and Gaebler 1992) stance which would be supposedly less bureaucratic and more catalytic. Day and Klein (1997) used this perspective to analyse organizational changes in the UK Department of Health in the 1990s, but found that in practice the department found it difficult to disentangle strategic and operational matters.

Nevertheless, an important general shift across UK government in the late 1980s and 1990s was expressed within the Next Steps (Jenkins et al. 1988) initiative which started a widespread process of such 'agentification'. Many operational functions were moved out from ministries to newly created and autonomized 'executive agencies' (Pollitt et al. 2004) which were endowed with a degree of operational independence.

Public agencies' search for autonomy is a well-established theme in the academic public management literature. It has long been suggested that while public agencies formally operate under the direction of their political principals, notably elected ministers, they informally often seek to protect their autonomy levels or even expand them. Selznick's (2015, reprinted) classic study of the newly established and controversial Tennessee Valley Authority in 1930s New Deal America explored how it sought to generate support and build its autonomy (or 'administrative discretion'). Selznick suggested there is a general quest for 'administrative discretion' in public agencies (2015, 65): 'management strives for discretion; a leadership seeks freedom of movement, a range of choice, so that it may more ably invest its day to day strategy with a long run meaning'.

How might we conceptualize the various levels of autonomy that types of public agencies in the UK public services might enjoy? Is it possible to create a typology of levels of administrative autonomy ordered by agency form? This question has already been considered in some recent strategic management literature on public-sector organizations. So Vining (2011) considers the extent of political influence found in different groupings of public agencies, which is seen as an important modifier of firm-based strategic management models as they diffuse into public agencies. Vining's (2011) typology suggests a hierarchy of politicization ranging from: (i) presidential or prime ministerial advisory units at the top; down through (ii) traditional ministries; and then

(iii) corporatized entities; and finally down to (iv) state-owned enterprises and public–private hybrids where political influence is weakest and scope for strategic management-style behaviour by agencies the greatest.

Adapting Vining's (2011) approach, we now put forward a 'ladder of autonomy' model which relates the degree of UK public agency autonomy to its underlying organizational form. We see the ladder as moving down from: (i) a non-ministerial department at the top; (ii) then a Non Departmental Public Body (NDPB); (iii) then a stand-alone executive agency; and (4) finally, reinternalization within a ministry so that the agency loses any separate institutional identity. How functions and agencies move up and down this ladder of autonomy may reveal the strength of their power base within government and how it may be shifting.

We now review some key characteristics of the different agency forms. A less visible, but perhaps more powerful option for autonomization (Pollitt et al. 2004, 106) than the conventional recourse to executive agencies is the creation of non-ministerial departments. These agencies are protected from direct ministerial oversight and are often headed by senior civil servants in those areas deemed to be ethically and politically sensitive. Current UK examples include the Charity Commission and the Supreme Court (HM Government 2016a) but the list of non-ministerial departments supplied by the Cabinet Office contains no exemplars from the health sector.

A second option is to create NDPBs (also informally known as 'quangos', or quasi-autonomous non-governmental organizations) which are not part of a government department but carry out their functions at arm's length. They can take either the form of executive NDPBs (e.g. NHS England) or advisory NDPBs (e.g. Human Genetics Commission) and usually have their own board. However, ministers remain ultimately accountable to Parliament for the actions of these NDPBs.

A directory (Cabinet Office 2012b), helpfully broken down by central department, listed thirty-seven different NDPBs relating to the Department of Health at that stage (admittedly some NDPBs were then in the process of being closed after the 2010/11 government-wide review of quangos with a view to reducing administrative costs), while Education had only three NDPBs in total. So this form has been extensively used in the health care sector and includes some important executive NDPBs, as well as many scientific advisory bodies which might well be expected to be prominent in the health field. Post-review, the Department of Health reported a slimmed-down number of thirteen executive NDPBs and eight advisory ones (HM Government 2016b) The executive NDPBs included at that date such major agencies as NHS England, Monitor, the NHS Trust Development Authority (since merged), the CQC, and NICE.

Executive agencies perhaps represent the next stage down on the agency autonomy ladder. While they often have a high-profile chief executive recruited from outside, a board with executive and non-executive members, and an annual report, executive agencies are seen as only 'semi-autonomous' (Pollitt et al. 2004, 107), as constitutionally they are still part of their parent ministry, unlike NDPBs. They often work to a performance contract agreed with their core department.

The number of executive agencies created by each central department varied strongly. The Ministry of Justice, for example, has created six such agencies (HM Government 2016c), including the important Prisons Service, but there are currently only two reported in the health care sector (HM Government 2016b), including Public Health England which is a significant example.

The other organizational form to consider historically and which was specifically evident only within the health care sector is the Special Health Authority (SHA) which either provided specialist clinical services or specialist support to the rest of the NHS. They could, in principle, be subject to ministerial direction like other NHS trusts, so can be seen as located down towards the bottom of the autonomy ladder. More recently, many SHAs were 'mainstreamed' in governance terms and ceased to exist, yet some migrated 'upwards' to become NDPBs in their own right (including after the 2010/11 cull). For example, the Health Research Authority was set up as an SHA in 2011 but then became an NDPB in 2015, increasing its autonomy level in our terms. Some SHAs, however, were instead absorbed: the National Treatment Agency for Substance Misuse, for example, became part of Public Health England in 2013.

Finally, and at the bottom of the ladder, there is the reinternalization of an agency within its home department, leading to its extinction as a separate administrative entity. For example, the politically visible and controversial borders and passports executive agencies have recently been reinternalized within the Home Office as the Border Force and the Passport Office, with the reassertion of direct political control within a classical Weberian bureaucratic hierarchy. Indeed, the Home Office currently has no executive agencies (HM Government 2016d).

So, we suggest that there are games of jurisdictional 'snakes and ladders' where agencies can change their formally designated status and move up or down the ladder of autonomy over time. NICE (founded in 1999), for example, moved up from the SHA level to designation as an executive NDPB in 2013, and also was given an expanded jurisdiction in social care (following the 2012 Health and Social Care Act). By contrast, service improvement agencies appear to have encountered more snakes than ladders in their career as bureaux.

## A BRIEF HISTORY OF THE (RECURRENTLY REORGANIZING) NHS SERVICE IMPROVEMENT FUNCTION

It is curious to note that so extensive and recurrent has been the pattern of agency reorganization that Wikipedia currently has a page titled 'defunct NHS organizations'. The history also suggests service improvement functions are in practice transferred to successor agencies rather than simply eliminated. We now outline a brief history of the (re)organization of the national service improvement function in the English NHS over the period 2001–16.

Pockets of what would now be termed service improvement-related activity were apparent in local NHS English organizations from the 1980s onwards. This activity was often associated with nationally funded experimental programmes (such as the two nationally evaluated business process re-engineering pilots; see McNulty and Ferlie 2002, 2004) but was small-scale and localized. Such activity began to move up to the national level when the National Patients Access Team was set up in 1998 as one of several change management teams located within the Department of Health (Ketley and Bevan 2007, 9), but as yet it was without its own separate identity as an agency or at a governance level.

*2001–05*: The NHS Modernisation Agency represented the first institutionalization of the service improvement function, now located within a distinct agency. In formal governance terms, it was an executive agency of the Department of Health so can be seen as enjoying moderate levels of autonomy in the ladder-of-autonomy model.

*2005–13*: In the second iteration, the NHS Modernisation Agency was abolished but the service improvement function then moved to the newly created NHS Institute for Innovation and Improvement, now located at one main site at Warwick University. It was set up in formal governance terms as an SHA, still with its own chair and non-executives, but in terms of the model used here this reincarnation marked a (small) move down the ladder of autonomy.

*2013–November 2015*: In the third iteration, the National Health Service Institute for Innovation and Improvement was closed and the service improvement function then migrated from Warwick to become NHS Improving Quality (NHS IQ), based inside NHS England's headquarters at Leeds. The agency lost its separate governance structure (e.g. its own board and non-executives) and was now subsumed within a larger agency (NHS England) which is an NDPB in its own right. NHS IQ texts suggested there was now an attempt to align service improvement work more firmly with NHS commissioners' general work-streams (perhaps indirectly implying that this extent of alignment had previously been weak). We suggest such internalization marked a big step down the ladder of autonomy as the agency now ceased to exist as a semi-independent entity.

*November 2015*: in the fourth iteration, NHS IQ was reabsorbed within NHS England as a lower-profile Sustainable Improvement Team. The NHS Five Year View (2014) also referred in broad terms to the need for 'further alignment' in what was now seen as a cluttered health innovation landscape.

The Smith Review (2015), led by a senior NHS manager, examined the future nature of national leadership development and service improvement activity in more detail. Its underlying principles were a reduction of activity done nationally, its redirection downward, and better integration of local health and social care systems. It was critical of the impact of NHS IQ (para. 69):

The NHS IQ resource is not sufficiently directed to or aligned with local priorities and deliverables, and therefore does not adequately support local organizations or local health and care systems. This includes not recognizing that many providers have a requirement to support their operational and financial performance (although it is acknowledged this was never part of NHS IQ's formal remit).

There was also a perception of an insufficient impact on either service improvement or higher-order service transformation work. Our interpretation of this text is that a dominant productivity and performance logic was now crowding out a secondary and softer quality logic (Ferlie et al. 2015), reflecting higher-order national policy shifts. The recommendation was for NHS IQ to be abolished but that its resources and expertise should be retained and reintegrated into a new and more locally orientated system architecture, through the new Academic Health Sciences Networks (AHSNs) which had a regional footprint and were in a staff rather than a line management role that could enable them to build local improvement networks.

The ladder-of-autonomy model advanced here, therefore, suggests the service improvement function has seen deterioration in its position in successive reorganizations and with a big drop in 2013 when the National Health Service Institute for Innovation and Improvement was abolished.

## NHS IMPROVEMENT—BUILDING AN ALTERNATIVE JURISDICTION?

Summer 2015 also saw the announcement of a new national agency called (intriguingly) NHS Improvement (formally created in 2016), based on the merger of Monitor (the sectoral regulator with a special focus on financial and governance issues), an executive NDPB, and the old Trust Development Authority (TDA) (also an executive NDPB). The TDA had supported and also performance-managed a significant number of NHS hospitals that had not yet obtained foundation trust status and now appeared unlikely ever to do so.

The new NHS Improvement organization is still in the early stages of its development at the time of writing but has closer institutional links to important sectoral regulators than previous service improvement agencies. It has been suggested that the leadership of the new agency would seek to move away from the (embedded) target setting/checking approach evident in previous agencies and regulators, to one which develops to a greater extent principles of system-wide collaboration and learning (Nuffield Trust 2015).

We ask: Will its core purpose instead turn out to be to restore financial discipline across a stressed system? How will it approach those secondary functions (perhaps including service improvement activity as well as a patient safety brief) which it seems to have acquired? '[I]t is welcome that patient safety now has a good home in a relevant location but NHS Improvement needs to resist the tendency to pick up functions that are not central to the role' (Nuffield Trust 2015). A major initiative it has launched takes the form of continuing support for Lean-based work first launched by the TDA, associated with the Virginia Mason model imported from the USA.

## SOME REFLECTIONS ON THE FAILURE OF SERVICE IMPROVEMENT AGENCIES TO CREATE A STRONG AND STABLE JURISDICTION

We conclude that NHS service improvement agencies failed to create a strong and stable jurisdiction over the 2000–15 period, when compared (say) to the greater success of NICE (set up in 1999) which can be seen as a long-lived and powerful agency with an expanding jurisdiction, as well as the main sectoral regulators (Monitor and the CQC). The closure of the National Health Service Institute for Innovation and Improvement in 2013 was an important decision point which marked a step backwards in terms of building a bureaucratic base and career.

The question which emerges is: Why? The first possible reason lies in these agencies' remoteness from the critical path of the NHS business, both nationally and locally, as several texts reviewed have hinted at or even boldly stated. These agencies are only advisory bodies and are not part of the core commissioning function or well integrated with NHS foundation trusts (which might well be arguing they should have autonomy in commissioning their own service improvement advice). Both CQC and Monitor, by contrast, are more central to the core business of the NHS. A political perception of poor performance may be fatal to the career of an agency—as in the case of the Borders Agency, now reinternalized into the Home Office.

Second, and more deeply, the quality-orientated agenda of the service improvement agencies fitted better with the period of buoyant NHS funding between 2000 and 2008, especially given the need for expert support in the push to implement the 2000 NHS Plan. After the 2008 financial crisis, however, and especially in the period of extreme financial pressure evident in 2015, they became marginal to an increasingly dominant productivity/efficiency logic (Smith Review 2015) being channelled down to the NHS field through Monitor and the TDA.

A third reason could well lie in the weakly developed literature and evidence base in the service improvement field, at least when seen in the conventional scientific terms which would be important to the clinical field. NICE, by contrast, has not only generated rapidly developing new forms of expertise, technical methodologies, or what have been termed 'grey sciences' (Ferlie and McGivern 2014) to guide its appraisal work, but also seems to have achieved strong engagement from senior clinical academics and also a range of voices representing patients and publics within its dense advisory structure. This enables it to engage in well-developed deliberative processes (Davies et al. 2006), which in turn help build legitimacy for its decisions.

## Theme 2. Service improvement agencies and their preferred management knowledge(s)

We now focus on a second theme: namely, the *content* of the service improvement knowledges in the texts produced or adopted by these specialist national health care agencies, now sometimes living only a ghostly existence in their archives. Service improvement work has developed as an important organizational and managerial activity within the English health care sector over the last twenty or so years, reflecting similar developments in other important countries and health care sectors, such as the USA. Service improvement work can in turn support major policy-led efforts in large-scale health service redesign. There are major subthemes within the developing service improvement literature relating to quality and productivity improvement, assuring patient safety and reducing medical error, and process simplification across the whole care pathway (see Berwick 1996).

Achieving and sustaining desired service improvement has not proved simple (Ham et al. 2003), given an observed 'improvement evaporation' effect whereby reports of short-term gains quickly erode with apparent regression back to the status quo. So, there is also a strong interest in this literature on approaches to change management which can contribute to the longer-term development of well-functioning health care organizations able to learn, create, and sustain desired change. These managerial activities have all been associated with—and supported by—a developing knowledge base which is examined in this chapter.

We will here test and develop our earlier analysis (Ferlie et al. 2016) of the circulation of management knowledges in the UK health care sector. We initially suggested there was a dominant pattern which consisted of the international and inter-sectoral diffusion of management ideas, tools, and techniques out from private sector-orientated texts written by faculty in elite American business schools and leading management consultancies into English and publicly funded health care settings. This pattern might intuitively be thought to be even better developed at the higher level of national agencies, given they may well enjoy more resources and better international networks than local sites. We conclude, however, that a more mixed pattern is found, with a surprising turn to novel and internally generated approaches (reflecting social movement theory), alongside the presence of more conventional change management techniques (such as Plan Do Study Act or PDSA; Lean).

## LONG-TERM CHANGES TO RECEIVED MANAGEMENT KNOWLEDGES IN THE ENGLISH HEALTH CARE SECTOR

We have already argued that the decade of the 1980s represented an enduring break point in the basic organization and management of UK public and health services. Our interpretation is that NPM-orientated and top-down reforms launched by New Right governments had disturbed the old pattern of professional dominance (Freidson 1970) and continuing incremental growth in budgets by introducing a mix of management and market-led principles of organization. We drew attention to the political economy of macro-level reforming in the UK public and health care sectors and its institutional effects.

While there is now a voluminous literature on NPM reforming—and even a whole handbook (Christensen and Laegreid 2011)—the effects of NPM reforms in eroding traditional public administration-based knowledge bases in the public sector were underexplored. We examined shifts in underpinning management bases in six local health care sites (Dopson et al. 2013).

But there is a broader question to be explored at the national level and over a longer period of time than was possible in these local sites within a relatively short-term research project. Do we see a 'long wave' of management knowledge diffusion occurring over several decades? To address this question, we here chart the diffusion of various general management-based knowledges—as opposed to traditional health sectoral or public administration-based knowledges—into the NHS, apparent from the mid-1980s onwards and also on a continuing basis. Using web-based and documentary sources, we specifically explore which knowledges were adopted and diffused into the English health care field by national service improvement agencies.

### Phase 1. The Culture Wave, 'Soft' Management, and the Management of Change

We see a first phase (say mid-1980s to 2000) of diffusion as being fuelled by the increased receptivity of NHS actors (specifically, the newly empowered cadre of general managers) to a wave of 'soft' generic management texts which explored newly fashionable ideas about organizational culture and change management. In the same period, the generic strategic management field also demonstrated a shift from its traditional focus on the design of formal structure to a newer concern for 'soft' notions of corporate culture, perhaps fuelled by the success at that stage of Japanese firms with their strong and collective value sets (Mintzberg et al. 2009, 276).

For example, Hughes's (1996) ethnography examined the move from reliance on conventional structural forms of reorganization to the adoption of more culturally based approaches to promoting service change in one Welsh District Health Authority in the late 1980s. This shift was consistent with a new managerial language of 'empowerment' and 'enterprise' and an attempted move away from old-style bureaucratic controls within an espoused 'post-bureaucratic' turn. Such novel managerial practices were supported by the extensive diffusion of American popular generic management texts from the early 1980s onwards into the NHS.

Hughes (1996, 292) states:

Culture management is a central theme in a series of popular business books well known to most NHS managers... one of the surprises of the 1980s was the way the 'soft data' of qualitative organizational studies gained credibility in the hard-nosed world of corporate management. The best-selling book of all time and a de rigueur addition to the NHS manager's bookshelf is Peters and Waterman (1982)'s *In Search of Excellence*.

Hughes (1996, 294) further suggests that the Peters and Waterman text went on to achieve high citation counts in the applied health management literature of the period. The authors of the text were two American McKinsey management consultants who were given funded research time by their company to write this influential and best-selling text. They connected with major American management academics in the course of writing. Their text presents a '7S' (as all the terms begin with the letter S) model of 'excellent cultures' but with the S for 'shared values' located at the core of the paradigm, whereas the more formal 'structure' is relegated to the periphery. The model is displayed in a vivid (and copyrighted) diagram (Peters and Waterman 1982, 10).

Hughes's 1996 case study found an attempted shift by local NHS management towards a symbolic form of management and an associated 'meaning making' style of managing, although the impact in practice was found to be less than the transformational ambitions of Peters and Waterman (1982). Rhetoric and story-telling became at least as important for them as traditional negotiation skills: 'the most important symbolic work is concerned with persuasion and identity construction; work that is accomplished largely through the rhetorical skills of senior managers' (p. 297).

Hughes (1996) suggests that the 7S model (Peters and Waterman 1982) appealed to NHS managers by supporting the exercise of symbolic management, giving them a privileged role as 'shared meaning makers' rather than casting them as mere bureaucrats. Its adoption also enabled NHS managers to display their own personal reorientation to legitimated private-sector models of management within a wider health care system under broader top-down pressure to shift in that direction. The career of Peters and Waterman's (1982) much-cited text is the first example of what was to become a broader and recurrent pattern: a text developed through the study of American private firms is later adopted by UK NHS management; the authors come from an elite American management consulting firm, or are American management academics in prestigious business schools; and the text is written in an accessible style, is well visualized, and has high global sales.

This cultural perspective also informed the research work of a team of UK academics based at the then Centre for Corporate Strategy and Change at the University of Warwick, led by Professor Andrew Pettigrew (including the lead author of this chapter, so there is a need to declare an interest!) in the late 1980s. In NHS-based research, they investigated the extent to which the new cadre of general management appointed around 1985 could be seen as having accelerated the pace of strategic change in fields supported by national health policy (e.g. hospital closures, mergers, and redevelopment).

Based on the comparative case-based study of four pairs of NHS District Health Authorities progressing similar strategic change agendas, Pettigrew et al. (1992) inductively developed a model of 'receptive and non-receptive contexts for change' through the analysis of observed local variation in the pace of change achieved. Like the 7S model, this model consisted of a number (in this case, eight) of different and mutually reinforcing factors—including a supportive culture—rather than relying on just one variable. It was also expressed in a visualization. Unlike the 7S framework, however, Pettigrew et al. (1992) did not accord culture a primary role but rather accorded each factor a similar weighting, with no one being seen as more fundamental than the other seven.

So the consultancy and academically based change management texts were by the early 1990s developing in both the private and public sectors, including in the NHS itself. As part of the wider expansion of the NHS research and development function in the 1990s, a National Coordinating Centre for Service Delivery and Organization research programme was set up with a strong interest in this area. It funded a codification (Iles and Sutherland 2001) of recent change management literature in an accessible guide, which was generally well received in the NHS management field.

## From 7S to the NHS Change Model

There is now an official and recently developed NHS 'change model' which has been outlined by NHS IQ (2013). The model was built up with extensive consultation with many NHS managers. It is presented deliberately as a non-linear approach which gets beyond early 'stage-like' models of planned change. It must also be said that its content—and indeed visualization—is consistent with the earlier models developed by Peters and Waterman (1982) and Pettigrew et al. (1992). It is pictorially presented as a multifactorial syndrome (eight forces) of both soft forces (e.g. leadership) and hard forces (e.g. measurement), but with common values ('shared purpose') placed at the centre. NHSIQ (2013) argued that equal weight should be given to all factors within a balanced approach to change and that in the past the 'hard' drivers had been more dominant than 'soft' ones, perhaps eroding intrinsic sources of staff motivation.

Martin et al.'s (2013) formative evaluation of the model based on a cohort of interviews with NHS managers found that in principle it was widely welcomed, particularly its awareness of the importance of 'soft' forces. It was however seen more as a broad framework than a precise model locally and not always applied in practice in a balanced way: the 'hard' system drivers, for instance, were very difficult to change within local projects.

There was still a question as to whether the wider and embedded organizational context could overwhelm the best intentions of the model's designers. Martin et al. (2013, 74) concluded:

Participants noted how the work of senior managers in organisations could do a great deal to legitimise the use of the Change Model, and to foster an organisational environment in which the thorough, patient approach advocated by the Model could be protected from short-termism and haste. However, organisational interest in the Change Model also risked corrupting it, turning it into a managerialist tool and prioritising compliance over commitment despite the eagerness of its designers to avoid this.

## Phase 2. Evaluated Local Organization Change Experiments in the NHS, 1991–2015

By the early 1990s, a few nationally funded experiments in major organizational change programmes in local NHS sites were appearing. The Department of Health also funded independent and academic national evaluations of these programmes within what can be seen as an early turn towards evidence-informed policy. These programmes often imported novel ideas widely discussed in the generic management literature about large-scale organizational change into the NHS and their implementation was sometimes supported by management consultants brought in to support the work on a project basis.

The first example refers to the Total Quality Management initiatives launched in various demonstration sites (1991–3). Total Quality Management was an incremental approach to quality-orientated service change which moved from Japanese to American manufacturing settings but later diffused into the NHS. These experiments were evaluated by Joss and Kogan (1995) who found the pace of change in NHS sites lagged behind their non-NHS comparators (patchy and somewhat disappointing impact was a finding which was to recur in a number of these evaluative studies).

These disappointing incremental experiments with Total Quality Management were followed by more radical and 'big bang' approaches based on business process re-engineering ideas in two sites in the mid-1990s (evaluated by McNulty and Ferlie 2002, 2004, in Leicester Royal Infirmary, and by Packwood et al. (1998) in King's College Hospital, London). It was thought possible that this more radical approach might achieve more transformational change than the earlier incremental Total Quality Management approaches. An influential business text (Hammer and Champy 1993) based on the study of work processes in American manufacturing sector firms again helped diffuse these business process re-engineering ideas into the UK and the NHS. External management consultants were brought in to advise NHS managers in the Leicester site on how to implement business process re-engineering ideas.

It became possible to undertake a 'compare and contrast' analysis across the evaluations of these different change programmes and start to build up a more synthetic knowledge base (see Ham et al. 2003; Locock 2003) about the impact of different organizational change strategies in UK health care organizations. Patchy rather than systemic impact appeared as a common finding across these early studies, with early transformational ambitions often not being realized in practice. Strong variation in impact between local clinical settings rather than a strong homogeneous effect was also found.

By the late 1990s, some of the expertise developed at local level in these change experiments helped inform the design of some national-level change programmes. The National Patient Access Team (formed 1998) was set up by the Department of Health to oversee the national booked admissions pro-gramme which had recently been introduced and was designed to tackle long-standing problems evident in some localities with consistently long waiting lists for elective conditions. It was one of several change management teams set up at the same time at the centre (along with the National Primary Care Development Team and the National Clinical Governance Support Team) (Ketley and Bevan 2007). Various NHS sites had not been able to solve their long waiting list problems locally, so the centre was now intervening (Neath 2007) with service redesign 'support'. The National Patient Access Team was a small team which combined clinical and managerial expertise, indeed drawing on experienced staff from the earlier Leicester business process re-engineering experiment (Ham et al. 2003). The National Patient Access Team then exten-ded its initial work into further waves of service redesign (e.g. cancer services). It also formed close links with the Institute for Healthcare Improvement (IHI) from Boston, Massachusetts, and adopted its quality collaborative models (Ham et al. 2003).

Ham et al.'s (2003) national evaluation examined the implementation of the new national booked admissions programme (1998–2003). So, this pro-gramme (and the evaluation) operated on a wider geographical scale than the earlier locally based studies. Ham et al. (2003) found not only strong variation in local impact (consistent with the previous work) but also suggested a novel finding of the poor sustainability of change. Despite initial claims of high impact, this impact eroded when it was tracked over longer periods: this decline was termed the 'improvement evaporation' effect.

Later NHS organizational change programmes of national or regional significance have sometimes been subjected to independent evaluation. For example, Erskine et al.'s (2013) recent empirically grounded exploration of the impact of the North East Transformation System, which had hoped to exert a transformational impact across what was a relatively small and self-contained regional health economy repeats analytic themes around local variation already discussed. It is of interest here because of its systemic ambitions. Another distinctive finding in this study related to the negative effect of the then structural reorganization at SHA level in draining focus and energy out of the programme.

## Phase 3. The NHS Plan and National Level Organizational Development Capacity, 2000–2010

The NHS Plan (2000) paved the way for ambitious national-level service improvement programmes across the whole NHS, drawing on the early experience of the National Patient Access Team in service redesign:

The Blair government made the national booked admissions program one of the centrepieces of its reform of the NHS and the National Patient Access Team extended new booking systems further in subsequent waves of development. The decision announced in 2000 to establish the NHS Modernisation Agency to lead an ambitious, system wide program of reform, incorporating the National Patient Access Team's work, signified the way in which the redesign of work processes had come to exercise a central place on the NHS agenda.    (Ham et al. 2003, 421–2)

So the successful implementation of the NHS Plan was seen as requiring a knowledge base and an organizational capability which could support desired significant change and service improvement: 'the NHS Plan launched in 2000 was probably the most ambitious and wide ranging organization development and change agenda ever attempted by any organization, in any sector' (Ketley and Bevan 2007, 3). However, the question of the plan's demanding implementation requirements was perhaps not accorded sufficient attention at the initial stage.

The NHS Modernisation Agency was formally set up in 2001 as an executive agency of the Department of Health to bring together earlier time-limited teams within a supposedly permanent agency (Ketley and Bevan 2007, 9). It drew heavily on some streams of business school-inspired change management work which have been already reviewed: 'it became apparent that the methods of process reengineering, Total Quality Management, continuous quality improvement, and "lean thinking" were directly relevant to healthcare' (Locock 2001; Ketley and Bevan 2007, 9). While Lean did not feature prominently in Buchanan et al.'s (2007) overview of the early work of the NHS Modernisation Agency, there was later to be more extensive use of Lean.

Yet the agency developed as a commissioner as well as a consumer of health management research. It developed its own applied research arm and tried to exercise wider 'thought leadership'. Its in-house and applied research arm (the Research into Practice team) investigated issues in organizational change coming up from the NHS field:

The Research into Practice team worked inside the health service, collaborating with the sponsors and users of research, rather than as a conventional external academic research team. The team was able through this approach to develop fresh insights that influenced practice at national and local levels in a rapidly evolving context.

(Ketley and Bevan 2007, 4)

So far, the pattern of management knowledge consumption presented appears to be largely orthodox, with the importing of successive American business school texts and models. On closer examination, however, this interpretation is not the whole picture. We now consider two examples of customization of imported models to the local needs of the UK health care sector.

Improvement models based on Plan Do Study Act (PDSA) principles and then larger-scale Breakthrough Collaborative models were imported from American texts (Langley et al. 1996) and agencies (notably from the IHI, with which strong links were established). But this diffusion process also shows evidence of customization of ideas to the health care sector context.

The IHI has been described by a staff member as follows (Kilo 1998, 2): 'IHI is a not for profit organization created in 1991 to help lead the improvement of health care systems and thereby increase their quality and value ... IHI strives to be an integrative force that brings health care professionals together to lead improvement'. Reflecting its origins, IHI counterbalanced the generic managerial literature by highlighting the need for clinical ownership and leadership of service improvement in health care and argued for a strong clinical focus in quality improvement work.

Commending the use of PDSA approaches to health care improvement, Berwick (1996, 622) suggests the adoption of 'small, clever, informative PDSA cycles that can often start within days or hours of their initial motivation. Large-scale lessons come as we link small-scale cycles cumulatively to each other'. The PDSA change cycle is a short-term and low-risk change management intervention which has some similarities with traditions of action research and organizational development. It is designed to stimulate both greater reflection and capacity to change in what are often stressed and operationally pressured work settings. Critics might argue that this technique tends to be over-consensual and incremental, and might well struggle to achieve radical or systemic forms of change. NHS Modernisation Agency Improvement teams were trained to implement rapid PDSA cycles (Ketley and Bevan 2007, 15), for example, encouraging nurses in redesigning and simplifying care processes, sometimes against initial physician opposition (Neath 2007, 160).

The Breakthrough Collaborative model was developed by the IHI and applied (to give one example) to the major field of cancer services redesign (Kilo 1998; Kerr et al. 2002) in the English Cancer Services Collaborative Programme. Kilo (1998) suggests that the Breakthrough Series model was developed by IHI as a response to increasing evidence that a decade of incremental continuous quality initiatives had failed to engage American physicians or demonstrate substantial impact. Breakthrough Series programmes still use PDSA cycles as a change tool but also create wider collaborative networks of between twenty and forty organizations working on the same topic at the same time to achieve wider impact. The collaboration works together for between nine and twelve months, mixing three two-day learning sessions with intervening action periods. A large open conference is held at the end of the collaboration to facilitate dissemination. There is also a strong focus on achieving a significant degree of change in a specific topic of real clinical significance, requiring some before/after measurement to assess progress objectively.

Kerr et al. (2002) reported early results from the service improvement work undertaken by the first cancer services collaboration launched by the National Patient Access Team and directly involving IHI support. The team worked on important clinically relevant areas including the reduction of delays across the care pathway. In Phase 1, nine managed cancer networks were involved, covering a population of 14 million, that then created forty-three project teams: 'we encouraged shared learning with two day residential meetings every six months, a web based list serve and regular teleconferences' (p. 164). In the first year, the networks reported substantial improvements upwards to the central team (but note that these were self-reports and over a short time period). In Phase 2, the collaboration was extended to all thirty-four English Managed Clinical Networks and new collaborations were started in cardiovascular disease, orthopaedics, and primary care. So, the collaborative programme can be seen as a major change technology widely used by the NHS Modernisation Agency.

The National Health Service Institute for Innovation and Improvement also appears to have made extensive use of Lean tools and approaches, drawing on the Toyota experience but also customizing them to the NHS. Its archived website (http://www.institute.nhs.uk/building_capability/general/lean_thinking.html) stated it had produced an NHS-specific package (the Lean Simulation Suitcase), at that stage available to purchase. The 'productive series' work packages represented many streams of work applying Lean ideas to different health care settings (e.g. the productive mental health ward). The website also contained links to various short articles written by the National Health Service Institute for Innovation and Improvement on applications of Lean to NHS settings.

This stream of activity was clearly continued by the NHS IQ. Its text on Lean (NHSIQ 2014) outlined Lean orthodox techniques (e.g. A3 thinking, ready visualization, statistical process control methods, current and future value stream mapping) that could be applied by NHS managers to manage 'towards perfection', eliminate waste, and increase service value. Disappointingly, there does not appear to have been a nationally commissioned evaluation of Lean (unlike earlier major organizational innovations), although Radnor et al. (2012) present the findings of an exploratory study based on four local NHS cases.

Some other examples which will now be explored, however, suggest a greater degree of knowledge pluralism than might have been originally expected.

## THE PUBLIC VALUE APPROACH: AN INTERESTING EXCURSION?

The 'public value' stream of public management writing is associated with the influential text of Mark Moore (1995), drawing on his extensive experience with executive education courses with American public managers at the Kennedy School of Government at Harvard (where he was located rather than Harvard Business School). Moore developed an academic collaboration with a group of UK public management academics then located at Warwick Business School (Moore and Bennington 2011). The National Health Service Institute for Innovation and Improvement was interested in learning more about this approach, and commissioned a systematic literature review on public value literature (the first such review at least in the UK).

Williams and Shearer's review argued (2011, 1):

Moore's central proposition is that public resources should be used to increase value in a way that is analogous to value creation within private enterprise. However, this public value would necessarily extend beyond narrow monetary outcomes to include that which benefits and is valued by the citizenry more generally.

It sees the public manager as exercising a more entrepreneurial and less bureaucratic role in enhancing the social value of existing public services through innovation.

The key heuristic in this school is Moore's (1995) 'strategic triangle' diagram where there are three dimensions which in his view should be aligned for public value creation to be achieved: (i) the value stream itself; (ii) support in the wider 'authorizing environment', notably including political support; and (iii) operational capacity within the public organization to deliver such improvements.

Its assumption of 'benign bureaucrats' has provoked a lively academic debate, with political scientists such as Rhodes and Wanna (2007) arguing for a reassertion of democratic political control over the expansionist and possibly self-serving bureaucrats that may be favoured by Moore's approach. It was also unclear how public value thinking handled tricky questions of power imbalances and strong diversity within non-cohesive communities. Williams and Shearer (2011, 15) concluded: 'without resolution of these, public value is likely to remain as a useful pedagogic tool for public administration but fall short of offering a broader theory of public enterprise and organization'.

After funding this literature review, the National Health Service Institute for Innovation and Improvement (2009) produced an online public value 'toolkit', which included health care-related tools (such as the public value stream heuristic) and two NHS-based case studies. However, it appears that public value models have since fallen out of favour: there seems to be no mention of them on the later NHS IQ website. The turn to public value can best be seen as an interesting but also as a time-limited excursion, which does not appear to have led to a sustained stream of work.

## THE NHS CHANGE DAY: COUNTER-CULTURAL AND SOCIAL MOVEMENT-BASED APPROACHES TO SECURING LARGE-SCALE ORGANIZATIONAL CHANGE

Since 2013 an annual 'change day' has been held across the NHS which promotes a radically different social movement-based approach to service improvement. The aim is to secure personal commitment to service improvement—rather than mere compliance—and to do so on a collective and mobilized basis. As the NHS IQ website states:

NHS Change Day is a grassroots movement that's about harnessing the collective energy, creativity and ideas of thousands of people to improve the care and wellbeing of people who use health and care services, their families and staff. Over the past two years thousands of people made pledges to change things. This year we want to inspire people to take action. Anyone can get involved, whether they work in or alongside the NHS or are a patient or member of the public.   (NHSIQ 2016)

Hilton and Lawrence-Pietroni's (2013, 12) account suggests, immodestly, that the 2013 NHS change day was the 'largest single improvement event in any organization in the world' which secured no fewer than 189,000 pledges (p. 4) on its online wall. They suggest it was deliberately designed to create one single day of collective action with a low threshold for participation, which (unusually for the NHS) did not require permission from senior managers and tried to unlock a willing commitment to act from the many participants enrolled. Their overall interpretation (p. 4) suggests that the national leadership team 'applied and adapted social movement theory, skills and practice associated with community organizing and made use of social media to secure voluntary pledges from NHS staff and patients to take specific innovation action on or around 13 March 2013'.

How did such a counter-cultural approach to securing organizational change come about in an organization which appears to be dominated by a late modernist search for perfect control and risk aversion? We argue that its history suggests that some staff in the NHS Modernisation Agency engaged in self-initiated reflection on the limitations of current programmatic change management approaches and also displayed an ability to search for and then apply alternative and very different models.

The NHS Modernisation Agency commissioned some 'blue sky' thinking from external academics which may well have proved influential in this reorientation. Bate et al.'s (2004a) review of the sociological and organizational literature on social movements was undertaken for the NHS Modernisation Agency. It explored possible implications for the (re)design of large-scale service change efforts in the NHS using a radically different framing. Social movements were a potential approach which could bring with them deep forces of emotions, identities, and beliefs which had the power of transformative change, rather than superficial compliance. They defined the key features of a social movement as follows: 'radical action, transformative events, collective action, voluntary associations and social relationships, organization and spontaneity, politics, conflict and durability' (p. 2). There were already examples of social movement-influenced approaches in the NHS such as the user involvement movement in mental health services, contests over childbirth, and health advocacy in HIV/AIDS.

Zald's sociological work on social movements and their expression within organizations is well known in academic circles (originally within American sociological writing) and was cited in the UK NHS-based work reviewed here (Bate et al. 2004a, 2004b), with a classic Zald and Berger article (1978) proving particularly influential. Zald (2005) suggests that the original article initially appeared to generate little interest after its publication, but that recently there has been a strong revival. He reflected on the (pleasant) surprise of strong interest from the NHS and the entirely unexpected movement of his fundamental ideas into a policy-related and applied domain in the UK. A conference was held in London in 2004 when some American scholars were brought over and met with senior relevant NHS personnel.

## THE TDA AND NHS IMPROVEMENT: BACK TO LEAN AGAIN AND THE VIRGINIA MASON PRODUCTION SYSTEM

NHS Improvement is still developing as an agency at the time of writing (early 2017) but it appears the new agency may develop with a quality improvement as well as a regulatory and performance management function. Such a capability might at a practical level help it damp down the number of critical reports coming from regulators (including the CQC which is mainly quality orientated) which then trigger complex and time-consuming 'turnaround' exercises.

As of 2015, one of its predecessor regulators (Monitor) was putting a significant number of supposedly autonomous and highly performing foundation trusts (e.g. King's College Hospital in London, following its enforced merger with another South London provider) into special measures or improvement regimes, as was the TDA which regulated the large number of hospitals that had still not progressed to foundation trust status (e.g. Worcestershire Acute Hospitals NHS Trust, following a critical report from the Chief Inspector of Hospitals). Why wait to put trusts—and even foundation trusts—into special measures, if preventive action can be taken?

Shortly before its merger with other bodies in 2016, the TDA had commissioned support from the Virginia Mason Hospital, Seattle, USA, over a five-year period in relation to five challenged non-foundation NHS trusts, including University Hospitals Coventry and Warwickshire NHS Trust (NHS Trust Development Authority 2015), with dramatic claims being made for the transformational impact which had been achieved in prior work: 'Virginia Mason estimated that on average nurses spent about 35 percent of their time in direct patient care. After transforming its systems this increased to 90 percent.'

This change programme will work on systematic approaches to quality and patient safety improvement as already developed in the Virginia Mason Production System, produced by a non-profit and regionally based health system in Seattle, USA. It is based on the principles of Lean and the Toyota Way, essentially repeating the more conventional approaches apparent in the change management of earlier service improvement agencies. In 2016, the TDA was merged into a new super-regulator (NHS Improvement), which now holds this Virginia Mason-related stream of work.

## Concluding discussion

Our first purpose in this chapter was to plot the problematic careers of a succession of national-level agencies in the service improvement field in English health care from the early 2000s onwards. Allcock et al. (2015) explored how national-level NHS agencies might seek to accelerate the substantial productivity and quality improvements desired by policymakers in the English health care system. They start by distinguishing (pp. 4–5) between possible intervention strategies. Type 1 strategies 'prod' local health care organizations using targets, direction, or performance management-based techniques, seen as a compliance-based approach using extrinsic motivation. Such approaches have been dominant in the past, and, we would add, could be seen as evident in the 'breach'-led approaches to regulation adopted by the field-wide regulators, Monitor and CQC.

Type 2 strategies, by contrast, offer proactive support to local organizations and can be seen as providing a different and more commitment-based approach which build on staff's intrinsic motivations. Type 2 strategies are more associated with the various service improvement agencies considered here.

Allcock et al. (2015, 19) argue that Type 2 approaches have been underdeveloped and that there is a need for a shift to a longer-term and more organizational development-orientated strategy (but we note that early NHS Modernisation Agency literature made exactly the same argument in the early 2000s): 'proactive support has potentially far higher relative impact in improving local performance and there is not enough of it, or hard thinking about support'.

The second theme explored in this chapter related to the analysis of what we see as the troubled career of the service improvement function in the English health care sector over the last fifteen or so years. We found an engrained pattern of continual agency turbulence, reorganization, and also a long-term erosion of agency autonomy and jurisdiction. Indeed, each reorganization seems to have pushed the agency housing the service improvement function further down the ladder-of-autonomy model we developed here as an analytic framing, in marked contrast to the success of alternative agencies such as NICE or Monitor.

How might we explain this disappointing career of successive service improvement agencies? In exploring this question, Allcock et al. (2015, 23) advanced three possible explanations. The first lies in the content of the work undertaken and its poorly understood knowledge base, which appears as less scientifically legitimate than that developed by NICE. The second is mixed or even weak evidence about the (at least short-term and direct) impact of such work and the extent to which in practice it was aligned with the NHS's critical objectives. The third possible reason is that there may be a clash between the menu offered by a national agency and the effects of an autonomization strategy for an increasing number of NHS foundation trusts that might expect to want to choose their own local support systems as autonomous actors, should they indeed feel they need them.

Are these explanations enough? Another factor (in our view) is the continually operationally high-pressured nature of the English health care system. Not only has service improvement activity been less central to the core day-to-day business of the NHS than meeting short-term targets and balancing books, but it became an even lower priority after the 2008 economic crisis when a dominant productivity and performance logic took precedence over softer themes such as quality.

From this perspective, there may have been a bias in the NHS system, at least since the early 2000s, towards too much exploitation activity and not enough exploration of knowledge. Utilizing a resource-based view (RBV) (Barney 1991, 2001) framing from strategic management, Gibson and Birkinshaw (2004) suggest successful firms manage to balance both activities, whereas we argue that the NHS has tilted towards exploitation and has weak exploration capacity.

Further, according to Hartley and Rashman (2010), leadership capacity significantly impacts on the creation and then the lateral transfer of knowledge in organizations. Such lateral knowledge transfer is especially critical for the solution of 'wicked' or adaptive problems that require novel approaches to both problem definition and solution (such as complex processes of service redesign). Such a 'leadership of learning' style is different from, and can often be in conflict with, the performance management goals of organizations: these call for a different kind of 'technical' leadership which is more suitable for problems that have been identified and resolved previously, and that were prioritized as a result of the shift in focus towards NPM logics (Ferlie et al. 1996) in UK health care (e.g. value for money, efficiency savings, and performance management).

Continued agency turbulence and the erosion of their autonomy and scope of jurisdiction may be the result of—and further reinforce—poorly developed leadership of learning capacity within service improvement agencies. This pattern can be seen as resulting from a combination of an increased shift towards performance management on the one hand, and a perceived political and high-level perception of the poor performance of a predominantly quality-orientated agenda within these agencies on the other—a 'soft' agenda that in any case no longer fitted with the managerial logic of the post-financial crisis period after 2008.

The third theme explored in the chapter was the adoption and diffusion of specific managerial knowledge bases by national service improvement-orientated agencies. There are both expected and also some unexpected aspects to this story.

The frequent use of PDSA, Lean, and 'productive services' can be seen as orthodox at least in our initial framing, according to which management knowledge bases from elite American business schools and management consultancies could be expected to be influential as sources of service improvement-related knowledge adopted by the NHS.

The case of the National Health Service Institute for Innovation and Improvement's importing of Moore and the public value school suggests what might be seen as a moderate shift away from the dominant pattern, as these models diffused from an American school of government (the Kennedy School at Harvard), rather than from the Harvard Business School. It can at the same time still be seen as 'strategic management' friendly. The case of the use of IHI's work also reflects a similar, moderate, shift to quality improvement models which have been customized for the American health care field.

The turn towards a more radical social movement-based approach by the NHS Modernisation Agency seems, on the other hand, to be an important and interesting exception to our original expectation. The knowledge base accessed came from a well-established but then rather neglected stream of work in (American) academic sociology rather than from the business school sector. Our provisional contention is that the commissioning of 'blue sky' thinking from external academics by the NHS Modernisation Agency then influenced the search for and choice of such alternative change management models by key senior Modernisation Agency staff. There was a shift towards a counter-cultural model of transformative change. It is also possible that social move-ment theory is a single idiosyncratic exception to the general pattern, which is now reasserting itself in the later adoption of a Virginia Mason-inspired cycle of work around Lean.

## IDEAS FOR A FUTURE RESEARCH AGENDA

So, the national agency level represents a fruitful level of analysis, in addition to the local case studies explored in other chapters, and is a level of activity which has been underexplored so far. What future questions might arise at this important national level?

Most obviously, researchers should continue to track the oscillating career of the national service improvement function. Some questions that can be explored include: How will the new body NHS Improvement (the merged super-regulator, created in 2016, which now holds the service improvement function) develop, and will it break or continue with the pattern of the past? Will alternative 'knowledge leaders' and knowledge leadership emerge in the service improvement field outside national NHS agencies, such as within consultancies or think tanks? For example, Martin et al. (2015) describe an attempt to revive the professionalized third logic as a post-managerialist change management approach, with their research being sponsored by a major independent funding body, the Health Foundation.

Another area that needs exploring relates to any changes in core knowledge content and the typical diffusion pattern as found within the domain of service improvement. For instance, will other home-grown or European models be developed or imported in the future? We do not seem to have discovered any significant diffusion of health care management models coming from Europe into the NHS in practice, despite the high performance of some of their health systems when benchmarked internationally. The models considered in this chapter are by contrast generally American inspired, albeit coming from some different American academic communities (including a surprise example of the sociology of social movements). There is a recurrent interest in the importing of models that seek to address at the same time issues of both productivity and quality, which often come from an operations management perspective, as broadly conceived. The recent interest in Lean fits this broader pattern well.

A final area that needs looking at is the transformation work now being carried out with five non-foundation trusts with the support of the Virginia Mason Hospital. This programme, rooted in the principles of Lean and the Toyota Way, appears to be relatively orthodox within the prism adopted here. It can be seen as a further iteration of the often-repeated cycle of importing organizational change programmes from American health care settings.

# 7 Case study 2

Think tanks and London's quadruple helix of public and health policy knowledge production

This chapter considers the role of think tanks in producing public policy knowledge. We will suggest such think tanks are located within a wider system of public and health policy knowledge production in the geographical zone of central London. The chapter first reviews the 'triple helix' model of knowledge production in the science policy literature, which suggests a 'spiky' innovation landscape globally, where capacity for strong science-based economic growth is geographically concentrated in a few favoured regions or cities. This literature has recently further considered the possible active role of civil society (as well as private firms) within a revised 'quadruple helix' model which is seen as of particular interest here.

The chapter will adapt this quadruple helix model to analyse a London-wide ecosystem of public/health policy knowledge production. We first briefly consider the role of government, universities, and also private firms in the management consulting sector. It then takes a more extended interest in the role of think tanks within this ecosystem. As they fall within the mainly non-profit sector, we suggest they may fit a quadruple helix model better than the prior triple helix prism. We see them as an expanding category of knowledge producer in this public/health policy field. They are geographically concentrated in central London, close to the centres of political power on which they are dependent in winning influence for their ideas through building political networks.

We present and discuss some political science literature on think tanks, before exploring how think tanks form a key element of a quadruple helix of public and health policy knowledge production in London. We then present a case study of how one London-based think tank effectively mobilized its networks to address the productivity question in the health care sector after 2010. The chapter concludes with some broader reflections about think tanks within this possible quadruple helix model of public policy knowledge production.

# Models of scientific innovation and growth: towards a quadruple helix?

Ferlie at al.'s (2017) review of academic literature on processes of knowledge mobilization in UK health care organizations suggested that the triple helix stream within the science policy literature is a promising avenue to explore. Etzkowitz and Leydesdorff's (2000) foundational paper on an early triple helix model suggested that innovations in science and technology fields are fostered by dense interactions between three institutional axes: government, universities, and private firms.

Influential variants of this model (e.g. 'triple helix 3') imply a semi-autonomous role for universities as major actors in their own right. Significantly, they are not seen as being heavily steered by a controlling government, although we suggest that such steering attempts might be more likely in New Public Management-orientated jurisdictions, such as the UK. In particular, research-intensive universities with a well-developed research base in science, technology, engineering, and mathematics (STEM) subjects are important knowledge assets likely to be of particular interest to private firms seeking to commercialize such knowledge. Science-intensive firms (e.g. in software, biotechnology, or nanotechnology) may wish to set up offices close to leading university campuses to establish closer personal connections with such institutions and their 'star' scientists.

Furthermore, some universities have recently developed a 'third mission' of commercialization, developing private income streams and contributing to national and regional economic growth, complementing the original academic missions of teaching and research. A subcategory of 'entrepreneurial' universities which stress such commercialization, such as the University of Warwick in England (Clark 1998), is emerging internationally. This group may also foster 'hybrid spaces' (such as technology transfer offices, spin-outs, and science parks) going beyond the academic heartland. These hybrid entities may be physically located at the expanding periphery of university campuses, close to but separate from traditional academic departments.

The knowledge intensiveness of the region or city is also seen as important in driving strongly varying levels of economic growth; there may be more and less knowledge-intensive regions which are on sticky and path-dependent tracks (Etzkowitz and Klofsten 2005) that are difficult to shift. For example, Silicon Valley in California is often held up as a pioneering region, globally visible from the 1970s onwards, in the rapidly developing field of software, as is the Route 128 industrial district in Boston, Massachusetts, in biotechnology. In the UK, 'Silicon Fen' to the north of Cambridge has been developing as a greenfield site for a significant cluster of biotech firms, with access to the leading-edge science departments at the University of Cambridge. Even here, it has been commented that 'Cambridge UK has generated a significant number of niche firms but has had difficulty in creating high growth firms, common in Silicon Valley' (Etzkowitz and Klofsten 2005, 244).

Many regions will not have the research-intensive universities and necessary stock of scientific and technological knowledge that the triple helix model suggests is critical. Concepts of 'smart cities' and knowledge-intensive regions suggest that the innovation landscape is spiky: only a few globally viable regions or cities are generated, which build on promising historical conditions and then 'scoop the pool'. 'Science city' initiatives involving government and other actors are evident in some high-profile cities (e.g. Barcelona; see Etzkowitz 2006) which seek to shift the inherited local pattern, to develop capacity, and to accelerate knowledge-based economic growth. The MedCity example is a similar initiative across London, in alliance with Oxford and Cambridge, designed to showcase its expertise in medical research globally. More recently, there have been attempts to bring 'society back in' (Leyserdorff 2012) as a possible additional actor to the early triple helix model. Schoonmaker and Carayannis (2013) propose the 'quadruple helix/mode 3' model of knowledge production to include an activated civil society seen as comprising the 'media and culture based public'. Carayannis and Campbell (2009) had previously suggested that in a knowledge-orientated society, a 'creative class' of highly educated workers shapes a public discourse that favours such values as a future orientation, the production of new knowledge, and innovation activity.

Schoonmaker and Carayannis (2013) adopt the definition of 'civil society' from the London School of Economics' Centre for Civil Society (2009): 'civil society refers to the arena of un-coerced collective action around shared interests, purposes and values ... (and) commonly embraces a diversity of spaces, actors and institutional forms, varying in their degree of formality, autonomy and power'.

As this definition is still very high level, we seek here to operationalize the concept further. Specifically, we argue that it refers not only to the emergence of a 'creative' social class (as suggested by Carayannis and Campbell 2009) in society, but requires that such forces be mobilized and institutionalized so that they become actors with some influence within the policymaking process. This position further suggests we need to analyse the role and activities of important 'third-sector' or non-governmental organizations lying between the state and the market which are not captured in the classic triple helix model.

While some such organizations may be party politically based or orientated to public campaigning activity, others which are highly 'knowledge intensive' are of particular interest. One example would be NGOs operating in scientific fields which may be controversial and have strong public policy implications (such as climate change or genetically modified foods). We argue that health policy similarly constitutes a knowledge-intensive arena which combines well-developed knowledge (widely defined, but certainly including social science-based research) with contested and controversial health policy issues.

In summary, this triple/quadruple helix literature suggests some important arguments to explore:

1. Scientific and technological innovation will be driven by interactions between the three helices of government, industry, and research-intensive universities. Novel hybrid spaces are likely to develop, linking the three axes.
2. Such systemic capacity may be path dependent and concentrated geographically within a few high-performing regions so that the region or city is an important unit of analysis. The regional eco-knowledge production system is likely to co-evolve rather than being directed in a linear and predictable manner by government.
3. A more recent quadruple helix model suggests a major role for an active civil society as well as private firms but these ideas need to be operationalized further. The notion of a 'knowledge-intensive' NGO as part of active civil society is important to explore.

To understand how think tanks create and mobilize their very distinct modes of knowledge production, we turn next to the significant role they play, not just within, but *for* civil society.


## The role of think tanks in civil society

A political science-based literature on public policy research institutes or think tanks points to their significant and potentially powerful role in producing and mobilizing knowledge between universities, governments, and industry. In providing links across the wider institutional landscape, they may fill gaps between sites of power (specifically, policymakers) and of knowledge (academics and other knowledge producers). Moreover, their future-focused knowledge orientation towards longer-term policy agendas may counterbalance the temporal tendencies of policymakers to focus on more immediate policy issues (McGann et al. 2014).

Weaver and McGann's (2009) analysis suggests think tanks are not just important sources of policy research, but operate as a key part of civil society. Arguing that one of think tanks' distinctive contributions to society is to catalyse both ideas *and* action as part of processes of democratization, these authors list what they see as think tanks' five critical roles in civil society: mediating between governments and the public; identifying, articulating, and analysing emerging issues; transforming problems and ideas into policy issues; providing an independent voice in policy debates; and providing a forum for the exchange of ideas and perspectives between stakeholders.

As Warren (2012) similarly argues, civil society functions through the social and physical infrastructure of a variety of associations and groups, including think tanks. Whereas these entities gain legitimacy through providing 'conduits of representation' for the interests, values, and voices of citizens, think tanks provide a critical role as specialists in public discourse. By analysing and transforming emerging issues in ways that provoke public deliberation, as well as by monitoring the activities and responses of public institutions, think tanks provide an amplifying (and potentially transformative) effect on these public issues (Warren 2012).

In an influential article, Weaver (1989) delineates three main models of think tanks, each seen as intermediaries in the knowledge production system: 'universities without students'; contract research institutes; and 'advocacy tanks'. Although each share certain characteristics of knowledge production and/or dissemination, the models can be distinguished by their orientation towards direct engagement and levels of two-way influence in relation to substantive policy issues. Whereas the models of more traditional think tanks emphasize intellectual independence and autonomy, all three models seek to provide solutions and recommendations (not merely analysis), suggesting a potentially powerful role that is targeted, whether directly or indirectly, at influencing decision makers.

Weaver (1989) proposes that this influence is exercised through four main activities: by being an important source of policy ideas (including peripheral ideas that only influence policymakers over the longer term); by providing critical analysis and commentaries on policy proposals or programmes (for instance, those of incoming governments); by being a source of embodied expertise for governments (as individual careers often circulate between think tanks and policymaking); and by media punditry (such as providing authoritative commentary on contemporary news items). By supplying not merely ideas and texts to policymakers, but sometimes also personnel, such influences provide various potential materials and routes for exchange, influencing and infiltrating 'permeable' administrative elites (Weaver 1989; McGann and Weaver 2009).

Such influencing activities raise important questions about think tanks' autonomy and potential critical distance from policymakers. Think tanks' reputations for autonomous intellectual thought are important because their knowledge claims hinge on their perceived legitimacy as independent institutions providing rigorous analysis and commentary. Yet McGann and Weaver (2009) argue that their autonomy should be analysed in relative terms, because think tanks' interconnectedness with other bodies and interest groups provides both advantages and disadvantages in their potential to 'speak truth to power'. Whereas some think tanks' analytic distance and objectivity can create tensions between academic rigour and policy relevance, others may be perceived as too close to government and funders, hence compromising scholarly objectivity.

Among the various models of think tanks, 'advocacy tanks' most obviously combine an overt (and sometimes ideological) lobbying focus with active salesmanship to 'spin' research for target audiences. Nonetheless, all think tanks operate by targeting policymakers as a potentially receptive audience. This influence may take place through various phases and routes into the policymaking process, including formal and informal meetings, briefings and seminars, as well as media influence through opinion pieces, analysis, and media appearances.

Overall, these scholars suggest we should pay attention to the issue-focused work of individual think tanks and contributions to a wider landscape of civil society. This 'noisy policy bazaar' of researchers, policy activists, and policy entrepreneurs can be characterized less by the ideals of autonomy and independence than the pragmatics of engagement and interaction between academia, funders, interest groups, and governments (McGann et al. 2014).

## How do think tanks mobilize knowledge?

Think tanks, then, are important organizations in the intermediary space between governments, universities, and industry. But how might we understand their influence within a wider knowledge mobilization process? Stone's (1996) analysis is anchored in her premise that 'ideas need organizations to mobilise them'. Moreover, she argues that, to grasp the influence of think tanks, we need to focus less on their direct interactions with government than on think tanks' efforts to mobilize knowledge at the *edges* of government. Indeed, she argues that it is unhelpful to analyse think tanks' direct impact on policymaking, when the focus of analysis should be on the diverse ways in which they bring together, link, and facilitate the mobilization of ideas and research across diverse interest groups and participants across multiple organizations.

In particular, Stone (1996) provides a convincing account of how think tanks are engaged in knowledge flows through two distinct (and potentially complementary) routes. The first is the existence of epistemic communities whose networks and influence flow through and beyond individual think tanks. Whereas epistemic communities are not necessarily centred in or driven by particular think tanks, their settings provide 'key locations' (Haas 1992, 31) or, as Stone (1996) puts it, act as 'switchboards' for such communities. Although community members may come from various organizational, professional, and disciplinary backgrounds, they are bound together by common ideas, normative beliefs, and values which form more or less shared perspectives on the causes of problems, the focus of their possible solutions, what expert knowledges are valid, and how this knowledge should be used.

Citing Haas (1990), Stone (1996) agrees that such 'consensual knowledge' involves: 'the sum of technical information and the theories surrounding it that command sufficient agreement among interested actors as a given time to serve as a guide to public policy' (Haas 1990, 74). Moreover, such communities display informal networks and institutional ties that provide a means of exchanging information, moral support, and solidarity. Their information flows and interactions include exchanges of email, journal articles, and discussions that between them create a form of 'invisible college' (Stone 1996, 88).

The second route is through policy networks, whose role in policy formation and implementation implies a more institutional focus on control over resources, including power struggles between competing groups. Such policy networks display relatively stable, interdependent relationships, bound together by common interests in particular policy fields, such as health care. Generally orientated towards policy stability and continuity, such policy networks tend to constrain change. Stone distinguishes policy networks as comprising powerful coalitions of favoured groups, policy makers, and other forms of control, principally coalesced around high levels of centralized power; this pattern contrasts with the coalescence of epistemic communities around themes and values of scientific authority, objectivity, and expertise. Such policy networks are important in analysing think tank activities, pointing to an alternative form of institutional influence, through more established and formal routes, where other issues of formal agenda setting and implementation capacity become important.

From Stone's (1996) perspective, think tanks are important sites that bring together diverse epistemic and policy networks in various ways. They may usefully be seen both as 'switchboards' that connect ideas, as key locales for agenda setting, and as potential 'springboards' that propel ideas into the wider policy domain. If her analysis suggests a rather indirect influence upon policy-makers, she argues strongly that this is nonetheless significant in understanding the reach and potential power of think tanks in mobilizing knowledge.

Indeed, an important aspect of think tank activity is building regional and international networks of knowledge. Stone (2000) later analyses this activity as a key mode of interaction which links three specific forms: interpersonal networks (individual exchanges and meetings through personal connections with civil servants, journalists, bureaucrats, politicians, and other policy researchers); organizational networks (which, beside their visible activities, may constitute clearing houses for sifting and coordinating what forms of knowledge, ideas, or thinking are current); and dispersed research networks often spanning multiple organizations, localities, and jurisdictions.

Intriguingly, Stone (1996) argues that the reach and influence of think tanks should be analysed through Foucault's notion of a power/knowledge nexus. Their power, in other words, is far less a matter of formal political influence, nor necessarily dependent on direct access to decision-making authorities, but instead depends on how think tanks operationalize their ideas through networks of influence across organizational boundaries. This ability to mobilize knowledge wields a significant degree of power and influence, making ideas available not just to policymakers and policy entrepreneurs, but simultaneously connecting them with the perspectives of diverse stakeholders across multiple groups. This connective nexus of power/knowledge provides think tanks with their distinctive position in civil society—making ideas available at critical times in the policy process (such as during times of critical uncertainty, when policymakers actively search for new but also available ideas).

Stone (2000) argues that their network interactions are key to understanding how think tanks penetrate political circles in practice, essentially acting as policy entrepreneurs. She gives the example of Kofi Annan, Secretary-General of the United Nations, who in 1999 convened a closed meeting of think tanks to guide UN policymaking. It is through network interactions such as this that think tanks operate far beyond local contexts, allowing them, in conjunction with others, to project ideas into policy thinking across regional and jurisdictional boundaries.

As McGann et al. (2014) comment, Stone's argument is that think tanks primarily concentrate on influential forms of engagement, rather than necessarily advocacy. Indeed, these views challenge the notion of think tanks as interest or advocacy groups, finding rather that they need interconnected engagement to exert influence upon government. Yet such engagement cannot be readily categorized as 'bridges' linking power (the government) and knowledge (social science research). Challenging what she describes as the myths surrounding policy think tanks, Stone (2007) argues that think tanks are not merely intermediaries between science and politics, but that knowledge and policy form a mutually constituted nexus. Think tanks provide the conceptual language, dominant paradigms, and real-world examples that may ultimately 'make it' into policy. Boundary-spanning networks provide think tanks with the power and knowledge resources to create influence across regional, national, and international levels of policy. This influence further requires actively building relationships that are essentially interconnected with multiple other parties. While this view contradicts the ideal of think tanks as autonomous and independent, it is precisely such positional power—lying at the intersection of diverse networks—that enables them to form, draw together, and 'prime' various forms of knowledge for policymakers, along with practical advice on implementation (Stone 2000).

In summary, we conclude with the following key points drawn from this brief review of the academic literature on think tanks. Think tanks are a significant and influential part of the public policy knowledge mobilization system. Through their networking activities, think tanks can be seen as an important part of civil society. The influence of their networks may be considerable and far-reaching, spanning both micro (person-to-person) and meso (organizational), so also potentially influencing macro levels of influence, debate, and policymaking. Furthermore, their vibrant networks create a potential role for individual policy entrepreneurs, or 'knowledge leaders' (Fischer et al. 2016) to connect, blend, and help mobilize ideas at various stages of the policymaking process.

More interestingly, this analysis suggests that think tanks may punch well above their weight in their potential influence on the policy process. When seen as significant switchboards and springboards for knowledge mobilization, their knowledge-focused activities at the edges of policymaking may exert greater influence than their positions as mere 'knowledge intermediaries' suggest. Especially when seen through a power knowledge lens, the activities of think tanks illustrate a powerful process of creating, assembling, diffusing, and mobilizing knowledge, potentially with significant influence on the policy process.

Returning to our argument about the role of think tanks seen as part of civil society, we now propose five dimensions to help analyse the extent to which a think tank could be seen as operating not just within but *for* civil society, in the particular context of UK health and public policy knowledge production. We suggest these dimensions may be useful as a possible 'ideal type' against which existing think tanks in this domain could be compared:

- In governance terms, a civil society-orientated think tank would be likely to be constituted as a not-for-profit organization governed by a board of trustees rather than being accountable to private shareholders as a public limited company or set up as a government agency within the public sector.
- In financial terms, it would preferably have an independent financial endowment to protect its autonomy or at the very least be able to attract funding from various funders to avoid overdependence on one or two large funders or donors which could erode its autonomy.
- In terms of activity, it would be likely to be both 'upwards facing' to policymakers and 'downwards facing' to rank-and-file constituencies. Such activities would be orientated to issues such as deprived geographical areas (in community development work), voices and perspectives of social movements (such as health service users), or epistemic communities (such as scientists), working with them to empower civil society interactions within the formal public policy world.
- Ideologically and discursively, the written texts it produces would be more aligned with network governance or Big Society ideas and the public good, rather than with New Public Management discourse.
- As a public interest-orientated organization, such a think tank would function by 'telling truth to power' and by offering public critique of official government policy in relation to important public/health policy issues, where necessary.

## The quadruple helix and public and health policy knowledge production in London

Having explored how think tanks function as a potentially key 'catalysing' element within civil society, we return to our focus on the quadruple helix of public and health policy knowledge production in London. In the following section, we first consider the major actors operating in this knowledge eco-system, before then presenting a case study of how one London-based think tank effectively mobilized knowledge across this quadruple helix to address emerging productivity issues facing the NHS.

## CENTRAL GOVERNMENT

Clearly, central government is a major actor in the quadruple helix, just as in the original triple helix model. In the UK case, core central ministries are located close together in central London and next to Parliament (reflecting the traditional and centralized 'Westminster and Whitehall' model of UK political institutions). These ministries include the Department of Health but also other central departments such as the Treasury (responsible for overall public expend-iture policy), and the Cabinet Office (responsible for public services reform). London is still by far the most important seat for government in England (however, the recent development of governments or assemblies in Scotland, Wales, and Northern Ireland shows a move to a more devolved system). Within England, the Department of Health and its operational agency (NHS England) have traditionally played a strong steering role from above.

Another direct role for central government in the domain of health care is to act as a customer for policy-related knowledge through its applied research and consultancy budgets. Again, its research budgets have been concentrated in one powerful research and development agency, the National Institute for Health Research, created in 2006, which has an annual budget of approxi-mately £1 billion (previously, devolved R&D budgets had been held at the regional level). The National Institute for Health Research funds a large number of different research programmes. Its Policy Related Research Pro-gramme commissions research to support policymaking in the Department of Health through various specialist policy research units operating at the national level, including one on policy innovation and evaluation.

A second and wider role for various ministries in central government is to build underlying infrastructure and capability across the London policy know-ledge ecosystem as elsewhere. It can, for example, make resources available, such as a ring-fenced national Higher Education Innovation Fund (HEIF) stream of funding to higher education institutions in London (and elsewhere) to support knowledge transfer activity. Another example is the use of public lottery funding to create an endowment for a new think tank located in central London, namely the National Endowment for Science, Technology and the Arts (NESTA), which pursues a pro-innovation agenda. This is a 'lighter touch' funding model than the direct commissioning of research units.

The quadruple helix model further implies that while government may be one funder, it does not have enough power to direct the knowledge production system by itself but rather has to negotiate with other actors. There may be alternative significant funders within a mixed funding model rather than one where government is a direct monopoly funder, as we will suggest.

## THE LONDON HIGHER EDUCATION SECTOR

Universities in London would also be expected to play a major role in the quadruple helix. As far as public and health policy knowledge production is concerned, STEM departments may generally be less important than social science departments, although departments of public health in medical schools may play an important role. However, research-intensive departments and academics in relevant social science and policy fields would be more attractive for policymakers to link to.

So how can we best characterize this sector? The London higher education sector is first of all a high-volume system. It has recently been estimated, using routinely collected Higher Education Statistics Agency statistics, that in 2014/15 London was home to no fewer than thirty-nine higher education institutions with a student population of about 370,000 (Londonhigher blog). It also contains some highly research-intensive higher education institutions. The recent ranking of universities by the *Times Higher Education* ranks four London-based universities—Imperial College, University College London, London School of Economics and Political Science, and King's College London—in the global top fifty (Times Higher Education 2017). These four key institutions all run masters' programmes in public or health policy and management which attract a substantial number of students, including international students. In addition, some single-subject institutions are widely recognized as very strong in relevant fields, including the London Business School in business education and research and the London School of Hygiene and Tropical Medicine (LSHTM) in public health.

University College London, the London School of Economics and Political Science, and King's College London each have large social science faculties, and indeed the London School of Economics is a specialist social science higher education institution with a strong academic presence in government and social policy. There are also large social policy-orientated research units, such as the well-known Personal Social Services Research Unit with a major branch at London School of Economics. The medical schools at University College London, King's College London, and Imperial College all have well-developed departments of public health. These schools have built up research capacity in the evaluation of health services, health services research, and in-service improvement. All three medical schools (and their wider higher education institutions) are an integral part of the three academic health sciences centres (only six of which are accredited in England) which cover the whole of London and which are seeking to develop translational research and knowledge mobilization (Fischer et al. 2013; French et al. 2014).

Both University College London and King's College London are large multifaculty institutions with a social science faculty alongside their arts and science faculties. (As already noted, London School of Economics is more social science based.) All three institutions are active in the public policy space, setting up bridging initiatives, for example, the King's Policy Institute, to build links with reflective policymakers and practitioners through seminars and events. These academic settings are geographically close to key ministries. Some individual senior academics have personal links with political parties, politicians, and the civil service and may be seconded for a period into government; in return, some reflective politicians or recently retired civil servants become visiting professors.

Imperial College is more a STEM-orientated institution but has a well-regarded business school with major research capacity in important and distinctive areas which fit with the institution's overall profile. These niche areas include technology, science policy, innovation, and entrepreneurship. Its medical school has a strong public health presence with a well-known global health policy institute.

All in all, we suggest the higher education sector in London offers major knowledge assets in health and public policy knowledge production, in terms of both high system volume and also high research intensity in key higher education institutions. Policy-relevant research capacity may be found distributed across business schools, other social science departments such as politics, government, and social policy, and also in the medical schools, notably their departments of public health.

## PRIVATE FIRMS: MANAGEMENT CONSULTANCIES

Within the private sector, management consultancy firms are here of particular interest. The sector has displayed long-term growth (McKenna 2006; Kirkpatrick et al. 2016), clearly evident within central London with well-known firms having their UK head offices there. Saint-Martin (2004) further suggests that the management consultancy sector has had a high degree of influence on UK government (when compared to France and Canada) and has proved resilient in repositioning itself to work with successive governments of different political colours.

London-based consultancies can perhaps be divided into generic and niche providers. Generic providers include major global firms such as McKinsey & Co. and Deloitte. There are also niche London-based consultancies, such as the Office of Public Management which specializes in public services assignments. Interestingly, on its website the Office of Public Management describes itself as a pioneering employee-owned public interest company in governance terms, rather than a private limited company or a professional partnership form.

While we lack precise data on the involvement of the main consulting firms in the UK health care sector, it appears to be substantial. Kirkpatrick et al. (2016, 525) argue: 'the activities mentioned so far point to how management consultants have become deeply involved in most aspects of the business of managing and organizing health care within the NHS'. They highlight the long-standing involvement of McKinsey & Co. and PA Consulting in strategic service reviews. GE Healthcare has recently been associated with work on Lean. The implementation of the 2012 Health and Social Care Act's reorganization of primary care was also extensively supported by management consultants. A previous chapter has looked at the consulting sector in depth so it will not form a major focus here.

## Health and public policy-related think tanks in London: an initial mapping and analysis

Having sketched the key actors operating in the government–university–firms triple helix, we next map the key civil society actors that potentially form the fourth helix. There are various think tanks that are highly concentrated geographically within central London, close to centres of political power. More recent foundations have sought to carve out a distinct niche in what is now a crowded field. Their central London base enables them potentially to build links with politicians, civil servants, and senior practitioners to achieve their aim of floating ideas and influencing public policy. Some are ideologically or politically aligned, while others adopt a more technical/rational mode of analysis.

These think tanks can be divided into three main clusters. We will present vignettes of twelve significant thank tanks which we divide into three clusters, based on our analysis of their public facing websites, selected publications, and texts. We will comment on their governance structure, their activities and/or influence in the health domain, and their exemplar types of texts.

Many of these think tanks are 'charitable companies' which means that they are both a private company limited by guarantee (so directors have only limited liability) and a charity. The same individuals often act both as directors of the company and trustees of the charity. Such entities have to file online annual returns to both Companies House and the Charity Commission (which can be downloaded and accessed as a useful source of information). It appears that their commercial activities tend to be subsidiary to—but help to finance—their more fundamental mission-driven work overseen by their trustees.

## CLUSTER 1. GENERIC AND POLITICALLY UNALIGNED THINK TANKS (3)

The first cluster consists of generically orientated and party-politically unaligned think tanks which work on the health care sector or the wider domain of public services reform from time to time, alongside a broader portfolio. The Royal Society of Arts (RSA) is the oldest foundation in the set. It was founded as early as 1754 as an institutional expression of the London eighteenth-century Enlightenment and is a not-for-profit organization with 28,000 Fellows (to declare an interest, both authors of this chapter are Fellows!). So, it is a membership-based organization. In governance terms, it is a charity with a royal charter with a board of trustees, as well as a Fellows' Council to represent the membership. The Fellows pay a subscription and help provide it with an independent financial base, along with income from some trading subsidiaries (RSA 2016). The RSA website characterizes its mission as to support the values of 'contemporary enlightenment' (reflecting its founding), along with social innovation and public policy-relevant research and ideas. The text's tone suggests it can be seen as ideologically progressive and reformist, although not associated with any one political party. It has three main research themes, one of which relates to strategies of public services reform.

Animating themes in this programme of work include decentralization, co-production with users, and a revival of democratic governance in local public services. It is also interested in supporting radical and realizable social innovation. Within the field of health care, the RSA is working with NHS England, NESTA, and the New Economics Foundation (two further central London-based think tanks) to promote the social movement agenda (as reviewed in an earlier chapter) in the NHS in what represents an interesting coalition. The tone suggests its value base is broadly aligned with the network governance narrative much more than with New Public Management (NPM) ideas.

The National Endowment for Science, Technology and the Arts (NESTA) is a recent foundation (1998) which works on social innovation, invention, the spotting of 'big new ideas', and the expanding digital policy space. It seems to favour disruptors rather than incumbents, as reflected in the core mission statement on the website: 'Nesta is an innovation foundation. We back new ideas to tackle the big challenges of our time.'

NESTA was initially funded from public money through a large endowment from UK national lottery funding. Originally set up as a governmental non-departmental executive body, it has recently been reconstituted (2012) as a charity with its own board of trustees and also as a private company limited by guarantee. Its annual report for 2015/16 (NESTA 2016) indicates that NESTA is formally the main operating charity, linked to the NESTA Trust (with about £16m in annual funding) and commercial subsidiaries. NESTA has worked with the Cabinet Office on strategies of public services reform, including social action-based approaches to innovation. It has also worked with the Behavioural Insights Team (of which it is a joint owner) on 'nudge' initiatives. NESTA has done some work on aspects of health policy, sometimes in alliance with the RSA, and also on the looming issue of antimicrobial resistance. In 2014, it launched the £10m Longitude Prize to tackle this threat, working with various partners including the BBC.

In 2015, it launched a 'Health Lab' initiative with the NHS:

which brings together a series of practical programmes in achieving systems change with the National Health Service (NHS), better use of technologies and more systematic approaches to peer to peer models of healthcare. The team also published an imaginative overview of how the NHS might look by 2030 with much more use of these different tools. We're convinced that their methods need to grow substantially if health systems are to avoid being trapped between rising demands and constrained resources. (Nesta 2016, 6)

This work included a stream on promoting digital health in dementia care. Key partners included the Department of Health, NHS England, the King's Fund, and the Health Foundation. The tone of the text is collaborative, with many partners listed working on specific projects.

The Michael Young Foundation was founded in 2005, but is directly descended from the Institute of Community Studies set up by Michael Young, the well-known serial social entrepreneur and institution builder, in the East End of London in 1954. Its website outlines its mission statement:

Our work focuses on the nature and form of structural inequalities and how we can best create the changes that will enable people to build resilient communities and lead more equal lives.

We do this by working alongside communities, using the tools of research and social innovation (new ways to meet social needs) to deliver national and international programmes, putting people at the heart of social change.

Its texts proclaim a strong and progressive value base, including a commitment to partnering with other relevant organizations. It is in formal governance terms again a charity governed by trustees and also a private company limited by guarantee. It also has various Fellows as associates.

Its annual report for 2016 (Michael Young Foundation 2016) indicates that it has no large endowment but is largely dependent on grants and earned fees (e.g. applied social research contracts). They have recently developed a transformation strategy to ensure better financial resilience. It is the only think tank in the group not located in central London but in the poorer East End of London. This choice may well reflect its strong history, not only of social activism but also of applied social policy research, including on local families partly undertaken there by Young himself (Willmott and Young 1957). Unusually, it is recognized by Research Councils UK as a bona fide independent research organization and specializes in ethnographic and qualitative methods.

While it is perhaps best known for its work on social innovation and social enterprises, its website describes several other core programmes. Its health and well-being programmes aim both to tackle health inequalities and to create sustainable and healthy communities. Its focus moves beyond NHS services and looks at wider social determinants of health inequality.

The foundation offers seminars and events, including co-design workshops, reflecting its participative values. The website indicates it partners with many collaborators both inside the UK (e.g. the Cabinet Office, London School of Economics, NESTA, and several research councils) and internationally (e.g. European Commission).

## CLUSTER 2. HEALTH SECTOR-BASED THINK TANKS, STILL PARTY UNALIGNED (4)

The second cluster to be considered consists of health sector-based think tanks still not aligned with political parties. The Wellcome Trust is a charitable foundation active in the broad field of medical and health care research, again located in central London. It is a registered charity governed by its board of governors. It has a major £21 billion investment portfolio so it has complete financial independence. Its website indicates that its mission is: 'to advance ideas'. Its four specified themes cover a vast range of territory going beyond: (i) understanding health and disease in biomedical research and (ii) improving health through encouraging innovations to wider goals of: (iii) engaging the public in conversations about health care through public engagement work and (iv) influencing health policy, including by helping create a collective voice for the community of science which can then better influence the policy process. It has supported the Department of Health in policymaking in areas it is expert in, for example, a policy review on accelerating the uptake of evidence-based innovations in the UK health care system (Accelerated Access Review 2016). While it is London-based and has links with the English Department of Health, Wellcome also has global reach and ambition and funds many projects in developing health systems.

The King's Fund can be seen as a medium-scale organization (with a 2015 budget of about £15 million) but is also the oldest in this group, founded in 1897 by the then Prince of Wales. In governance terms, it is an independent charity governed by a board of trustees and has a royal charter. The main sources of its funds are its own substantial endowment, which provides about a third of its income, and also money from NHS organizations, which use its leadership development or organizational development programmes or attend fee-generating events. There is also funding from corporate partners, including GlaxoSmithKline.

King's Fund typically seeks to develop a bi-partisan and consensus-building approach to current UK health policy issues: its website states that 'our vision is that the best possible care is available to all', avoiding strong political or ideological alignment. It provides independent research and analysis of current UK health policy, undertakes applied research for health care bodies, produces reports and publications, blogs, and events with well-known speakers, and delivers health care leadership development programmes and consultancy in organizational development. It historically has had close links with MPs, the Department of Health, and the NHS management field as it is a well-known sectoral 'insider'. Its main streams of work lie in health and care services, leadership, systems and organizations, patients, people, society and policy, and finance and performance. While there are streams of work on the themes of volunteers and health inequalities, many of its texts demonstrate an expert and rather rationalist approach to health policy and it seems less influenced by social movements from below than some other think tanks.

The third example is the Nuffield Trust which again is a registered charitable trust governed by trustees, and also a private company limited by guarantee. It was founded in 1940 as the Nuffield Provincial Hospitals Trust and later renamed the Nuffield Trust for Research and Policy Studies in Health Services in 1988 to reflect better its core purpose, with the 'Nuffield Trust' chosen as its working name. It lies on the applied research end of the think tank spectrum. It has some distinguished Senior Associates from the academic and policy worlds whose advice it can draw on. It has a strong research focus on health policy, notably on health economics, markets, and financing. It has published applied research widely on NHS productivity and currently has a health care quality research project jointly with the Health Foundation. It is a smaller trust with an income of about £3 million, with roughly £2 million coming from its charitable endowment and £1 million in contract research and project work (e.g. the evaluation of the North West London Integrated Care Programme with London School of Economics).

Fourth, the Health Foundation is a more recent foundation (2003) with the benefit of a very substantial endowment (currently valued at £900 million) from the sale of the PPP insurance group, so it has no need to engage in further fundraising activity. In governance terms, it is a charity governed by its trustees. It co-owns the *BMJ Quality and Safety* journal, which is an important academic publication in its field. Its work tends to be focused on quality and service improvement issues, being a substantial research commissioner in those fields. A major theme is promoting the engagement of front-line clinical staff in positive organizational change. Its 2015 expenditure was about £28 million (Health Foundation 2015). It works with partners, such as the King's Fund on the NHS transformation fund, or NHS Improvement on quality improvement initiatives.

## CLUSTER 3. GENERIC AND MORE POLITICAL THINK TANKS (5)

The third cluster consists of politically aligned but generic think tanks which undertake work on public services reform or health policy, as well as on other sectors and issues. Some of their texts display a more political and ideological style of writing; others combine a strong value base with technical analytic skills and a more academic style. They vary in the extent to which they are formally aligned with one political party.

The oldest example is the Fabian Society (founded in 1884) which is constitutionally affiliated to the Labour Party as a Socialist Society, although its website also states: 'The society is however editorially, organizationally and financially independent of the Labour Party and works with a wide range of partners of all political persuasions and none.'

The website defines its guiding values as follows:

We are not a doctrinal organisation but the Fabian tradition informs how we think and what we do. No other think tank has an adjective of its own. Our commitment to Fabianism means we believe in the fight against inequality, the power of collective action and an internationalist outlook. We believe in social progress, evidence, expertise, rationality and long-termism. We advocate gradualist, reformist and democratic means in a journey towards radical ends. We are a pluralist movement and create space for open debate.

It is a membership-based organization with individual members who pay subscriptions and elect its executive committee which governs the Society rather than the more conventional board of trustees (as the Society cannot be a charity, having explicit party-political objectives). There are currently seventy local Fabian societies in the UK which extend well beyond London, although its head office is in central London. Their annual report indicates commissioned research is also a major source of income, although its total budget is only about £700,000. It has a range of partners, including with various trade unions (Fabian Society 2017).

The Society has five central work-streams, including one on public services and communities with a strong interest in questions of social integration and health localism (given the recent devolution of responsibility to some cities and regions in England). Its online presence showcases many written texts, including the traditional form of the pamphlet.

The Institute of Economic Affairs (founded in 1955) is by contrast a right-of-centre think tank, historically more aligned with elements within the Conservative Party. It was an influential source of outside and on occasion radical advice to government in the Thatcher period. Formally, it is an educational charity and an independent research institute limited by guarantee (so it files at Companies House as well as the Charity Commission). It is governed by a board of trustees. Its website states:

Ideas and policies produced by the Institute are freely available from our website for any individual or organisation to adopt, but we do not 'sell' policy. The Institute is entirely independent of any political party or group, and is entirely funded by voluntary donations from individuals, companies, and foundations who want to support its work, plus income from book sales and conferences. It does no contract work and accepts no money from government.

Its overall positioning is to be suspicious of 'big government', favouring free market-based policy solutions and strong property rights. It adopts an economic mode of analysis, applied to different policy sectors. As well as face-to-face events (such as its annual Hayek lecture), its lively website offers new modes of communication, such as tweets, blogs, and TV podcasts, as well as more traditional downloadable discussion papers. Its publication policy is that these papers should be blind peer-reviewed before publication so it retains a strong academic base and culture, and has a distinguished Academic Advisory Council to assist it with this blind peer-review task.

A recent annual report indicates a budget of about £2 million per year so it is relatively small scale. Its income comes mainly from donations, with some funding from sales of publications and events. Unlike many think tanks, it accepts no money from government, a policy which can be seen as consistent with its principles. It positions its overall work programme as follows:

Continuing themes are over-regulation, much of it stemming from the European Union; systemic problems in the welfare state, including social security, education and health services; infrastructure deficiencies; and other aspects of government interference. The Institute of Economic Affairs has recently embarked on a major project (the Paragon Initiative) to critically examine every aspect of government activity from an economic perspective and propose major reform.

As part of the Paragon Initiative, a recent discussion paper (Niemietz 2017) argues that UK health care spending seen as a proportion of GDP has moved up from 5 per cent in 1990 to 10 per cent now, which is not grossly out of line with comparators. However, UK health care spending is disproportionately loaded onto the public purse. The UK private sector is much smaller than in many other health care systems and with a more rigid boundary with the public sector. UK private insurance levels remain low when compared internationally. It is also not clear whether the NHS can achieve the 'heroic' productivity improvements now expected of it.

The text then argues that much current NHS spend goes on the very elderly (over 85), a demographic group projected to expand in the future. So, there are substantial upward pressures on public expenditure in this key sector. The suggestion is to move from a 'pay-as-you-go' to a 'pre-pay' system similar to pension funds where people of working age build up a reserve fund over their working careers for their old age which would be protected from short-term government decisions. While people would not be able to access these funds directly (Niemietz 2017, 38) and the NHS would act as their custodian, these funds would still be defined as private property with certain rights.

Founded in 1988, the Institute of Public Policy Research (IPPR) was originally close to New Labour and a key part of the modernizing centre left of the 1990s It has been described as not so much as a 'think tank' but rather a 'pink tank' (Toolky 1992). It is formally a registered charity governed by a board of trustees, with income of about £4 million a year, according to its latest annual report and with a commercial trading subsidiary set up as a private company. It describes its mission as follows: 'Our purpose is to conduct and promote research into, and the education of the public in, the economic, social and political sciences, science and technology, the voluntary sector and social enterprise, public services, and industry and commerce.'

It undertakes policy-orientated research for a wide variety of funders (private, public, and third sector), many of them smaller scale projects. Its website declares it to be a 'progressive' think tank but also states that it never accepts funds from political parties.

Devolution is a strong theme. A recent publication by the IPPR (Quilter-Pinny and Gorsky 2017) explores the recent devolution of health and social care responsibility within England (e.g. the recent experiment in the major northern city of Manchester whereby a £6 billion health and social care budget has been devolved to its local NHS and local authority). This is a potentially important development in extending devolution to English regions and cities (King's Fund 2015a, 2015b). The IPPR publication includes short essays from well-known academics and experts, along with an initial commentary. This work was sponsored by the Wellcome Trust, a major London-based science-orientated foundation (as already reviewed), and with an academic collaboration with the Centre of Public Health at LSHTM. Consistent with its long-standing support for devolution, the IPPR is unusual among think tanks in having branches outside London: in Edinburgh, and also Manchester which takes a special interest in public policy issues in the North of England, such as poor transport links.

Demos (founded 1993) is a registered charity (and also private company limited by guarantee) originally seen as close to New Labour but which now describes itself as a leading 'cross-party' think tank. It is governed by a board of trustees. Its website indicates a commitment to a strong and multidisciplinary research presence alongside a more devolved and bottom-up politics:

Demos has always been interested in power: how it works, and how to distribute it more equally throughout society. We believe in trusting people with decisions about their own lives and solving problems from the bottom-up.

We pride ourselves on working together with the people who are the focus of our research. Alongside quantitative research, Demos pioneers new forms of deliberative work, from citizens' juries and ethnography to ground breaking social media analysis.

Its 2017 annual report indicated that its annual income was only about £1 million, with a small deficit arising in the year (Demos 2017). The funding came overwhelmingly from charitable activities and there was no large endowment. The trustees were actively preparing a financial recovery plan.

Demos currently has four core policy areas including one on welfare and public services, covering health and social care. This work seeks to propose solutions to major social policy challenges including public services reform. Its recent reports on health care issues (e.g. measuring the financial impact of motor neurone disease) can be seen as thoroughly researched, substantial in scale, and relatively non-ideological in tone.

More recent think tanks include ResPublica (founded in 2009), which describes itself on its website as a non-party-political organization:

Our ideas are founded on principles which move beyond the current political dichotomies of left and right. We favour the pursuit of the common good and the development of real wealth that promotes human flourishing. Our work—which includes policy innovation, research, publications, events and commentary across a wide range of policy areas—is framed and directed by three key programmes: Society, Prosperity and Virtue.

ResPublica offers various services, including events, publications, 'thought leadership', and consulting. There is a strong value base, for example, in its notion of a 'virtuous' rather than a hedonistic consumer society. The mode of writing is more literary than narrowly technical. It is associated with so-called 'Red Tory' thought which rejected the neo-liberal inheritance. ResPublica tends to favour post-liberal, communitarian, and third-sector solutions which move beyond the old state/market binary. It is specifically (and again unusually) associated with a book influential with the then leadership of the Conservative Party under David Cameron (Blond 2010). As explored previously, this book helped potentiate a novel Big Society approach to public services reforming. This narrative moved beyond privatization and New Public Management-based reforms in its support for staff-owned mutuals as an alternative organizational form.

This text (Blond 2010) has a specific chapter (chapter 10) on public services reform. It advocates a so-called 'civil state' with strong and vibrant professions (p. 239): 'in order to put a virtuous society at the centre, we require not only a mutualist civil economy, but also a civil state in which professional responsibility has been restored to individuals and collegiate groups'. This argument is radically different from the NPM view that the public services professions form an opaque collusion system against the laity. A need to re-engage front-line public services staff with positive organizational change had been created by dysfunctional NPM reforms (driven by the over-influence of public choice theory) which led to ever-escalating and pointless audit and accountability regimes (p. 140).

A recent pamphlet on the future of the professions (Blond et al. 2015) develops this argument further with three examples of teaching, law, and medicine. So, the focus goes beyond but includes health care. This text suggests that the professions currently have failed to uphold their founding principles (this may be because of the overdominance of NPM reforms). The dehumanization of patients in the NHS—and the failure of the medical and nursing professions to protect the basic safety of patients—had been notably highlighted by the Francis Report (2013) on gross failures in patient care in Mid Staffs NHS Trust.

They then argue that within the health care sector (Blond et al. 2015, 2): 'When professions fail, the state steps in to regulate, and that all too often compounds rather than addresses the problem. In health, centralisation often leads to more fragmentation: as targets focus solely on the point of crisis, attention drifts from wider issues and the goal of holistic care recedes still further.' These micro interventions are dysfunctional, as elaborating rules just creates the need for even more rules to resolve ambiguity and combat the gaming by the professions to appear to meet targets. Instead, the medical profession should regenerate an internal sense of purpose and vocation and recover a vision of holistic care. The ultimate sanction for unacceptable behaviours should be being struck off by the self-regulating professional body.

ResPublica is in governance terms a private company limited by guarantee rather than a charity. It therefore has directors rather than trustees and files returns at Companies House rather than the Charity Commission. Recent files uploaded there (ResPublica 2017) suggest it may have cash-flow problems and it entered into a voluntary agreement with creditors in 2017.

Overall, then, we see a strong concentration of knowledge producers in the UK public/health policy field, tightly clustered within central London. Spanning across the quadruple helix of government, universities, private industry, and civil society, these diverse groupings of knowledge producers should permit—at least in theory—strong potential for interactions and exchange between various actors. To explore in further depth how such interactions might operate in day-to-day practice, we next turn to our case study of one knowledge-producing health policy think tank and its links with the wider UK public/health policy field.

# A case study of knowledge production in a health policy think tank in London

Beechwell was a think tank with a well-established reputation for rigorous and independent analysis of the English health care system. Overall, its use of management knowledge could be seen as not merely as using or mobilizing existing knowledge, but also as actively creating new knowledge through its own research. As an intermediary organization, spanning both academic research and applied organizational advisory work, its approach to management knowledge included an array of methods and also media-focused publications, designed to stimulate policy and organizational interest and potential applications. Our interest in Beechwell's engagement with QIPP arose through initial interviews here, which described some researchers' rather independent efforts to actively influence the QIPP policy agenda.

## A NETWORK-BASED KNOWLEDGE 'SWITCHBOARD'

Perhaps unsurprisingly for a think tank, staff often identified themselves as being autonomous and independently minded in their ideas. Involving a diverse group of committed and often passionately engaged individuals, Beechwell employees had diverse career routes, typically also working as academic researchers, management consultants, health care professionals and managers, or policy advisers from government or other policy-related NGOs.

We've got people from CQC, NICE, people who worked at the BBC, all sorts of different backgrounds—people who are good expert writers, field researchers, data analysts...

Accordingly, staff members' professional networks spanned many agencies, and contributed to what staff described as the wider 'Beechwell community'— including health services and policy communities.

What characterizes people is a strong desire to be both in and out at the same time...the whole organisation is littered with very independent practitioners. It's a jazz band rather than orchestra, loosely connected people with strong values who want to make a difference. We may not agree about the route but it doesn't really matter. So, a culture across the organization, of passion and wanting to make a difference.

Professional identities can be interlinked with such wider communities (which are sometimes a source of future as well as previous employment), serving as important sources of ideas and knowledge. Accordingly, staff described a strong felt sense of Beechwell as a heterogeneous mix of diverse backgrounds and influences, bound together by a strong value base and rationality focused on improving the English health care system.

Individuals (are) there both in their own right and as members of Beechwell, it's much more family-like...it feels it...you get people in a room (and) it works.

This variety of influences, shaped by a primary purpose of tackling challenges facing the health system, also shaped how management knowledge was thought about— not as an end in itself, but as a means of actively driving change in health care.

So, what are the issues, big issues out there which may be big and everybody knows they're big or they may, in our view, be important but nobody's doing anything on them...

The issue of relevance...people want to work here rather than an academic institution because they value knowledge that makes a difference...We don't just want to just produce ideas, we want (to change) things...to make some practical difference.

Even more traditional academic researchers described a shift in their orientation towards knowledge that was stimulated primarily by pressing or foreseeable issues in the emerging health care and policy environment. Researchers described being driven far less by theoretical questions than in addressing emerging challenges. Indeed, abilities to identify and respond to such challenges tended to be highly valued and were seen as a source of career advantage within the think tank and policy context.

> The people who have been most successful have come up with original ideas … people who are kind of creative, more aware of the outside context … Those who kind of do horizon scanning, pre-empt developments … big thinkers, big picture people.

Accordingly, staff described a rather elastic and diffuse notion of evidence as researchers deliberately sought out and drew upon more heterogeneous and varied sources of knowledge, often taken from their wider communities and stakeholder organizations.

> So being a 'do tank' … (we look) not only to the published sort of systematic review evidence, but a more diffuse evidence base about what is going on … that was relevant to people leading healthcare organizations. For our work to be as practical and relevant to them as it was to Westminster policymakers, (because) you can influence policy but it can have almost no impact on what's going on the ground.

Such horizon scanning was regarded as important not just as a means of detecting emerging issues and perspectives within the health care system, but as part of a pragmatic commitment to creating knowledge which could be responded to, so providing workable solutions for diverse stakeholders. While Beechwell staff were motivated by rigorous analysis and independence of thought, they also emphasized their primary purpose as serving the health system as critical friends and advisers, sensitive to the experiences of health care professionals and managers.

> There is a way of thinking, which I suppose is about engagement and understanding … trying to get alignment between heart and head … There's a massive assumption in the field that what was blocking (change among medical consultants) was something cognitive and practical, but actually they were furious and terrified.

This close engagement with the field is not merely a source of empirical insights and ideas, but provides significant understanding of the health system as a potentially receptive context for management knowledge. Beechwell's external orientation can be seen recursively as being both receptive to emerging issues of concern, as well as deliberately assessing and promoting the field's absorptive capacity (Cohen and Levinthal 1990) for mobilizing management knowledge and practicable solutions. As the following policy adviser suggested, this engagement with the health system attempted to create new, rigorous yet timely knowledge just 'ahead of the curve', to shape both policy and practice.

Our independence is really critical for us... our influence and bringing about a high-performing health care system... getting that translated both into policy and into practice. I think we'll lose a trick if we spend all of our time doing three-year research projects and becoming more like an academic institution, because actually life moves so quickly in the NHS. However, we still need to be academically credible and do rigorous and robust work—we don't want to become a [management consultancy]—style everything's done in three months... rehashing evidence. So, we've got a difficult balance to take.

Overall, staff described iterative cycles in this knowledge production process, moving from field sensitivity to creating knowledge, crafting messages and techniques for publishing them, and working with stakeholders to actively stimulate potential impact.

But the key issue is what we do about it... we don't conclude by saying we found this—we conclude by saying so what?! (And I'm bashing the table!) We have to interact with lots of people... present our work to a wider range of stakeholders... What we're trying to look for is as much the people who are the audience we're trying to reach, to (ask) does this get our messages across? Have we got the right messages? Are there other things here you would find interesting?

## FROM SWITCHBOARD TO SPRINGBOARD: THE MOBILIZING EFFECTS OF KNOWLEDGE LEADERSHIP

Whereas individual researchers may stimulate and generate ideas within their own communities, they also serve as significant conduits for bridging knowledges across diverse policymaking and health systems. Unsurprisingly, we saw this pattern operating among the most senior members of the organization whose knowledge leadership role (Fischer et al. 2016) illustrated how ideas may be actively mobilized across diverse policymaking, commissioning, and provider aspects of the health system.

The Chief Executive is hugely in touch with the NHS, is out a lot, and spends lots of time in NHS organizations... with a portfolio of (the CEO's) own... A lot of time travelling in the NHS, very concerned about the cross-fertilization of knowledge of people in the community, combined with the policy experts and getting that dialogue going at the sort of high level.

Overall, such network-based engagement means that the notion of think tanks as knowledge 'switchboards' is not merely an internal aspect of their work, but can be seen as an important part of their external function—by linking together and potentially enabling conversations spanning diverse strands of health policy and the wider health care system. As they engage in micro-level action, think tanks connect diverse networks and communities, potentially stimulating discussions among various external groups. Such multiple opportunities for engagement function to anchor individuals within wider knowledge networks, so providing potential sources of ideas, while also being a significant organizational resource for mobilizing management knowledge at meso and macro political levels.

As several respondents observed, senior-level directors and especially the chief executive were visibly engaged with the external policy environment by actively connecting and spanning government, health care organizations, universities, and other think tanks. Such activity was seen as a powerful means of combining long-term engagement with stakeholders, providing a rich source of knowledge, and helping in mobilizing knowledge, ideas, and influence between these diverse settings.

So, there is a strong centre of power . . . the chief executive's (policy engagement) has always been its own island of activity in the bubble of the policy world, talking to the (Minister) of this world, the (Department of Health) stuff and doing the high, international bits and pieces . . . Very adept at these network-like influences and getting you in contact with other people . . . (to) have those conversations with the Minister, you know.

Importantly, our analysis of such leadership engagement is that it is not merely providing advocacy or a means of lobbying and political influence. Instead, we find think tank leadership is powerfully engaged in commissioning and conducting high-profile research activity that becomes highly significant as potentially 'dynamising' (Mazzucato 2013) sources of knowledge and influence in their own right. As a senior stakeholder commented:

You may have said that (Beechwell) would collectively commission some piece of analysis, but that hasn't been the case. (The CEO) went off and commissioned it himself . . . you've got this sort of slight mix (of leadership activities) where (the CEO) asked these five people to go off and do some work looking at different aspects . . . (of) policy work.

As we have argued before (Fischer et al. 2016), such knowledge leadership involves effortful and personal engagement with research ideas and other people and operating agentically through deliberately connecting and mobilizing knowledge through relations with others. As in this case, senior organizational leaders were involved not merely as conduits of research, but were powerfully engaged in stimulating and producing high-visibility research, actively connecting it to critical areas of influence and potential points of intervention in the health system.

## THE ANALYSIS OF QIPP—HOW A THINK-TANK 'SPRINGBOARD' MOBILIZES KNOWLEDGE WITHIN THE PUBLIC POLICY QUADRUPLE HELIX

In considering how these network-like, micro-level arrangements can create potential organizational springboards, the example of research into the QIPP issue provides some intriguing insights into the way both individual researchers and think tanks themselves interact with other agencies in competing for policy impact. Here think tanks recognized themselves as operating in a crowded arena, where a number of agencies—management consultancies, government departments, research institutes, and other think tanks—competed to produce noticeable, impactful ideas.

In the overtly politicized context of the QIPP issue (as considered earlier), such competition for authoritative knowledge is hardly surprising. The influential Wanless Report (2002) previously examined evidence on likely scenarios for the UK health care system, drawing on an international panel of academic experts. In their efforts to provide similarly authoritative management knowledge for policymakers, diverse London-based research institutes and consultancies produced reports focused on QIPP, often in close collaboration with other agencies.

Thus, McKinsey & Co. (2009) worked with the Department of Health to produce a financial analysis of a likely funding gap of £15–20 billion. The University of York's Centre for Health Economics (2017), produced numerous published reports examining variations in the productivity and efficiency of the NHS. In conjunction with the Institute for Fiscal Studies, the Kings Fund similarly produced a series of reports examining scenarios and analysis on the financial climate, their consequences, and options for future funding. The Nuffield Trust collaborated with both the Institute for Fiscal Studies and the London School of Economics to examine funding pressures on the NHS in what it terms 'a decade of austerity' (Roberts et al. 2012).

In this emerging landscape, the production of authoritative texts is clearly important, but how do these emerge from think tanks' day-to-day 'switchboard' activities to produce the kind of impactful 'springboard' effects that think tanks seek to achieve?

As one think tank director described, the team's initial interest in QIPP arose from emerging discussions with doctors and managers whose personal experiences and reactions to QIPP provided an early indication of its potential impact on health services:

(This) has just evolved from interesting conversations. We've been really interested in what doctors are saying (about financial pressures)...and really hearing alarm bells. Of course (my team) gather information all the time from people telling their stories and we don't make as much use of that as we could do, (so we then talked) to some leaders of the teaching hospitals who are really worried about (QIPP).

The team's early interest in the perspectives of health professionals and managers on QIPP prompted them to explore more broadly. Interestingly, the think tanks we spoke to described the need to make an impactful contribution to policy. As one manager described, it was not sufficient that issues are experienced as locally important, but that the potential analysis should chime with a wider group of stakeholders, with potential for wider policy and health system implications.

I think people want to be convinced that (this) is a high-priority issue ... We always get approaches from people, 'could we do an enquiry ...' Well I'm sure it's very important, but is it a big enough issue (with) wide implications, great resonance?

So, what are the issues, big issues out there that (may be) important but nobody's doing anything on them ... It was clear a few years ago that the good times wouldn't last, (but what are) the implications of that for the NHS?

Furthermore, an important dilemma for various think tanks was the need to clearly differentiate their own contribution from that of other agencies. At a time when other organizations were also working on QIPP (in particular McKinsey & Co. was working with the Department of Health on financial analysis), think tank researchers were motivated to find a distinct angle or niche that could differentiate their work and create knowledge that would potentially produce change in the health system.

We actually had quite a lot of trouble thinking what we would do that these other people weren't doing ... In fact, there's a lot of work by researchers (at other think tanks) ... so we felt well there are other people better placed (than us and with) more knowledge ... Management consultancies and McKinseys do (some of this) work too. So, we had quite a bit of trouble thinking, what we'd actually do.

As one researcher described it, their analysis and recommendations sought to carve out a distinctive niche where the think tank could be (and be seen as being) distinctively impactful.

We're not a lobbying organization, but we do want to change things, otherwise what's the point?

So, we find here a search for management knowledge that is inherently tied to its mobilization. Such endeavour went beyond efforts to mobilize individual reports, but represented an enduring attempt to activate and energize a stream of management knowledge focused on influencing health care policy.

There is actually a very clear role that the chief executive's playing ... and has clearly been hugely captivated by the experience of some of the (most effective healthcare) organizations. And that is a thread ... you won't write a (policy) paper these days without it appearing somewhere (in the policy world), so that has been very powerful.

However, we suggest the most significant impact of think tanks lies less in their individual contributions than in the interactions between these texts in co-producing not merely influential ideas, but a cumulative body of knowledge (in the form of authoritative texts), thereby representing a significant influence within and by civil society. Indeed, we suggest the example of QIPP illustrates the role of think tanks in surfacing and mobilizing knowledge in ways that may then be mobilized in other strands of the quadruple helix. As one senior stakeholder (a management consultant) commented:

It was a bit frustrating that having done this (consulting) work you could never talk about it because of course it was sort of quite confidential... And so actually being able to have (think tank) reports that you could talk about... was very useful... Very helpful in terms of, you know, having that data from an organization that is perceived as objective, and then particularly as we got close to the general election... to have something from a non-party political organization saying that there is a financial crisis.

Despite wider interest in think tanks' individual reports on QIPP, respondents commented that the internal research focus was necessarily crowded out by other, competing policy items pressing on the NHS at that time. In particular, a major policy white paper, *Liberating the NHS* (Department of Health 2010a), produced a dominant wave of activity responding to the government's vision for health care. Accordingly, research activity within think tanks was—at least in the short term—diverted towards this rapidly progressing policy agenda.

Of course, that has now taken a more dominant role and so (our research) has lost traction because a lot of energy that had to go in to responding to the need of the environment... But clearly now it's coping with the organizational change... and we've been quite heavily engaged in responding.

Despite the original research on QIPP appearing to lose momentum and organizational attention *within* particular think tanks, we find, intriguingly, a continuing and growing wave of activity *between* think tanks through rather informal networks of committed researchers. Importantly, this activated a continuing stream of publications, with several think tanks collaborating to create a powerful and coherent voice on the impact of QIPP on health care. As part of a response to the UK government's 2015 Comprehensive Spending Review, the Nuffield Trust, the Health Foundation, and the King's Fund (2015)—all think tanks based in central London—created a powerful joint submission to the Health Select Committee of the House of Commons which provided an authoritative view, based on their cumulative analysis of QIPP and its effects since 2009:

The outcome of the 2015 Spending Review will profoundly shape NHS and social care services in England over the rest of this decade. Our three organisations have come together to provide the Health Select Committee with a clear, objective, and independent view of its implications...

(Nuffield Trust, Health Foundation, and Kings Fund 2015, 1)

It is important that the government is honest with the public about the implications of the settlement for what the NHS and social care can deliver. Both services are now set for a decade-long funding squeeze which will see spending as a share of GDP [Gross Domestic Product] fall and leave the United Kingdom behind many other advanced nations on this measure of spending. In the face of unprecedented financial pressures and rising demand for services, this is not sustainable. We reiterate the call we all made before the Spending Review for a new settlement which places health and social care on a sustainable footing for the future.

(Nuffield Trust, Health Foundation, and King's Fund 2015, 13)

We suggest the case of QIPP indicates the most significant impact of think tanks lies less in their individual contributions than in their wider work of mobilizing knowledge between think tanks and the other strands of the quadruple helix of public policy knowledge production in London. When combined, these texts provide a compelling body of evidence and build expert consensus within an influential nexus of management knowledge, which is strongly interconnected across the health care system. This power/knowledge nexus illustrates the influence of think tanks and their role as part of mobilizing an active civil society within the quadruple helix of public policy knowledge production.

## Do the London think tanks operate as civil society organizations within a quadruple helix?

We now return to our earlier dimensions which we suggested might define an 'ideal type' of think tank in the UK public/health policy field, functioning as a civil society-orientated organization. To reiterate, we see such functioning as important when considering their role in the quadruple helix model of knowledge production, because such think tanks should operate not merely within but *for* civil society.

We reprise our original assertions against our later review of think tanks' websites and documentation, augmenting our assessment through the particular lens of the case study. We had initially argued that the following dimensions would be important:

1. In governance terms, a civil society-orientated think tank would be likely to be constituted as a not-for-profit organization governed by a board of trustees rather than being accountable to private shareholders as a public limited company or set up as a government agency within the public sector.

Looking across the twelve think tanks considered, most demonstrate a major element of a not-for-profit model of governance which includes registered charity status and accountability to a board of trustees. Two (RSA and the Fabians) further demonstrate an element of a membership-based mode of accountability. A number exhibit a mixed mode of governance which also includes status as a private company limited by guarantee. This mechanism appears to protect relatively small-scale commercial subsidiaries which then support the core mission activity overseen by the trustees. One only example (ResPublica) appears solely to have a public limited company-based form of governance.

2. In financial terms, it would preferably have an independent financial endowment to protect its autonomy or at the very least be able to attract funding from various funders to avoid overdependence on one or two large funders or donors which could erode its autonomy.

The Wellcome and the Health Foundation have the benefit of very major endowments; King's Fund, the Nuffield, and NESTA have smaller but still substantial endowments. Documentation from some other think tanks, however, reported some financial anxiety which might potentially lead to an overdependence on short-term NHS project work.

3. In terms of activity, it would be likely to be both 'upwards facing' to policy-makers, as well as 'downwards facing' to rank-and-file constituencies. Such activities would be orientated to issues such as deprived geographical areas (in community development work), voices and perspectives of social movements (such as health service users), or epistemic communities (such as scientists), working with them to empower civil society inter-actions within the formal public policy world.

There appeared to be a variable pattern on this dimension, as some think tanks appeared to be strongly Westminster and Whitehall centred (IPPR and the Fabians were interesting exceptions with a strong out-of-London presence). The Michael Young Foundation's long history of working with deprived communities further stood out as a strongly downwards-facing style. The Wellcome Trust's work with the broader science community is also of interest, as was the RSA's work with its own large-scale fellowship.

4. Ideologically and discursively, the written texts it produces would be more aligned with network governance or Big Society ideas and the public good, rather than with New Public Management discourse.

The language and key words used by a significant cluster of think tanks indeed appear more compatible with 'bottom-up' network governance (RSA, Demos, IPPR, Fabians, Health Foundation, also to some extent Wellcome) or Big Society ideas (ResPublica, Michael Young Foundation). No think tank displayed the narrow managerialist language of the NPM, although the Institute of Economic Affairs remained an outlier in its attachment to market-led (but rather non-managerialist) ideas in a broader field which appeared generally indifferent or even suspicious of them.

5. As a public interest-orientated organization, such a think tank would function by 'telling truth to power' and by offering public critique of official government policy in relation to important public/health policy issues, where necessary.

Particular examples of such 'truth telling' were evident in the united front between various London think tanks on the major issue of QIPP and also the Wellcome Trust's strong involvement in the Accelerated Access Review which was critical (if rather more implicitly) of previous policy direction. But these examples were relatively rare.

Overall, examples of each dimension could be found, sometimes in significant clusters. So, the framework could be operationalized and helped highlight the presence of an additional type of actor to those considered in the triple helix model. However, real-world think tanks (unsurprisingly) did not always correspond to the ideal type advanced but also contained hybrid elements. More and more intensive work in this area would be fruitful to explore which think tanks correspond most closely to the ideal type.

## Concluding discussion

Think tanks, first, should be seen as significant public and health policy knowledge producers in their own right. Moreover, we argue they play a major role that punches above their weight within wider system of public and health policy knowledge as they seek to (and on occasion are able to) win substantial influence on the UK health policymaking process.

We have, second and more specifically, argued that think tanks are an important part of what we see as the spatially based London public policy knowledge 'ecosystem'. There is a high concentration of key actors in central London whose networks may be dispersed, yet also interconnected, and which operate across a relatively small geographical area close to political power centres. Knowledge exchanges across and between these networks are actively mobilized through the day-to-day work of think tank employees, but think tanks (and especially their leaders) also establish embedded relations with diverse policy, academic, and health care provider communities.

Third, we argued (on the basis of an early analysis, although augmented by our case-study analysis) that a significant cluster of the think tanks examined showed some key features of civil society-orientated organizations. The implication is that the triple helix model is by itself too narrow and that the later quadruple helix version is helpfully additive.

Fourth, we suggested that the type of knowledge produced is distinctive. Many of the think tanks examined deliberately sought out and attempted to exploit distinct niches of expertise. They were focused on addressing pressing policy issues, orientated towards producing utilizable and pragmatic knowledge and directed towards prompting change across diverse audiences of public policy and health service stakeholders. Accordingly, we see distinct texts and technologies (such as blogs, pamphlets, and Twitter feeds alongside reports, stakeholder roundtables, and conferences) which were crafted to rapidly inform and shape thinking among key audiences. These communication modes are often integrated with processes of knowledge production that reflect an intent to achieve local absorption and wider knowledge mobilization.

So how do think tanks compare with other knowledge producers examined in this book? Relatively unencumbered by the profit motivation, confidentiality clauses, and client contracts that characterize management consultancy projects, think tanks can access, draw upon, and publicly report various data, knowledge, analyses, opinions, and recommendations which draw attention to critical issues of public importance. As we have seen, such motivations are not value neutral in terms of their intended impact, nor academically aloof (as in, say, the case of university-based research), but motivated by the desire to make a distinctive, notable, and timely contribution to shaping policy ideas and debates. Think-tank knowledge production may thus have a distinctive voice and tenor which is deliberately crafted to amplify and mobilize knowledge across diverse sets of stakeholders. As one senior stakeholder suggested to us, they may be able to publish findings in controversial and difficult areas (such as QIPP) where government or commissioned research or consultancy agencies may be either reluctant or unable (because of confidentiality clauses) to publicize.

Whereas much literature reviewed focused on the role of individual think tanks, our analysis suggests that this organization-specific focus rather misses the point. At least as far as our study of the London health policy ecosystem is concerned, some of the major impact of think tanks arises through their interconnectedness with other agencies, especially with other think tanks, universities, and other bodies as they operate within broad coalitions. Seen from this perspective, think tanks function less as particular types of research institutes or 'universities without students' (Weaver 1989) than as key knowledge mobilizers, activated through their formal and informal networks, functioning within, and for, civil society.

As Edwards (2012, 8) also suggests, their importance lies far less in their individual functioning than in the various and multiple ways in which they interact with other think tanks and civil society groups, and the institutions of government and industry: 'in complex civil society assemblages, ecologies, or "eco-systems," which vary widely in their details from one context to another. As in a real, biological eco-system, each element is related to the others and gains strength from the system's diversity and organic growth'.

Indeed, we found such exchanges and 'assemblages' strongly evident in our example of how health policy think tanks operated initially individually, and eventually through overt collaboration between think tanks, in a critical response to QIPP.

Returning to the academic think-tanks literature reviewed, we also find persuasive Stone's (1996) analysis of 'power/knowledge' relations arising through think tanks' networks of influence. Indeed, these networks provide access to knowledge resources as well as representing a valuable conduit for exercising influence. However, the main significance of this power/knowledge nexus is that think tanks' networks are themselves a major source of their influence. Their interconnected networks act less as a simple conduit or 'switchboard' for knowledge exchange, than as a way of producing the relations and conditions that help 'dynamise' (Mazzucato 2013) processes of knowledge mobilization across diverse organizations and strands of what we see as the public policy quadruple helix in London.

In conclusion, while think tanks have been the subject of previous interesting academic studies, we still need to understand more about the interconnections between them and other public policy partners and how their networks operate to help constitute the knowledge ecosystem apparent within the domain of public policymaking. We see these relations less as dependent on formal structure but rather as a looser and more heterogeneous mix of actors operating in various ways as a broader policy-related community over time. Indeed, the notion of 'epistemic communities' (see Haas 1992; Knorr-Cetina 1999; McGivern and Dopson 2010; McGivern et al. 2016) helpfully suggests potential ways to explore the informal interactions of think tanks with public policy partners and their potential to connect with powerful sources of political and government influence.

In terms of future research, much of the material for the chapter has been taken from think-tank websites and annual reports and so is necessarily rather 'flat' in character. Our case study of a London think tank provided illustrative material which uncovered interactions and institutional alliances between various other agencies. However, this important area could be usefully explored in further qualitative work or through a social network analysis. From a knowledge leadership (Fischer et al. 2016) perspective, board interlocks at trustee level would, for instance, be an interesting area to explore empirically. Further theoretical as well as empirical work on how civil society-orientated think tanks operate in practice would usefully extend our exploratory analysis of the role of think tanks in the knowledge production quadruple helix.

# 8  Case study 3

Management consulting knowledge
and English health care organizations

In this chapter, we address a case study of a management consultancy-led project to redesign the delivery of primary health care services in a UK region, which aimed to make substantial efficiency savings as part of the QIPP agenda (discussed in Chapter 4). This micro-level case study provides a rare and interesting insight into how management consulting knowledge is mobilized into health care organizations at local level.

## Management consultancy in the public services

Public-sector management consultancy accounts for an estimated 12–19 per cent (Gross and Poor 2008) or 21 per cent of overall consulting revenue (Management Consultancies Association 2016), US$57 billion globally (Kennedy Information 2008), with only banking and finance a bigger sector (O'Mahoney and Markham 2013). In the year 2014–15, the UK public sector spent an estimated £300–700 million (down from a high of £1.2–1.7 billion in 2009–10 (National Audit Office 2016) and £1.1 billion (down from a high of £1.8 billion in 2009) on management consultancy (Management Consultancies Association 2016). Two-thirds of government expenditure on consultancy was on the transformation of ICT and service delivery programmes. Yet only 38 per cent of management consultancies' government income is classified as 'consultancy'; consultancies also earn income by supplying 'temporary workers' to government (National Audit Office 2016).

Many consultancies have thriving health care practices. For example, the NHS spent £640 million on management consultancy in 2014 (Oliver 2014). Three-quarters of consultancy work was conducted by just six global management consultancy firms—PWC, Deloitte, KPMG, Ernst & Young, PA Consulting, and McKinsey & Co. McKinsey & Co. has played a particularly significant role in influencing the development of NHS policy and reforms since the early 1970s (McDonald 2014; Kirkpatrick et al. 2016). More recently, McKinsey advised the government on NHS reforms outlined in the 2010 Health and Social Care Bill (Rose 2012; McDonald 2014; Kirkpatrick et al. 2016) and developed the Quality Improvement Productivity and Prevention (QIPP) national-level policy (McKinsey & Co. 2009) as discussed in Chapter 5.

Thus, management consultancy is important because of both the scale of public service spending on it and because consultants played a key role developing and importing managerial ideas associated with New Public Management (NPM) into public services. Indeed management consultants are more generally key agents in the commodification and diffusion of new managerial 'fads and fashions' (Abrahamson 1996; Suddaby and Greenwood 2001) which are often associated with best-selling management books written by consultants. For example, *Reinventing Governance* (Osborne and Gaebler 1992), written by two management consultants, affected how politicians thought about public services, leading to changes in how they were organized around the world (Saint-Martin 2004; Ferlie et al. 2016).

Management consultants' role in and effects on public services and health care are controversial (Saint-Martin 2004; Kirkpatrick et al. 2016). A recent National Audit Office report (2016, 4) concluded that, 'when used well', consultants are an 'important source of specialist skills and capabilities' that government departments do not have and are 'essential to making that transformation successfully'. Yet Hood (1994, 138, cited by Saint-Martin 2004, 19) describes consultants as part of 'a self-serving movement designed to promote the career interests of an elite group of new managerialists ... who colonized the public management from outside'.

Critics like Craig (2006) argue that consultants promote ideas that serve their own commercial interests rather than the public's best interests. For example, during new Labour's NHS modernization, consultancies like KPMG, Deloitte, and PWC advised clients to sign up to private finance initiatives as the best way to build and run health care infrastructure while being deeply invested in private finance initiatives-related consultancy work. Private finance initiatives turned out to be far more costly and problematic than health organizations were led to expect (Craig 2006). Rose (2012) critically argues that, in particular, McKinsey & Co. 'hijacked' health system reforms to serve their own interests. Thus it has been suggested that 'McKinsey seems to be setting the rules of the game in relation to the Government's health Bill and then benefitting from the outcome' (Hansard 2012, cited in O'Mahoney and Sturdy 2016).

So, are management consultancies promoting management texts and ideas, and mobilizing knowledge in ways that are usefully shaping health care thinking and systems, promoting ideas serving their own interests, or doing both, or something altogether different? Despite its scale and significance, there is relatively little research on management consulting in health care and the public services more generally, and what research there is tends to provide macro-level overviews of the sector (Saint-Martin 2004, 2012; Sturdy et al. 2009). Therefore, micro-level case studies of management consultancy in practice, such as the case here, are useful and important in deciphering consultancy's effect on health care specifically and public services in practice.

## Management consultancy and knowledge mobilization

Management consultancy is knowledge-intensive work, providing an interesting context in which to explore the book's theme. We can broadly think about two models of consultancy, as well as a third critical perspective on consultancy (Nikolova and Devinney 2012).

Process consulting involves consultants 'helping' clients find their own solutions to problems (Schein 1969), facilitating social learning (Nikolova and Devinney 2012), which relies on a balanced and constructive two-way relationship between consultants and clients (McGivern 1983).

The expert consultancy model involves consultants, with expert power over clients, diagnosing and defining clients' needs for knowledge/expertise, and then transferring what they judge as appropriate specialist knowledge/expertise from previous projects to new clients (Czarniawska-Joerges 1990; Berglund and Werr 2000). Thus, the expert model of consultancy is less collaborative than process consulting, with consultancies mobilizing knowledge for and to clients, downplaying the diversity and plurality of knowledge and the importance and legitimacy of clients' own knowledge (Sturdy et al. 2009; Nikolova and Devinney 2012).

Critics of expert consultancies suggest that consultants transfer knowledge by standardizing expertise, knowledge, methods for diagnosing problems and solutions (Sahlin-Andersson 1996; Werr 2012; Wright et al. 2012). Sahlin-Andersson (1996, 80) describes this as an 'editing' process, in which consultants 'dis-embed' stories about successful organizations from their setting, representing them in a standardized model that focuses attention on key features of successful cases and 'invites comparison and imitation by other organizations'. Yet, Sahlin-Andersson (1996, 80) notes, 'situational and time specific features and unplanned elements are seldom mentioned'. Consultants then 're-embed' edited and standardized models in new settings by reformulating new stories that focus attention on aspects relevant to new contexts, while ambiguity within models allows them to mean different things to different groups, appealing to diverse interests.

The ambiguous nature of management consultancy, involving projects being co-constructed by consultants and clients, also makes consulting projects difficult to evaluate (Alvesson 2001; Sturdy 2011). Furthermore, while project members usually focus on completing specific tasks, from the perspective of permanent organization, projects' success often depends on their contribution to longer-term business outcomes (Lundin and Söderholm 1995; Burke and Morley 2016). Thus, as Czarniawska-Joerges (1990, 149) warns, consultancy projects can only be judged by 'observing the effects, especially when the consultants are no longer there' and 'if there isn't some sort of anchorage and no one responsible for pushing things ahead consequently, everything collapses rather rapidly like a house of cards'.

Impression management and persuasion may be as important as demonstrating tangible results from projects or solving clients' problems (Czarniawska-Joerges 1990; Fincham 1999; Berglund and Werr 2000; Alvesson 2001). Consultancies often develop strong organizational cultures, shaping how consultants think and behave to ensure they give a favourable impression to clients (Alvesson 2001; Gill 2015). Alvesson and Robertson (2006, 211) describe global management consultancies as 'standardizing' consultants to ensure that they make the right impression with clients, producing 'subjugation of subjectivity . . . premised on elitism' which 'provides a sense of ontological security in an ambiguous, fluid working context' and counters consultants' doubts about their own analyses (Alvesson and Robertson 2006, 221).

Kieser (2002) argues that hyper-expert groups addressing very specific problems, including consultants and academics, may exacerbate problems because they disregard the larger complex system in which they are situated. He describes management consultants (and academics) as closed, self-referential communication-based social systems, unable to understand communication within different (client) systems. Thus, Kieser argues, consultancy clients are doomed to become cynical about consultants when projects fail to deliver the results consultants promised.

Yet the idea that consultants can so easily and repeatedly manipulate clients and continue to sell ever-failing projects is simplistic (O'Mahoney et al. 2013). Good relationships between consultants and clients are important and much consulting work relies upon long-term relationships and repeat business (McGivern 1983; Fincham 1999; Nikolova and Devinney 2012). Thus, we may need to consider other reasons clients hire consultants.

Consultants may be brought in for political reasons—to drive, legitimate, and overcome resistance to agendas, policies, and organizational changes senior managers have already decided. Consultants may also be hired to take the blame for painful or negative outcomes (Fincham 1999; Sturdy et al. 2009). In the context of the public sector, consultants can also be blamed for failed government policy, providing clients with protection from attack from political adversaries (Saint-Martin 2012). Clients may, more simply, hire consultants to provide an external perspective on issues that they cannot understand or address, drawing on expertise unavailable in their organization (Nikolova and Devinney 2012).

Accordingly, we can think of consultants as providing what Benford and Snow (2000) describe as 'diagnostic frames', explaining what has occurred and why, 'prognostic frames', showing what should be done, and 'motivational frames' to compel action. Heusinkveld and Visscher (2012) suggest that consultants' strategies for framing management ideas and knowledge depend on both the 'dispositional' characteristics of consultants and 'interactive-situational' features of their clients' sites, including 'organizational settings' and relationships between consultants and clients, time pressures, and the cognitive and socio-political complexity of problem situations. McGivern et al. (2017) highlight the way consultants' short-term time frames may often lead them to frame projects in simplistic terms, enabling the delivery of project outcomes by close deadlines.

Framing plays a role during organizational change more generally, yet we need to know more about how frames are enacted and received, and their effect on change implementation (Bartunek et al. 2006). Research on framing has often prioritized the perspectives of senior managers and change agents, focusing on how to overcome resistance to change, but may overlook ways in which subsequent divergent interests and interpretations affect implementation. A clear frame is a vital ingredient for organizational change (Kotter 1995). Yet there is a risk that by diagnosing clients' problems and proffering solutions in a standardized way, expert consultants may suffer from 'frame blindness' (Haas et al. 2015). Hence, expert consultants may ignore or be unable to see complexity or other perspectives affecting projects, which are likely to lead to unintended longer-term project outcomes.

Strong clear singular frames may downplay the political nature of management consultancy. Indeed Dewulf et al. (2009) note a conceptual confusion in the framing literature between 'cognitive frames', which represent schemas structuring understanding of phenomena, and 'interactional framing', involving ongoing dynamic interactions, conflicts, negotiations, and collective alignment of meaning. Accordingly, framing involves both figuring out and agreeing what is going on among multiple stakeholders and how stakeholders interpret frames may be affected by different historical and contextual factors (Bartunek et al. 2006; Buchanan et al. 2007). Yet framing is also a political process, often involving divergent, competing, and conflicting interests and interpretations, and a way of exercising power. In conditions of uncertainty, actors may attempt to transform their own cognitive frame and related interests into the organization's predominant frame, while making others think that their frame reflected 'reality' and everyone's best interests (Kaplan 2008).

Middle managers may resist organizational changes that threaten their interests and often understand local contexts and how other factors are likely to affect change implementation better than senior managers or external consultants. Thus, the outcome of organization change often depends on relations between change agents (external consultants and senior managers) and change recipients (middle managers). So dialogue between them may be necessary for sustainable change (Balogun and Johnson 2004; Rouleau 2005; Huy 2011; Thomas et al. 2011).

Reflecting our earlier argument about the importance of an equal relationship between consultants and clients (Schein 1969; McGivern 1983; Nikolova and Devinney 2012), Tsoukas (2009) argues that the creation of new knowledge in organizations requires 'productive dialogue' between stakeholder/actors who understand the phenomenon in varying ways due to the different contextual backgrounds framing it. To develop a new common understanding of the phenomenon, Tsoukas argues, actors need to reflectively distance themselves from customary ways of understanding the phenomenon and then relationally and openly engage with others in a dialogue about the different background frames. Then, by combining, expanding, or reframing their understandings, conceptual breakthroughs can be achieved.

However, Tsoukas (2009) warns that if engagement is 'calculated', and actors enter dialogue to maximize their own interests or protect turf, dialogue is likely to be unproductive. Drawing on Tsoukas's (2009) ideas, Thomas et al. (2011) illustrate such problems. They found that 'oppositional' power–resistance relations, involving senior managers and consultants imposing change and middle managers and other employees resisting them, produced 'calculated engagement' and 'degenerative dialogues', which led to the imposition and reproduction of existing knowledge.

We ask whether it is possible for management consultants and managers in client organizations to engage in productive dialogue and combine, expand, and reframe how they view clients' problems and develop new knowledge, contextually appropriate and sustainable solutions. We explore some of these issues in the case study that follows.

## Elmhouse Consulting case study

Elmhouse is an elite global management consultancy. The consultants we interviewed described the consultancy as 'careful in recruitment, about the types of people we hire' (consultant), only employing the best candidates from elite universities and organizations. They also noted that 'different' people tended 'not to enjoy working in the company' (consultant) and to leave quickly. Similarly, an Elmhouse partner noted 'diversity, which, if you think of as ethnic or religious or gender . . . we are world-class but what strikes me is how different people can be and yet utterly the same'. So Elmhouse consultants were elite in terms of their abilities and achievements but in a homogeneous way, which we suggest meant they tended to view the world and organizations in the same way.

Consultants described being under considerable pressure, receiving intensive performance 'feedback twice a year, and then after every project' (consultant). Elmhouse's 'up and out' performance management system was likened to the Olympics where 'sometimes you don't get a gold and get kicked out' (Elmhouse academic adviser). Consultants typically lasted two years in the company.

Such pressures in turn affected how Elmhouse generated and used knowledge. One consultant commented: 'we work in four-week timelines . . . we never get to the depth of understanding [academics do]'. Another consultant describes:

You can get to the 80% answer . . . in 20% of the time . . . Spending 80% of my time refining 20% of the answer is no longer value adding . . . The world is changing . . . just because you publish something . . . doesn't mean that it's true forever . . . What . . . doesn't ever change in Elmhouse is the process that we use to get to answers.

An Elmhouse consultant commented: 'Knowledge really tends to come from what we've done here before', that Elmhouse had 'got into this habit almost of relying on the Elmhouse Model as a way of thinking' and 'persuading people that things are important'. This suggested that Elmhouse rarely engaged in 'double loop learning' (Argyris 1976) to develop new frames. Thus, consultants' accounts reflected accounts of consultants' use of standardized knowledge and impression management as important elements in management consulting.

Consultants demonstrated a 'quasi-religious' belief in Elmhouse, with the consultancy likened to a religious movement with 'certainty in their viewpoint . . . that they're doing the right thing' (consultant). They were 'awfully optimistic . . . we know how to save the world . . . it's almost like a motto, and only Elmhouse can do this' (consultant). An academic Elmhouse adviser commented: 'Elitism . . . has led to . . . a feeling that we don't need other folks, because we're doing this better than most people anyway for our own purposes . . . audiences and . . . standards . . . [Elmhouse] are not used to recognizing that there are other standards and purposes'.

Thus, while consultants were all extraordinary in terms of their high abilities, their sense of elitism might lead them to dismiss alternative frames and forms of knowledge at odds with the Elmhouse frame. Our data thus reflected descriptions of expert consultants dismissing plural knowledges, including those of clients (Sturdy et al. 2009).

In sum, intense performance management led consultants to frame clients' problems and solutions in ways that could be quickly diagnosed and resolved. Elmhouse's strong culture and elite identity enables consultants to persuade themselves and clients of the superiority of Elmhouse's expertise in diagnosing and resolving organizational problems, and dismiss alternative ways of framing them.

## THE ELMHOUSE PROJECT

As discussed in Chapter 5, following the 2008 global financial crisis and consequent strain on government finances, in early 2010 the English Department of Health introduced a Quality Innovation, Productivity and Prevention (QIPP) Programme in the NHS, which aimed to make £20 billion of efficiency savings (from an overall NHS budget of then approximately £106 billion) during the period 2011–14. Twenty per cent of savings were to be made through redesigning primary health care services. The Department of Health gave Strategic Health Authorities (SHAs) a deadline for producing plans to redesign primary health care and make efficiency savings by September 2010. Most SHAs hired management consultancies to advise them how to do so (National Audit Office 2011). We examine one such example.

Elmhouse set about diagnosing ways of making QIPP efficiency savings using an organizational change model which we refer to as the Elmhouse Model; the model was outlined in a book written by Elmhouse Partners. The book was structured around a clear memorable pneumonic, which involved identifying a number of steps for organizations to undertake: (i) setting ambitious but realistic goals; (ii) assessing the organization, its performance, and its underlying mindsets by benchmarking particular organizational features against comparative organizations; (iii) developing a narrative to convince people of the need to change; (iv) establishing incentive mechanisms to promote and sustain change; (v) developing change management skills within the organization; (vi) leadership and role modelling by senior managers; and (vii) evaluating and monitoring performance and progress throughout the change process.

The book was based upon academic sources, experience, and evidence from Elmhouse's consulting work. A consultant noted: 'The evidence base that underpins the Elmhouse Model I think is hugely compelling . . . when you stand up and you say [to clients] look, organizations that do this are three times more likely to succeed . . . here's the [evidence], we have a database of 650,000 entries.'

We note from the book's methodological appendix that the Elmhouse Model was based upon a huge dataset. However, the book contained no information about *how* authors' analysis and change model emerged from data. Indeed, an interviewee noted that the book's authors made 'conclusions . . . about some association between variables, but don't explain the association . . . They've got very good evidence in here, but they don't display it'.

Nonetheless, an Elmhouse partner commented: 'The book itself is a powerful thing . . . we're no longer having . . . framework wars where different bits of the firm would each view transformation in a different way. We have one unified coherent point of view . . . we've got everyone singing off the same hymn sheet.'

So, again, the book encouraged consultants to view management ideas and frame client organizations in a singularly coherent way.

## FRAMING THE NHS'S PROBLEM AND SOLUTION

Health care managers in regional primary care trusts (PCTs) were aware of severe financial pressures on the NHS. They believed that historical 'difficult relationships' between local primary care organizations and GPs, with 'everyone in isolation trying to meet their own individual objectives', were 'bankrupting' primary care organizations (PCT manager). Consequently, for six months preceding the QIPP project, PCT managers had been engaged in dialogue with local stakeholders, particularly GPs, to develop a bottom-up, region-wide 'transformation partnership'. PCT managers diagnosed the NHS's financial problems as due to fragmentation, requiring the complex systemic solution of an integrated health system, which demanded long-term dialogue with a range of relevant stakeholders.

Under pressure to produce a plan for QIPP-related efficiency savings by a Department of Health deadline, SHA managers observed that 'debate and discussion was going on for some time without reaching a conclusion' and 'weren't confident... [PCT] managers were starting to analyse the challenge quick enough' (SHA manager). SHA managers can be seen as framing QIPP as 'make or break' (SHA manager) for the NHS in the region. They commissioned Elmhouse because they had 'fantastic insight and analytical abilities... the capacity... [to] make progress far quicker than we could ever have on our own' (SHA manager).

Elmhouse framed the NHS's problem and solution in standardized terms, which brought 'a sharper focus... [on] absolute numbers' (PCT manager). A project consultant commented: 'How do you organize your services better so that you can absorb that increase in activity?... It's about uniformity... it doesn't actually demand any real innovation, what it demands is the systematic application of what's already known to be best practice.'

Elmhouse consultants 'benchmarked' local PCTs' performance against national data relating to comparable organizations to work out potential productivity gains. Their analysis suggested that PCTs could achieve QIPP efficiency savings targets through service redesign and by improving their performance and productivity in line with the 'upper quartile' of PCTs nationally. Elmhouse proposed that regional health services be redesigned around a number of 'care pathways' and developed 'golden rules' for service redesign and 'prescriptions' for making organizational change.

In sum, we note PCT managers' and Elmhouse consultants' very different diagnostic and prognostic frames.

# FRAMING LOCAL CHANGE IMPLEMENTATION

Elmhouse ran three 'forums' for regional PCT managers and clinicians. In the first forum Elmhouse consultants outlined the case for change in the NHS, drawing upon examples of private-sector organizations that succeeded (or failed) as a consequence of taking (or not) Elmhouse's recommended approach. They then explained their regional diagnostic 'benchmarking' analysis, prognostic 'prescriptions' for change, and 'golden rules' for service redesign, leading, and motivating change.

Elmhouse consultants gave PCT managers a PowerPoint-based 'template', which 'everyone had to fill out...that standardized what people were being asked to do...[made] clear what was being required...[to] convince people to change' (consultant). PCT managers were instructed to complete the template, compare the Elmhouse benchmarking analysis with local data, 'confirm or deny' (PCT manager) whether the proposed redesign and productivity gains were possible. They also had to hold a 'stakeholder workshop' in which to discuss their plans with and get 'buy-in' from local clinicians and other stakeholders before the next forum (ten working days after the first forum). PCT managers perceived this as an extremely short time frame and described working late evenings and weekends to meet deadlines.

In the second forum, PCT managers shared their initial vision for the design of local health systems, discussed its implications for local health care delivery with Elmhouse consultants and NHS managers, and received feedback. PCT managers then went away to further refine their analysis and service redesign model and hold a second stakeholder workshop before a final forum four weeks later.

In the final forum, PCT managers presented their refined analysis and service redesign plans and then 'prepared for action', with Elmhouse providing final training about how to manage the process. The deadline for PCT managers to deliver their final draft plans was set for thirty-four working days after the first forum and the end-of-project 'final review and handover' one working day later.

Elmhouse's standardized, structured, and short framing, and limited opportunities for dialogue frustrated PCT managers and primary care clinicians. A PCT manager described Elmhouse's 'golden rules' as 'semantically disabling' and 'prescriptions' for change as 'rules against which people were measured'. A GP complained: 'Golden rule to a GP, who's trained in critical appraisal skills, appears patronizing...whose rules are they and why are they golden and do they stand up to critical appraisal?...That frame is particularly toxic.' A PCT manager also suggested: 'The problem is...Elmhouse's frame is their organization...trying to run an organization from outside...We got into an analytical framing before...a more creative understanding of do we really understand this problem...[from] multiple perspectives.'

A PCT manager commented, 'dialogue didn't happen'. A GP added: 'We had more depth in understanding the potential method of change than was apparent in the conversation from Elmhouse... The Elmhouse conversation... left a feeling of impossible disengagement' between those who had developed the analysis and NHS managers and doctors who 'have to go away and practically try and deliver the change' and 'good people [PCT managers and local clinicians]' were 'looking extremely disengaged and distressed or puzzled' and 'would get into a huddle outside' the main conference meeting to question the 'disconnect between rhetoric and reality'. Lack of dialogue 'didn't help with ownership' and meant that plans did not 'make sense locally' (PCT manager). A local doctor commented: '[The] outline financial model was based on a series of very quick turnaround... cost estimates... but the general conversation back among the troops was... Chief Executives felt under increasing pressure to prove that the maths could work... by the time it got down to delivery it was... fantasy that services could work on the budget proposed.'

PCT managers described 'struggling' to align Elmhouse's analysis of potential cost savings with its own local data and how 'there was [£x] million sort of missing... it wasn't clear where that saving was going to come from', PCT managers were 'bridging a gap by putting in things that everybody wasn't necessarily signed up to' and that nobody outside the financial department 'had any idea of those numbers whatsoever' (PCT manager). Another PCT manager commented 'Elmhouse's analysis would mean closing ten wards... risked a complete loss of credibility with local clinicians'. Another PCT manager argued that Elmhouse 'didn't understand the context' or NHS accounting rules so 'the whole context of that savings opportunity was lost; that rationale didn't work' (PCT manager).

Doubts about the credibility of Elmhouse's analysis led to 'local resentment of the QIPP programme' because it was 'difficult to get behind the Elmhouse figures' and 'everyone wanted... to challenge their validity' (PCT manager). Yet NHS County's managers felt unable to openly challenge Elmhouse's framing and so accepted it, unable to devise a better way of analysis within the project time frame. But rather than being about service quality improvement, PCT managers framed QIPP as a rationale for cutting costs: 'The message [was]... you've got to save £[x] million... We don't mind if it's different from the Elmhouse analysis... but you've got to come up with alternatives... you're not allowed to come back with a figure that's not £[x] million' (PCT manager).

The 'final review and handover' project meeting noted: 'though consensus has not been reached, [local NHS organizations] are fully aware of the scale of the challenge and recognise that a solution must be found'. The meeting presentation concluded: '[The regional NHS] is now moving towards the fourth phase in its QIPP journey—full scale local implementation' beginning 'tomorrow'. Some interviewees commented on a sense of 'relief' when Elmhouse 'went away' and how the pace of change implementing the Elmhouse analysis then slowed but after 'an intense period for a relatively short period of time . . . what's happened after is equally important . . . there's still an awful lot of work to do' (PCT manager).

The last phase of the Elmhouse project also coincided with a government announcement of the planned abolition of SHAs and PCTs, distracting NHS managers from the QIPP project with the prospect of losing their jobs. In sum, again we see differences between Elmhouse and PCT managers' and local clinicians' frames for the analysis of their local context and expectation of dialogue, which undermined local ownership of implementing the proposed change.

## FRAMING THE PROJECT OUTCOME

Interviewees retrospectively viewed the Elmhouse QIPP project outcome in contrasting ways. An Elmhouse consultant noted: 'I do factually know from conversations with the SHA that all the plans got signed off, so eventually it did happen'. An Elmhouse partner argued that rather than Elmhouse's solution being flawed, the national-level policy abolition of SHA and PCT made implementing Elmhouse's plan impossible. Discussing PCT managers' difficulties implementing the Elmhouse plan, an Elmhouse consultant who worked on the project commented: 'The NHS' problem is not that [NHS] people don't know what the right thing to do is . . . [but] making change happen is like wading through treacle because everyone has to be aligned . . . resistance to change and cultural cynicism . . . a million reasons why not . . . It's bullshit . . . an excuse'.

SHA managers were generally pleased with the project. One commented: 'In a very quick space of time we'd got to the point where we'd looked at redesigning the system in order to develop the potential savings . . . It got everybody on the same page, challenged mindsets, helped us move to a more common mindset', but cautioned that 'the big time lag in health care in moving from the analysis to the delivery . . . that's the big problem'. Another SHA manager noted: The proof is still in the pudding . . . we're still waiting to see how the NHS faces up to the challenge as we go into . . . delivery', adding that Elmhouse's frame

fitted well with our [SHA] strong delivery focus . . . a very structured and focused programme . . . [But] fit with reality? . . . Elmhouse doesn't necessarily think that the politics of a situation is a limiting factor, when actually it is . . . it takes the NHS as a whole so long to make some of the changes . . . as soon as the Elmhouse team have gone . . . momentum slips.

PCT managers were critical of the project. One argued that the QIPP project had actually slowed and 'derailed' local health care system transformation by undermining dialogue with clinicians and their ownership of change:

[The QIPP project] slowed us up from where we would have been with the transformation programme . . . We were concerned about our local transformation partnership being derailed because we'd worked on it on a bottom-up ownership basis and suddenly now we've got to come up with a set of QIPP plans in this deadline and we hadn't got time to talk to the clinicians.

Two years after the project (in late 2013), we reinterviewed two NHS County PCT managers and an NHS doctor about the longer-term impact of the project. One PCT manager commented:

[NHS County] engaged with the suggestions Elmhouse were putting forward but at a pretty early stage we understood that there was no way we could deliver . . . [the] reality gap between Elmhouse's high-level analysis and what [NHS] people in their hearts and minds would ever believe . . . Today . . . I don't think we've achieved [efficiency savings] anything like what was indicated . . . Elmhouse . . . perhaps chose to ignore some of that implementation difficulty . . . weren't . . . hearing . . . messages about how difficult it would be implementing the analysis.

For PCT managers, lack of dialogue about redesigning the local health service was at the root of the problem. One PCT manager noted: 'I am . . . aware having been around quite a long time that . . . a consultant is someone who comes in with a specific task . . . [but] you need . . . strategic thinking space and . . . political permission to do these things.'

The abolition of SHAs and PCTs complicate our ability to assess whether the project achieved its aims. However, national reports on QIPP (National Audit Office 2011, 2012; House of Commons Public Accounts Committee 2013; King's Fund 2014) suggest that the NHS (including the SHAs that were studied) achieved efficiency savings targets without a reduction in service quality. However, most efficiency savings came from freezing NHS pay and tariffs paid to hospitals, reducing the number of NHS managers, and making the easiest savings first, with relatively little progress in redesigning and *transforming* health services; only 7 per cent of efficiency savings were made through service transformation against a target of 20 per cent (House of Commons Public Accounts Committee 2013). Furthermore, making these efficiency savings may have damaged NHS staff morale and motivation to make further efficiency savings (King's Fund 2014). So efficiency savings may be less sustainable than headline figures suggest. We suggest that differences between the framing of management consultants, SHA and PCT managers, and local clinicians and limited dialogue may have undermined sustainable service transformation.

# Discussion

From the start of the Elmhouse project, differences were apparent in how PCT managers and local NHS clinicians, SHA managers, and Elmhouse consultants framed the problem they were addressing and its solution. PCT managers were engaged in a slow-moving, long-term regional 'transformation partnership', involving dialogue among multiple stakeholders to address what they perceived as a complex problem in a fragmented health system. SHA managers hired Elmhouse for their capacity to work fast, focus on numbers, and apply a standardized analytical frame which would enable them to produce a plan for making QIPP-related efficiency savings by a Department of Health deadline (for a more detailed analysis of the interaction and effects of these different groups' time frames, see McGivern et al. 2017).

During the project, differences emerged between the approaches of consultants and health care managers to interaction and dialogue. Elmhouse initially appeared to engage in dialogue with local stakeholders, arranging three change forums in which to discuss plans for implementing change. However, early in the project, PCT managers and local clinicians became frustrated by Elmhouse's focus on persuasion and 'structuring' dialogue and by 'semantically disabling' PowerPoint templates they needed to complete. One PCT manager noted that Elmhouse's 'people, they're outstanding and I learned a heck of a lot from them. But almost their organic knowledge, their creativity is crushed out by this need to turn it all into bloody PowerPoint'.

Thus. a sense of 'impossible disengagement' undermined any possibility of 'combining, expanding or framing' (Tsoukas 2009) Elmhouse consultants' and PCT managers' understanding of the problem the local NHS was facing. Instead Elmhouse consultants, confident that their own elite expertise and knowledge was superior to that of PCT managers and local NHS clinicians, imposed their own top-down frame, which PCT managers and local NHS clinicians resisted because they did not understand how the Elmhouse Model could work in the face of opposition from GPs. Finally, PCT managers appeared to accept the Elmhouse plan, with the final project and QIPP deadlines looming and a lack of better way for delivering efficiency savings, although its subsequent implementation appeared limited.

Thus while initial rhetoric and stakeholder workshops suggest that different parties were interested in engaging in productive dialogue and co-constructing ways of making efficiency savings with NHS managers and clinicians, PCT managers and local NHS clinicians quickly came to feel that Elmhouse consultants were not receptive to the points they were making and the nature of the dialogue became more 'calculated', which as Tsoukas (2009) predicts, led to the development of a plan for efficiency savings based upon the Elmhouse Model, which appeared to be implemented in a limited and perhaps superficial way. Indeed, the project we studied reflected Thomas and colleagues' account of meaning making during an organizational change workshop framed by 'oppositional power–resistance relations' and defensive 'calculated engagement', which produced conceptual closure, sterility, stand-off, and the reproduction of existing incommensurable frames (Thomas et al. 2011). Thus 'framing contests' and politics (Kaplan 2008) appear to undermine the development of new knowledge in organizations.

Our case study highlights differences between the frames and forms of knowledge 'expert' management consultants and managers and clinicians in NHS primary care value and use. Therefore a lack of 'epistemic fit', as we have discussed elsewhere (McGivern and Dopson 2010; McGivern et al. 2016), between standardized knowledge used and valued in management consultancy and that in primary care may undermine its mobilization in health care. As a result of the project, as Elmhouse noted, PCT managers and local clinicians perhaps became more aware of the scale of the financial challenge the NHS is facing, which shifted their mindset, as an SHA manager noted.

Thus, longer-term engagement and productive dialogue between consultants, health care managers, and clinicians evolve (Tsoukas 2009) through a development of balanced relations between consultant and clients (Schein 1969; McGivern 1983; Nikolova and Devinney 2012) more akin to a process model of consulting which may be more effective in sustainably mobilizing new knowledge in health care. Yet without wider power relations in health care systems becoming more facilitative (Thomas et al. 2011), we may see an ongoing pattern of knowledge being mobilized in a way that is loosely coupled (Kitchener 1999; Hinings et al. 2003) and half-hearted, with unintended and suboptimal consequences that do not address the real challenges facing health care.

# 9 Case study 4

## The high impact of private-sector management knowledge in an independent-sector provider

In this chapter, we present one of the empirical cases in our original study and review the role and high impact of management knowledge in the Oakmore site, which is a specialist health care provider in the independent sector. We see it as an example of a third-sector social-enterprise organization, having charitable status but working closely with the government to provide a service not currently available within the NHS. In Chapter 3 we highlighted the impact of the 2008 global financial crisis in introducing a government-wide austerity programme, QIPP, into the NHS. This change programme facilitated the importing of operations management-orientated, team-based texts and knowledges into Oakmore. The CEO in this case was alert to changes in the macro environment and was active in repositioning the organization he led to cope. The case evidences the importance of agency in knowledge mobilization.

Specifically, we consider the impact of the 'balanced scorecard' (Kaplan and Norton 1996) in transforming the organization's practice and financial position in a period of austerity. The balanced scorecard is a management tool which takes a holistic view of an organization and attempts to translate a company's vision/mission statement into the practicalities of managing the business better at every level of the organization. This management text is aimed at practitioners and would not be rated highly according to evidence-based management criteria such as randomized control trials or quasi-experimental methods, yet our empirical data suggest that the impact on practice was high. As the market intensified with post-QIPP cuts, the scorecard proved to be a useful tool that fitted with the new context. In this case we see clinical and managerial forms of knowledge being successfully combined by a highly skilled chief executive and his management team. This case provides particular insights into the various supporting factors that need to be in place for a management knowledge text to have a high impact on more micro-level organizational practices in a health care setting, including active and skilled support from top-level leadership.

# Private-sector involvement in the National Health Service

Although publicly funded, the NHS utilizes a mix of providers from a variety of sectors—private, charitable, and now social enterprises—for delivering health care services, which are still free at the point of use, to consumers. The private sector has been integral to the effective functioning of this system since its early days, for instance, through services relating to dentistry, eye care, and prescriptions, and the independent contracting of most general practitioners (GPs) who serve as gatekeepers to the service but are not publicly appointed by the government. In addition, although most hospitals, whether voluntarily or publicly funded, became part of the NHS at its inception in 1948, a few (including Oakmore, the subject of this chapter) remained independent.

Nonetheless, the debate around whether the NHS is moving towards greater privatization has gained momentum in recent years, especially since the New Labour reforms that led to the overall corporatization and adoption of private-sector management principles in the provision of health care in the late 1990s (see the discussion in Chapter 3).

One way of understanding the extent to which privatization has taken place is by employing the conceptual framework proposed by Powell (2007)—the 'mixed economy of welfare'—to trace the shifts in the NHS, based on consideration of the three dimensions of provision, financing, and regulation. Such an analysis indicates that 'while some trends such as user charges ... date from the early NHS, others such as extensive outsourcing and the Private Finance Initiative ... date from later periods, and broadly support the generally accepted view that privatization has increased in recent years' (Powell and Miller 2016, 113). When analysed based on type of service provided, mental health and community care reflect a stronger extent of privatization than others (Powell and Miller 2016, 113; also Thorlby and Arora 2016).

Supplemental to this broad view are observations around the increased incidence of 'hybrid' forms of health provision that are not clearly either public or private but that represent a new form of regulated 'publicness' (Powell and Miller 2016, 113) within the system. The introduction of private-sector techniques and the related outsourcing of hospital management to corporates is one example in this regard; and the turn towards semi-autonomous, social enterprise-type foundation trusts is another.

A country-wise breakdown of the extent of privatization in the UK reveals that it is only in England that the use of private providers within a system of publicly funded health care is encouraged, with no competition between public and private providers in Scotland, Wales, or Northern Ireland (Bevan et al. 2014). The evidence for increased privatization in the English NHS is most notable in recent reforms resulting from the enforcement of the Health and Social Care Act, introduced by the Conservative–Liberal Democrat Coalition government in 2012.

This led to a significant restructuring of the National Health Service and an attempt to make the NHS more 'responsive, efficient, and accountable' through six legislative changes: clinically led commissioning; greater voice for patients; new focus for public health; greater accountability both locally and nationally; streamlined arms-length bodies; and provider regulation to support innovative services (Department of Health 2012, 1).

The last of these is the one considered most controversial in the debate around privatization—the introduction of a more diverse provider market including charitable and independent-sector providers as a means of (further) creating a 'fair playing field' (Department of Health 2012, 1) in which patients are able to choose a preferred provider from among a variety that operate at NHS cost. Additionally, the King's Fund and Health Foundation have recently proposed the creation of a 'transformation fund' for earmarking resources for the strategic changes required of the NHS to keep up with changing population needs and related service demands. One aim of this fund is to also focus on greater service delivery innovation by reaching out to non-NHS organizations, such as the third and private sector as well as social care partners, to meet service demands adequately (Health Foundation and King's Fund 2015).

As of 2016, there are 1,243 independent-sector health care providers contracted by NHS UK to deliver health care services—this number includes only the large private-sector companies and does not count other non-NHS smaller private companies that receive occasional referrals from GPs (NHS Digital 2016). Aside from these, there were about 548 private hospitals (465 owned and managed by private companies, and 83 private patient units within NHS hospitals) and between 500 and 600 private clinics in the UK as of 2013 (Competition and Markets Authority 2014).

The total commissioner spend on the independent sector (including independent-sector treatment centres, private providers, and social enterprises) slowly increased from 2010 to 2015, and represented 6.3 per cent of the total spend in 2014–15 (British Medical Association 2016). The total commissioner spend on voluntary and other sector providers has remained largely the same since 2011–12, and represented 3.1 per cent of the total spend in 2014–15 (British Medical Association 2016). The total purchase of health care from non-NHS providers, however, has shown an increase and rose from 8.9 to 9.4 per cent of the total spend in 2013–14 and 2014–15, respectively.

## Hybrid organizations and social enterprises

Organizations can be categorized as belonging to one of three sectors: public, private, and what is known as the third sector which includes all voluntary and community organizations (whether or not they are registered charities) and other social enterprises, mutuals, and co-operatives which are independent of government. Hybrid organizations can be defined as 'organizations that possess "significant" characteristics of more than one sector (public, private and third) . . . [but that] have "roots" and . . . primary adherence to the distinctive principles . . . of just one sector' (Billis 2010a, 3).

Depending on the nature of overlap and interaction between the three sectors there can be nine possible hybrid forms, with each sector taking on up to three forms of hybridity. For example, a hybrid organization with adherence to the principles of the public sector can take the public/private, public/third, and public/private/third forms (Billis 2010b). The extent of hybridity and pace of transition from a non-hybrid to a hybrid state can be conceptualized as 'shallow' versus 'entrenched' on the one hand, and 'organic' versus 'enacted' on the other (Billis 2010b).

Entrenched hybridity differs from a shallow form in that it results in permanent changes in the governance and operational structures of an organization—a third-sector body can, for example, receive grants or contracts that require it to take on paid private- or public-sector employees and establish a complex hierarchical structure around them in order to deliver its services. 'Enacted' hybrids vary from 'organic' forms in being established by an external organization as an entity with an independent legal structure (e.g. a trading subsidiary within a charity) as a result of an immediate change, rather than as a gradual, organic shift in shape and form over a number of years (Billis 2010b).

Social enterprises represent one type of hybrid organization that are based, to a large extent, on the adoption of market principles by third-sector organizations. They have been described as becoming more business- and client-driven through activities that focus on 'revenue-source diversification, fee-for-service program development . . . private-sector partnerships, and social purpose businesses' (Dart 2004, 414). These types of organization are defined as 'business[es] with primarily social objectives whose surpluses are principally reinvested for that purpose in the business or in the community, rather than being driven by the need to maximise profit for shareholders and owners' (Department of Trade and Industry 2002, 7).

# Revenue-source diversification: fee-for-service programme development

Government policy has tended to support the growth and development of the social-enterprise sector in England. The Labour government spearheaded this shift through the early 2000s by establishing the Social Enterprise Unit as part of the Department of Trade and Industry in 2001, and the Social Enterprise Investment Fund as part of the Department of Health in 2007 (Hall et al. 2012). This was followed by two significant contributions by the 2010–15 Coalition government in the form of Big Society Capital—an independent social investment institution launched in 2012 (Cabinet Office 2012a)—and the introduction of a Social Investment Tax Relief of 30 per cent to those investing in such enterprises from 2014 (Cabinet Office 2015).

More recently, the Conservative government published its 2016 social investment strategy which has three broad aims: 'using social investment to transform public services, growing the social economy, [and]strengthening the social investment marketplace' (HM Government 2016e, 19). The social-enterprise sector has been especially key in supporting the delivery of services under the English national health system. Its engagement has been promoted by successive governments through a number of policy initiatives, such as the 2008 Transforming Community Services programme and the 2011 Right to Provide initiative, which highlighted the advantages of social enterprise-type service models to NHS purchasers (Hall et al. 2012).

The hybrid nature of social-enterprise organizations can offer advantages as well as disadvantages. The former entail greater financial flexibility around, for example, how business is undertaken and profits are invested; the latter relate to uncertainty around sectoral positioning that can undermine levels of trust with stakeholders within a context of high government dependence and regulation (Hall et al. 2012). Additionally, transitioning from a third-sector to a social-enterprise form can be expected to significantly affect 'organizational structure, culture and practice' (Hall et al. 2012).

## Oakmore Healthcare

Oakmore Healthcare is a long-standing private charitable trust offering a wide range of specialist services. At the time of the study the organization offered nearly 1,000 beds and employed more than 3,000 staff. The organization is run from the spacious main site where two-thirds of the patients are accommodated, most in modern purpose-built accommodation. Other patients are spread between three smaller sites in different areas of the country. Although Oakmore is a private facility, nearly all its patients are NHS funded.

The organization's history suggests that since its establishment in the nineteenth century it has always aspired to be in the vanguard of the acquisition and application of new knowledge about its clinical specialty, and hundreds of papers have been written and published in professional journals by Oakmore clinicians. However, management of the charity had always been in the hands of a mostly voluntary board of governors with little turnover of membership, a chief administrator (later known as chief executive officer), and a succession of medical directors. In addition, for most of its history there had been a relatively stable market environment. Hence, until the early 2000s there had been little appetite for either acquiring new management knowledge or indeed engaging in strategic change to enhance the financial position of the organization.

With the turn of the century both the environment and the trust began to change. Not only was there an increasing degree of financial stringency within Oakmore's biggest customer, the NHS, but a new and dynamic medical director was appointed who was himself a 'hybrid' manager-professional (McGivern et al. 2016), being a doctor with long clinical experience in Oakmore's specialist field but also an avid consumer of management knowledge and management development courses. He regularly scanned management journals for useful articles, especially on change and leadership. He also sought executive education courses and conferences that explored the complexity of leadership outside health care contexts and was particularly intrigued by organizations as complex systems and the practice of adaptive leadership (Heifetz and Laurie 1997). An authoritative figure, his job title was quickly extended to include that of Acting General Manager and, on the retirement of the long-serving CEO two years later, the posts were combined, leaving the now medical director/CEO in sole charge.

The new incumbent was well aware of the need to engage with and anticipate future macro policy trends. He took the view that the organization needed to expand and increase its capabilities to survive in an increasingly competitive health care market. Over the years new executive and non-executive management blood, selected specifically because of their knowledge of the hard commercial realities that needed to be tackled, was brought in at board level and the organization gradually changed from 'a slightly old-fashioned trading charity' into a business-like and profitable enterprise. Profits were used to improve services and the number of beds on offer more than doubled, with new hospital premises operating from four different geographical sites. In addition, salaries of senior management staff became comparable with other major organizations in the private sector.

Although the CEO's position was one of great strength, he had been clear from the beginning that this turnaround could not be achieved without finding ways to convince a workforce made up largely of people who had always been primarily orientated towards looking after the patients in their care, that a focus on making the organization both successful and profitable was not necessarily at odds with its charitable aims. His strategy was to change the culture of the organization through the top-down introduction and application of management and commercial knowledge, while at the same time trying to show them that business success was ultimately for the benefit of patients: 'We've now got to the state that people understand that occupancy equals new hospitals, it took a long time for them to understand that.'

## THE BALANCED SCORECARD: A RESPONSE TO MACRO CHANGES

As discussed earlier, the CEO was proactive in his engagement with macro-level trends. He quickly picked up the significance of the QIPP agenda, arguing locally that it was not simply a cost-reduction strategy but involved quality assurance and improvement possibilities. His interest in models of perform-ance management and measurement chimed with the QIPP agenda. This caused him to further seek knowledge about operations management and team-based texts from the private sector. As one manager pointed out, it was no longer sufficient to have 'a culture where some patients came in and some staff were employed and there was a budget which was a rollover from last year'. The CEO partly positioned his response to QIPP consequences around the 'balanced scorecard', a text suggested to him by one of his senior managers following the latter's use of the model in his master's thesis. It 'provided some nice, clear graphs of, you know, number of patients and income costs and surplus and staff sickness and staff turnover, and made it very visible', and the CEO and his board seized on this framework as a way of both helping with management of the organization and establishing Oakmore's credibility as a commercial enterprise.

To use the balanced scorecard approach, an organization must ensure knowledge of: the financial status of the organization; how the organization is currently structured; the level of expertise of their employees; and customer satisfaction level. Once the specific and quantifiable results are analysed, the leadership of the organization can utilize the balanced scorecard approach to improve the areas where it is seen to be deficient. The management systems set up according to this approach must be 'specific, measurable, achievable, realistic and timely' and fit in with the organization's strategic plan. Presented as a collection of key performance indicators, a version of the balanced scorecard was available in database form on the intranet, where it was known by most staff as 'the Matrix'. Staff entered data, and had different levels of access to the information it held, depending on their seniority. The data gathered could either be used directly (e.g. bed occupancy, staff sickness days), or as an indicator of a need to collect further management information. The scorecard provided staff with a welcome and useful way of looking at data: 'We actually look at the scorecard now and we'll say, so for example if incidents are going up in one area, actually is there a training requirement in that area or have we missed something . . . has their training fallen below ninety-five per cent in that area?'

Managers interviewed clearly felt that this tool had helped to make the case for change, particularly with clinicians who were used to weighing clinical evidence: 'their [clinicians'] whole life is all about evidence base and what is the evidence for these different treatments and these approaches to rehabilitating and helping patients recover.' So, the balanced scorecard was seen as a management tool which offered data-based and therefore apparently objective evidence to convince any sceptics and, in one manager's words, 'justify what we're doing'. The evidence from the balanced scorecard was often supported by a narrative designed to persuade: 'My team obviously provide evidence, whether it be numbers or whatever, and I then work that up into a narrative which, you know, it's the facts, is the narrative built on that and the narrative used to explain why one's doing something. So, I think that's using evidence, isn't it?'

At the time of our study, Oakmore was undertaking an in-depth review of their current version of the balanced scorecard, first with the aim of refining how the data were presented to different internal and external groups according to their needs. So, for internal consumption:

What's a key performance indicator that we need to see at a board level and what's management information which doesn't need to be seen at that level which is a bit more detailed? And so, we've kind of, we've got some new indicators that have come in and we've got existing ones and we've taken some out at the moment.

This was also to meet the requirements of commissioners following QIPP:

We need to link how we're being measured externally to how we're measuring internally. So, we have our KPIs that manage and review our performance to do with occupancy and budgets and everything else which is looking at the organization, at a business side of things, but we need to be linking what the customers are looking at from an operational customer perspective . . . rather than just internally looking.

The second aim was to align the scorecard better with Kaplan and Norton's (1996) intention that it would be used as a strategic tool for improving quality and efficiency.

What you do is you take your strategy and there's, I think there's a very clear process that Kaplan and Norton defined for trying to figure out how you map that strategy on to KPIs. And what I see a lot of out there is people doing a lot of the KPIs, you know, what's our total in KPIs, and they're all sitting there discussing which KPIs are important, whereas actually that's an end result of discussing what the strategy is and how you best represent that in the areas you want to look at, and then KPIs just fall out of the picture. And there's almost a concentration at the wrong end of the process because they haven't really looked at the issues.

There was a sense that, once this overhaul was completed, to use the term 'balanced scorecard' to refer to its management information system might no longer be entirely appropriate. Already, in the words of one respondent, it seemed 'like yesterday's phrase'.

## OAKMORE: A CONTEXT RECEPTIVE TO MANAGEMENT
## KNOWLEDGE IN AN ERA OF AUSTERITY

Crucial to making progress was establishing a cultural change towards a more business-orientated ethos. Although using systems such as the balanced score-card offered many benefits from a senior management point of view, individual clinical staff sometimes saw them as, at best, a distraction from what they saw as their 'proper' task, and, at worst, a source of pressure to perform which they found difficult to handle. Gradually, though, as the senior leadership team emphasized the existence and increasing intensity of competition, staff began to see the benefits of complying. As one manager commented:

Very slowly the ward staff are... [improving] at getting the information on [the matrix]... they need to understand that if you don't... let the commissioners have... [the information] within the timeframe there is a huge, big, fat penalty and it will come out of your ward budget. And it seems to be working a treat, you know, financial penalties always work... As soon as you're losing money off from your ward that changes everybody's opinion on how we're going to do things.

While the balanced scorecard was clearly the most widely used performance indicator, there was also ongoing monitoring of staff performance through supervision, appraisal, and career development. There was an extensive training programme, which in part had the aim of educating and persuading staff who did not easily espouse the new culture: '[we] put a training package together and said, what... I want you to articulate to your staff is why we make money, and as a charity the key part of that was we make a margin not to give to stakeholders or the taxman or the shareholders, but it's to invest in the future patients.'

In addition, the training programme covered many other aspects of staff development. Many of our interviewees, particularly those with a clinical background, had been at Oakmore for a considerable time and, until relatively recently, had succeeded solely by drawing on their professional training. Training events proved to be valuable spaces for knowledge sharing with other professional communities and useful forums for increasing the understanding of the interdependencies of work and the constraints on others. Learning opportunities, for example, the highly valued and bespoke leadership training course based on Franklin Covey, were adapted and integrated into a framework for organizational learning and were frequently tailored to meet individual requirements. This flexible approach proved important in drawing established professionals into new conversations: 'if we have a workshop and somebody would prefer a one-to-one session for whatever reason, we're happy to deliver that in a one-to-one setting.'

Nearly all those interviewed at Oakmore had experience of the in-house training on offer and spoke about it with a degree of enthusiasm: 'the opportunities for personal development are just, are very good. And so, there's just, you know, there's plenty of opportunity to go on to the courses and spend time doing stuff'.

Yet another important supporting factor in the implementation of the balanced scorecard was the investment in technology. Oakmore's respondents were generally enthusiastic about utilizing all forms of new technology for communications. Not only was the internet felt to be essential for communicating with the outside world and accessing up-to-date information from various sources, but its local organizationally bounded version, the intranet, was also crucial in the day-to-day running of the organization itself. This allowed a ward manager to look at, for instance, the peaks and troughs of bed occupancy over time and to gain a 'meaningful understanding' of the data rather than saying 'well, overall we're three beds down'.

Use of the balanced scorecard had helped shift conversations away from the professional/clinical domain and towards management and business knowledge in a productive and acceptable fashion. The framework also helped demonstrate the importance of more commercial knowledge in contributing to the growth of the business. The separate languages of these knowledge bases appeared to have been blended in everyday interactions and work.

The first language is really about, particularly about current patients. The business language is about freeing up resources for future investment in healthcare and the people at the coalface don't really understand that too well. I think the questions about translating, the solution to that first is the common frame of the common language of the charity, so our core marketing, a core message about the charity but also our core vision, vision for our staff is the charity. And so, the common language becomes the mission of the charity is to treat as many people as possible and we don't exist if we don't fill our wards.

Many staff had initially found it particularly hard to reconcile the twin objectives of providing the best possible care for patients and also profiting from the enterprise. Marketing concepts, for instance, had been treated with particular caution (one respondent referred to the function of marketing being seen as 'the evil M word'), appearing to some to be wholly concerned with bringing in more business and therefore making more money. However, even this most controversial of the three knowledge bases evident at Oakmore, the language and practice of commercially driven initiatives, seemed to have been accepted by the majority of staff.

The leadership of Oakmore purposively highlighted in their communications examples of the way clinical, management, and commercial objectives can actually work together in practice, the classic win–win situation. An example of this was an initiative called the enhanced support scheme. In essence, this initiative involved more intensive therapy combined with more frequent monitoring of certain patients' progress by a multidisciplinary team, with treatment decisions regularly recorded. This scheme was welcomed by clinicians, as it represented an improvement in practice which would benefit the patients; it was welcomed by commissioners because they had better information about why such expensive care was being provided; and the organization benefited financially, both because expenditure on care could be justified and charged for and because regular review meant that staff did not need to be intensively deployed for longer than necessary.

The appointment of non-executive board members, selected specifically because of their knowledge of the hard commercial realities that needed to be tackled, provided a counterbalance to the more traditional views of how a charity should behave. They engaged with the changing agenda of QIPP in a direct and decisive manner in the board discussions. They also were aware of and made use of the freedoms associated with the charity and independent status of Oakmore.

## Discussion

Oakmore faced an increasingly difficult commercial environment as the system experienced efficiency and quality pressures in the form of QIPP. Furthermore, the 2010 white paper on health care reform introduced the doctrine of 'any willing provider', highlighting the extension of the principles of patient choice. Commissioners were also becoming more and more reluctant to make referrals to organizations operating outside the NHS.

We've entered what is a very difficult climate in a very strong position. So very small borrowings, a price that makes us lots of money . . . There's a new Executive in place which is much more business-like . . . the clinical part's always been pretty good, and the commercial parts of the charity are performing pretty well now. So, we're in quite a strong position against some very weak competitors.

Yet despite these pressures, Oakmore was our strongest site for management knowledge use and positive impact. Oakmore as a private provider arguably enjoyed more freedom to fashion an organizational context that coped with the macro changes it found itself a part of. However, the success of the balanced scorecard in helping facilitate growth in a climate of austerity was strongly influenced by the agency of the CEO who, as a leader, sensed and coped with the many changes the macro environment threw at him. Since the early 2000s he had provided a new vision of what Oakmore might become and much needed leadership to a long-serving board of governors. With the board augmented by new members with private-sector management experience, the CEO was in a position to challenge, where necessary, the traditional attitudes of many of the clinical staff and impose top-down change throughout the organization.

Arriving at a time when social-enterprise organizations generally were becoming more business-like in their approach, the new CEO had recognized that Oakmore's reputation for clinical excellence was no longer sufficient to ensure it retained its place in an increasingly competitive market. The financial imperatives of running an organization which not only delivered a valued product, but did so profitably, meant that clinical and management knowledges as well as more commercial knowledge were required. His strategy was to change the culture of the organization through the top-down introduction and application of management knowledge, sensitively and respectfully blended with existing clinical knowledge.

Demonstrating this cultural change to various external audiences, Oakmore's extensive list of published clinical research papers had been augmented over recent years by several papers more concerned with the organizational management of a large health care facility than with strictly clinical issues. In addition, the words and tone of the organization's media messaging, while it continued to espouse key features of the organization's original external persona—provision of excellent services and the image of the 'good employer' that cherishes and develops its staff—was drawing on a more managerial style of language. In particular, narratives made a point of stressing the virtue of the organization's charitable status in enabling the reinvestment of profits into service improvement, thus effectively combining two different and potentially conflicting sets of values into a cohesive package.

The Oakmore case highlights the importance of learning and development processes in supporting culture change, effective communication across multidisciplinary groups, and the effective use of management knowledge. The investment in these types of learning processes seems to have been effective in reshaping the attitudes and values of many staff in support of the organization's objectives. We see in this case the power of an alignment and integration of management development, training, well-developed incentive systems and a strong culture that embraced learning and knowledge sharing.

The case evidenced the importance of embedded agency in achieving organizational change. The academically curious CEO personally embodied and created an organizational form that was able to blend management, medical, and commercial knowledges, and straddle formal codified management knowledge and experiential relational knowledge. He sought management knowledge about leadership outside his familiar context of health care and sought opportunities to mix with leaders from other sectors to explore and learn from their change efforts. He and his senior team made what was a changing organization even more receptive to the discipline of the balanced scorecard. His interest in complexity, scenario, and systems management knowledge alerted him (and others) to the need to repurpose the organization in light of political changes, budgetary austerity, and QIPP. His skill in synthesizing management knowledge and filtering knowledge to make it more accessible is also an important part of the high impact of the balanced scorecard.

The Oakmore story demonstrates the importance of formal knowledges being complemented by a range of other sources of more experiential knowledges, for example the training and development activities. Learning and development events served as useful spaces where multidisciplinary conversations could happen and interdisciplinary dialogue took place. The blending and hybridization of knowledges moved the organization from a narrow focus on the immediate needs of individual patients to a position in which a commercial and business-like approach in support of improving facilities and increasing capacity was no longer tolerated but valued and celebrated by the majority of staff.

# 10 Knowledge leadership

## Securing organizational change

Mobilizing research-based management knowledge into organizational practice is an important, yet elusive dimension of a developing knowledge economy. This chapter introduces and explores empirically *knowledge leadership* as an important process for mobilizing management-based forms of knowledge to stimulate organizational change, developing related ideas we have discussed elsewhere (Fischer et al. 2016). Drawing on our six case studies, we focus here on the work of six particular managers (one from each organizational case) whom we describe as exemplifying powerful practices of mobilizing research-based knowledge into organizational practice.

Whereas much of our focus up to this point has addressed broader institutional and more macro-level perspectives on the production and consumption of management knowledge, in this chapter we consider how the work of local 'knowledge leaders' embedded in our sites engaged with, and sought to influence, wider organizational (and in some cases, macro-level) processes of knowledge mobilization.

We situate our analysis within the literature on organizational processes and practices, focusing in particular on how individual agency may engage with research-based management knowledge not merely as ideas, but through the world of material objects in the form of texts, technologies, and devices (Orlikowski and Scott 2008) concerned with the translation, exchange, and mobilization of research-based knowledge (Rashman et al. 2009; Currie and White 2012; Oborn et al. 2013; Swan et al. 2016).

Much prior scholarship on forms of knowledge management has tended to focus on rather upstream processes of knowledge production (Scarbrough 1996; Nonaka and Teece 2001) and knowledge-intensive firms (Alvesson 2004; Starbuck 1992). Situated leadership in such settings, for instance, may create ideal conditions for local, autonomous, and self-organized knowledge creation (von Krogh et al. 2012). Accordingly, the idea of 'knowledge leadership' has previously been used to describe supportive climates for learning, innovation, and development (Viitala 2004).

Yet knowledge leadership may focus not merely on such facilitative practices aimed at providing supportive climates, but with the more agentic and effortful work of mobilizing research-based knowledge into organizational practice. In our previous research (Dopson et al. 2013; Fischer et al. 2016) we have studied how local knowledge leaders operated, striving to activate and mobilize management research at micro levels within their local settings. Largely motivated through their individual, agentic, and often personally meaningful, orientations to such research, their localized practices may be analysed as specific ways of operating on codified research:

Mobilising codified knowledge into practice entails effortful processes of *transposition* in which individuals are personally involved in converting management research into its utilisation, practices of *appropriation* in which certain elements are selectively used and deployed, or *contention* involving codified knowledge being actively engaged with yet deliberately undermined, as a means of advancing subjective 'truths' and alternative ways of knowing.   (Fischer et al. 2016: 1565)

In this chapter, we shift our analytic lens to explore how such attempts at local knowledge leadership can operate to 'dynamize' change at more meso and macro levels and contextual changes impact local leadership action. All knowledge leadership, we suggest, involves agentic practices through which individual leaders strive to animate research. As leaders' personal identities and practices become meaningfully engaged and entangled with the work of knowledge mobilization, interpersonal and political stakes within their settings increase. Knowledge leadership essentially involves agentic efforts to act upon and shape organizational settings—mobilizing knowledge as a technique to powerfully secure organizational change. Knowledge leadership is thus also crucially mediated by the organizational and sectoral contexts which these leaders engage with and are part of, as evidenced in the previous chapters.

# Bottom-up examples of knowledge mobilization

## IMPROVING ORGANIZATIONAL SYSTEMS FOR HEALTH CARE QUALITY

Our first example focuses on the early stages of the inception of organizational change within the context of a new and emerging academic health science centre: a recent meso-level organizational innovation designed to improve knowledge flows, thus creating openings for local activity. Peter was a medical consultant with an enduring interest in both academic medicine and management science. He held a Ph.D., based on his clinical specialty in biological medicine, and had an MBA from a leading business school. Interestingly, Peter sought to combine and apply his dual interests to improving organizational systems for health care quality, using an applied research focus on operations management.

A distinguishing feature of his applied research focus was his determination to improve the quality and consistency of health care provision across what he regarded as isolated 'silos' within his organization. His efforts to do so nevertheless isolated him from medical colleagues who saw his efforts at having 'gone over to the dark side' by attempting to steer practice through managerial perspectives and systems: 'Other people . . . can't see it because it's not really being applied in healthcare—they're saying, we're not (a supermarket), it's not (a consulting firm). So, it's very hard to be a lone voice saying it.'

Drawing on process engineering literature, with a particular focus on queueing theory and flow management (previously developed within acute physical health care), Peter attempted to develop and test these ideas to improve patient flows and pathways in his mental health care setting.

That to me is the failing really of (this) organization that you've got these boroughs . . . you've got that huge variability, a variability that just shouldn't be happening . . . not allow(ing) learning to happen across the borders. I find it foreign and frightening . . . 'Oh well we're not going to do what they're doing in (a neighbouring district) because we're very different.' Yes, but what are the similarities?! There must be some similarities so (how can) we learn from the similarities and work out what they are?

In order to develop a compelling rationale for his work, he sought to anchor his methods in an established research literature, as a means of 'get(ting) to the operations management heart of the organization': 'I guess I bring management theory into practice . . . The first thing (I'm) doing is going out to literature to check that the methodology would come from an evidence base . . . on every, every occasion.'

He then used this evidence to craft a compelling argument for change through collecting and comparing activity and outcome data, and supported this using qualitative interviews he conducted with health professionals and managers across his organization.

Actually, when you're making (organizational) changes you're going on data, you're using evidence to make a decision, so you're not just going on opinion. To me that's part and parcel to the research you're doing in the foreground, why you're going to do that change, how you might do the change, and collecting the data and measures to see the change work. Whether that be financial data, or activity data, or outcome data, whatever it is, but you're measuring something and gathering evidence as to why you need to make that change and how you're going to make it change and make an improvement.

To persuade hospital executives and medical colleagues of the need for change, he established a proposal in the form of a report which he presented to the hospital board, arguing for an evidence-based case for organizational change, established by linking it to his analysis of flow data in his organization. 'We need to show the evidence because I think (otherwise) you lose . . . the doctors.

Doctors come from numbers, you know, as scientifically trained, they might just see numbers.'

Yet his efforts to establish such a persuasively evidence-based case for organizational change provoked strong reactions among colleagues. Whereas hospital executives were (mostly) persuaded by the data, it was met with heated confrontations with district managers and some medical colleagues, a number of whom expressed direct anger and resentment at Peter's efforts to drive change.

Very defensive from the managers . . . it could be perceived that I'm threatening them, showing knowledge that maybe they don't have . . . taking on their job and telling them how to do it . . . My [project] was one of the biggest things that caused a lot of upset . . . [Managers] found it very hard and one of them said he couldn't see me for a while because he felt so angry . . . even three years on!

Despite such negative reactions among some colleagues, Peter's efforts to introduce research-led change were influential within his organization and supported by senior managers. His initial proposals to the hospital board, focusing on service improvement, were often returned requesting further work, yet these were ultimately taken up and used as a basis for reorganizing patient flows in the organization.

Oh it was definitely taken up . . . we did run a project locally following on from the report, trying to improve things, and in fact they invested in an outside consultant to come in to give the extra resource to help that work . . . there was a difficulty and tension between leadership and, you know, what was to be achieved . . . I guess the two of us, myself and the consultant involved, weren't pushy enough with the senior managers . . . to break down the barriers to get the change happening . . . they were too distant from it.

Interestingly, despite Peter's later reflections about failings 'lying on both sides', his conclusions that they had not been 'pushy' enough led him to redouble his efforts to mobilize change in the face of tensions and resistance. His personal convictions and growing insights about navigating politics led him to explore further means of engaging senior leaders and clinicians to develop his approach.

In summary, we see in this example efforts to directly translate evidence-based knowledge on operational management into a planned programme of organizational redesign. Significantly, such research was directly and overtly tied to local data and metrics on patient flows which Peter used to justify and assess the need for change, comparing these metrics with his subsequent efforts to monitor, evaluate, and report degrees of compliance across his organization.

According to Peter's personal account, we find a process fraught with emotional tensions and unexpected local confrontations which threatened to derail his project. Analytically, we see the technical aspects of assessment, monitoring, and reporting as operating powerfully on differences between professional groups (most notably in this case, between doctors and general managers), cutting across long-established divisions between geographical districts and subunit divisions in the Academic Health Sciences Centre. In particular, by combining management research with data from across the organization, he assessed and made visible significant local variations within the Academic Health Sciences Centre, which the hospital board then felt compelled to take notice of and (eventually) act upon.

## STIMULATING LOCALIZED, INTERDISCIPLINARY EXCHANGE AND INNOVATION IN A POLICY THINK TANK TO ADDRESS SYSTEMIC ORGANIZATIONAL ISSUES IN HEALTH CARE

Our next example focuses on boundary spanning and mobilizing knowledge across disciplinary silos in a health policy unit to create, and disseminate into wider practice, more innovative and synthesized forms of knowledge. James was a senior policy manager in a policy think tank. He held a Ph.D. in information science. He had a long-standing interest in using research drawn from management and organizational psychology to inform and implement transformational organizational change across boundaries in complex organizational systems, especially health care.

A distinguishing feature of his approach was a combination of actively seeking to understand the state of the current and emerging literature ('That's really, really important to me. If I don't know what's being written, then I have a fear') with an action research orientation to seek and develop local solutions.

I work a lot with leadership dimension of policy . . . and that really formed the guy I am . . . You can say, I'm going to lock myself in a loft and I'm going to (research) . . . and that's how most people work. Or you can say, I really want to help people at their jobs . . . (Well) I want to be the guy who helps these people do a better job (by building) relationships with people.

Hence, instead of searching for and applying more generic management texts, James actively sought out and strove to transpose lessons from wider related research fields, such as the sociology of science and the military literature. His approach to driving change was to stimulate ways to challenge prevailing notions of top-down change in health care organizations. In particular, he sought to challenge and 'humanize' what he saw as managers' technical approaches to delivering QIPP agenda.

People have really persistent and deep professional identities. And new ways of doing things, you know, they undermine those identities . . . These are important issues, right? You're explaining it to these (directors) and they're: 'well I want to know how it transforms technology, how do I meet the QIPP agenda' . . . And you realize, these guys are not leaders, they're managers. This is utter bullshit!

Accordingly, he sought to actively challenge dominant models of management thinking in change and quality improvement models (often drawn and applied from Ford, General Motors, or other such multinationals), and attempted to stimulate managers to draw upon alternative sources of knowledge to stimulate change.

I don't think there's really ever been an organization as big and as complicated and as dysfunctional as the NHS. You can't rely on the normal texts. People start quoting Peter Senge, Jack Welch, all this stuff, and you say to yourself, what are you talking about? You're comparing apples with oranges—this doesn't work here and it never will . . . You have to think of some other way of doing it.

In his efforts to mobilize wider research, he sought to stimulate interdisciplinary working within his own organization as well as in clients, seeking to stimulate ideas and debates as a precursor to initiating change. He argued for boundary spanning as a means of transforming ideas and new thinking, rather than coordination or collaboration between 'stale ideas': 'What you're really looking for when you're working across organizational boundaries, you're not looking for coordination and you're not looking for cooperation, what you're really looking for is really transformation, I really want to get a kind of transformative way of working.'

He drew upon the sociological literature on boundary spanning, especially Leigh-Star and Griesemer's (1989) work on how amateurs and professionals worked together in a museum at Berkeley, through boundary objects at the interface, which he regarded as increasingly important in his work mobilizing ideas. As he described it, the social tensions run 'behind the scenes' in terms of who owns the flow of resources.

What you really want to be able to do is to say where is the tension, you know, what's at stake, you know, what do we believe in . . . and one way of doing that is by making those differences explicit, and the boundary object is a way of making those differences explicit . . . If you're working, say in aeronautical engineering, the boundary object could be the technical prints, because they will have a very different meaning (to the engineer) than it does to the person who's trying to sell the airplane to British Airways, right? So, you can see clearly what the differences are . . . what the trade-offs are going to be, but you'll be able to understand how the other guy thinks.

Interestingly, he applied this to his own work ('I can't spend time wondering what the boundary object would be . . . well let's make the boundary object the contract between us, what do you want, what do you expect to get out of this?') and sought to make explicit expectations between parties and the dynamics operating at the level of 'boundary objects'. He used this internally to create debates, bring in alternative ways of thinking and to stimulate what some colleagues referred to as exciting 'bun fights' during meetings across divisions.

His efforts were designed to generate, and indeed produced, energized debates along with mutual engagement and potential to generate new insights and initiatives. His ability to stimulate meaningful discussion was often welcomed by colleagues who participated in lively discussion. Yet James was aware that his ability to energize dialogue could place him in a potentially awkward and tension-filled position between conflicting perspectives and interests.

How do you know when you choose the right boundary object? One way is by making differences explicit, raising tensions—in a sense you're making problems for people. You step back and say, 'Look at the problems I've created for you, what does this tell us?' And you just have to wait for them to calm down, because there's a hell of a lot of emotion in organizations.

Whereas in his external consulting work with other organizations, he actively drew upon differences to stimulate discussion and reflection, which he facilitated ('if you say, we are working together, and these are the rules of the game...you could act as a facilitator to direct that attention'), he described this overt 'third-party' position as a consultant as a missing dimension when attempting to work similarly in his own setting: 'It's hard to say, why are you so upset? They'd want to wring your neck...I discovered what you need to do is to back off [a bit], so you've got to be really, really careful, recognizing the traps...the best thing to do is just kind of lay back, subside a bit and be patient.'

In this example, we see James actively seeking out and attempting to apply rather marginal and unconventional sources of social science research which he saw as relevant to specific organizational contexts. Analytically, this case is interesting because of the overt focus on affective-political dynamics as a potential catalyst for stimulating and mobilizing interest in research-based ideas. More intriguingly, in James's specific efforts to stimulate interactions (and potential learning) across divisional and organizational boundaries, he positioned his own practices as a disruptive—and potentially integrating—technique for mobilizing research: 'If you're in your own organization and you're trying to...work across boundaries and it's creating tensions... nobody wants to do it.'

James deliberately sought to integrate these through his own activities as a clearly identified 'boundary object'. His approach sought to combine and blend these activities with diverse parties across organizational boundaries, so 'bringing ideas to life' in ways designed to stimulate meanings. Although powerful as an approach, James's account suggests his middle-manager level within his organization meant that the early impact of organizational change proved harder to handle and sustain without clear support from his senior managers.

# ENERGIZING CROSS-BOUNDARY COLLABORATION
# IN A LOCAL HEALTH CARE COMMUNITY

Ben was a clinical director of Willowton Primary Care Trust (PCT). Trained as a medical doctor, he had long-standing interest and experience in creating organizational change in health care systems, gained from prior experience of working with local communities in the UK and overseas. He had a deep personal interest in using social science theories of emergent change in complex, interorganizational settings. He held an MD (Doctorate in Medicine).

A distinctive feature of Ben's use of management knowledge was his strong engagement in participatory methods. Intending to stimulate and equip staff and community groups to better understand and change their organizational contexts, he combined conceptual models and practical frameworks to develop locally designed solutions with strong ownership by participants. He described his approach as helping participants to reconcile conflicting paradigmatic interpretations, to bring them to 'a shared kind of narrative'.

I became very frustrated with the paternalism of medicine and (its) seeming certainty of science inside medicine . . . [Its] contemporary ways of thinking about the structure of the world, the nature of identity, construction of health care systems and so on, were not very helpful. But the really big influences came . . . where the mismatch between my observations and the available theory made it into a quest rather than idle interest. I had a couple of almost visceral experiences that brought (this insight) down to reality . . . [sensing] very deeply that these people [were] as trapped as each other, inside their [interpretive] systems.

Ben described this 'quest' as having stimulated an intensive search for related ideas derived from organizational change, complexity, and systems theories which he integrated into a model that he developed over a period of several years and published as a textbook of transformational organizational change.

What I have done is construct my own theories about all of this which . . . I've largely written up in to my book which puts that in the public domain. And I continue to gravitate towards . . . and make friends with people with those kinds of [complex systems] ideas . . . I'm afraid it's still too far ahead of the times . . . I get, to a different kind of language . . . that is very uncomfortable for most academics to relate to because it strikes at their entire discipline . . . The same thing goes on with managers in the health service [who] find this deeply discomforting—where's the beginning, where's the end and how do you manage it?

Indeed, he recognized that his strong focus on context tended to be at odds with his colleagues' increasing interest in evidence-based models of change that were locally promoted and developed through training initiatives, secondments, and locally circulating research texts. Conversely, he was deeply sceptical about claims of evidence, refusing to accept academic texts that were not specifically framed and justified in relation to the specific contexts from which they originated. His strong phenomenological orientation led him to engage critically with academic texts and other forms of codified knowledge, interrogating and testing them against his own and colleagues' personal experiences.

Well the notion of evidence, of course I seriously contest . . . Evidence-based management actually is a de-contextualized notion of evidence; therefore, I dismiss the entire lot . . . This inability to make that translation is [because] all this kind of rubbish that you get from the [practitioner journal] and the [research institute] is taken as unopposed fact. There is no other place to go to for ideas . . . solely to act as a counterpoint.

Consistent with this approach, in Ben's efforts to stimulate change, he did not seek to circulate or widely publicize his own book. Arguing that decontextualized theory is simply ineffective ('if people learn it before they need it they can get it wrong'), he drew selectively on certain ideas, introducing them to participants engaged in the change process as and when he felt the situation specifically required it: 'So, this is why theory is incredibly important. If the theory can be broadly accepted . . . and [achieves] what society wanted it to do, then yes, it can (be effective). But it's a waste of time [just] talking to people about it, [because] they cannot "get it" until they're engaged in it.'

Accordingly, he insisted on a developmentally focused approach, attempting to stimulate deeper understanding and leadership abilities among potential change agents already embedded within the settings.

I kept on running into the same kind of problem: that management theory needs to be available [just] when people need it. So, at very early stages in peoples' careers, expose them to very modest ways of understanding leadership and their role as leaders . . . giving people managerial theoretical understandings in response to their needs . . . Well, the role of academics actually inside all of this has to be rethought, to be more responsive and engaged in this [work].

In his efforts to stimulate meaningful interagency collaboration at Willowton PCT, he deliberately focused on working with one of its most deprived communities to stimulate a research-focused service improvement through collaboration between community members, health and social care agencies, and academic researchers. As he described it, he actively sought to embed and rhetorically justify his project within policy initiatives ('looking for chinks of light'), while mobilizing sustained engagement to assist in this work from an array of individuals sympathetic to his project from a range of local organizations.

The reason why that was important was, as it was put to me, 'nobody can do anything with [this place] . . . it is a basket case, and nobody will ever be able to make it any different'. So, I was offered something that was a place of despair; everyone had tried everything (and) it couldn't possibly work. There's a tremendous mismatch between the ideas (and) things I do and the structural realities of the NHS, (but) that is overcome if [this work] can be siloed somewhere in a pilot project—something nobody else really cares very much about.

As one senior executive described it, although the direction and increasingly positive outcomes of this project were valued within Willowton, the increasingly austere fiscal environment produced significant local consequences and constraints on support for the project's more emergent design and focus. Whereas members of the senior team were personally supportive and acknowledged Ben's efforts ('I happen to regard it as essential, because that's the way in which you're going to get the change'), there was growing concern about the project's strategic alignment with top-down structural changes imposed by government. For example, the PCT was reorganized, a supportive CEO left, and there was increased pressure to produce savings leading to a loss of traction of the existing activities.

It's quite difficult to sustain all of this as times get tougher and tougher and tougher . . . I'm trying, you know, to see things from the lens of the ground rather than the lens of where I sit. It's absolutely essential . . . but we can't afford to not concentrate all our resources, all our capacity, on a certain limited number of things . . . Somehow, we've got to make sure this is really connected to making the kind of strategic change that we need to make . . . it's certainly (not) totally starting [as the NHS] requirement you go away and do it in a dutiful way.

In this case, we find Ben's approach to actively seeking out and using social science research was closely tied to his personal experiences and epistemological framing (elsewhere we have described a related notion of 'epistemic fitting': McGivern et al. 2016). Conversely, he tended to engage critically with formal, data-driven evidence both as a means of driving alternative theorizing, and to stimulate more innovative ideas and solutions among colleagues. Although he had carefully codified his theorizing and techniques of organizational change in his textbook (published by a leading academic publishing house), an interesting aspect of Ben's use of knowledge is that he downplayed the significance of this text, seeking instead to engage others in dialogue about their first-hand experience.

Analytically, we find Ben's primary anchoring in social science research was an epistemological stance which he translated into his well-developed model of active participant engagement. Sensitive to potential power dynamics within his organization, he deliberately sought out a neglected and failing area which he saw as having the strongest potential for rapid organizational development. Intending to rigorously drive practice-based theorizing (informed by his prior research and textbook), he promoted techniques of engagement within this selected setting. He did so, in part, by deliberately undermining and suppressing what he openly criticized as 'decontextualized', policy-orientated academic texts.

# Top-down examples of knowledge mobilization

## STIMULATING TOP-DOWN TRANSFORMATIONAL CHANGE IN A THIRD-SECTOR ORGANIZATION

Our example focuses on the process of successfully implementing a systemic approach to change in a large and growing organization, using a process of organizational transformation. This case is discussed more fully in Chapter 9. Clive was a medically trained CEO, with a Ph.D. in his medical specialty and an MBA. He took an active interest in seeking out and applying management ideas, in part sourced through executive education activities, and through reading management textbooks from leading academic publishing houses. He sought to incorporate such ideas into his approach to leadership, using a complexity perspective on organizations as open and emergent systems.

A distinguishing aspect of Clive's research focus was his interest in using management ideas to stimulate the transformation of a traditional organization. Oakmore Healthcare, as described in Chapter 9, was a long-established and independently run specialist medical charity. Clive sought to change its long-established patterns of hierarchy into a more dynamic and flexible setting, focused on adaptation and growth in what he saw as a rapidly evolving external market. His strategy had been to change the culture of the organization through the top-down introduction and application of management knowledge.

[I have] a different model which is a kind of complexity-systems model where I wander around seeing where there are emergent patterns, encouraging some patterns to form and squashing others...You're looking for a fit between ideas that are triggered in your mind by skipping through management [literature] with problems and patterns that triggered your mind by looking at stuff in the organization. Putting them together in a very sort of chaotic way and then getting that, 'oh that's what we need to do...'.

He sought to 'deconstruct hierarchies' by disrupting established power positions, drawing selectively on management ideas to justify 'ranking and yanking' areas of poor performance and to drive a new commercial focus on bed occupancy rates.

As the new CEO, I had a meeting with the senior clinicians and managers, and the oldest of them said to me 'what's your agenda here', in this rather suspicious way: kind of, challenge the new guy. I found myself saying in a sort of Thatcherian tone 'occupancy, occupancy, occupancy'. Well there was this short of shocked silence [in the boardroom].

Clive's approach to initiating change reflected his broader openness to management ideas. He embraced the concept of the balanced scorecard (Kaplan and Norton 1996), the subject of an MBA dissertation by one of his direct reports. This stimulated his interest in reading further ('I was kind of digesting the management stuff pretty quickly') and using this as a methodology:

So, I read up a little bit about Kaplan and Norton at that time and it seemed . . . that if you focused, if you figured out what was really important to drive the business forward and . . . if you repeatedly paid attention to a particular matter, then the staff you managed would pay attention to it and regard it as serious and do something about it. So that seemed to me to make sense. Now the first indicator on the sheet was bed occupancy—just like hotels or anything else, so that's where I'd got to in my first few weeks.

Clive's interest in management ideas and texts led to many discussions with colleagues who shared his intellectual curiosity. In particular his interest in and utilization of the balanced scorecard stimulated one senior manager, with a background in accounting, to do further reading to help craft key perform-ance indicators to the organizational context. As this colleague described:

I try and go back to the original research . . . There's a very clear process that Kaplan and Norton defined for trying to figure out how you map that strategy on to KPIs. (Yet) what I see a lot of is people . . . discussing which KPIs are important. Whereas actually that's an end result . . . a concentration at the wrong end of the process, because they haven't really looked at the [strategy] issues . . . Presenting themselves as experts, without really understanding where the book had come from in the first place . . . The more fundamental [ideas], you know, none of [these people] were doing strategy maps or anything like this.

Clive then drew upon and assimilated these 'foundational ideas' into his own model which he developed, producing written frameworks, templates, and reporting systems that he then introduced to influence thinking and drive and monitor reform, using the organization's standard reporting mechanisms. In this example, we see affective-political dimensions of change channelled through reporting mechanisms designed to surface and monitor change. 'Since then I've looked at the occupancy figures every week. I'm just hammer-ing down on (them) all the time. I have a simple management theory that if I pay attention to it, everybody else just has to keep at it.'

Interestingly, while Clive's efforts to establish such a persuasively evidence-based case for organizational change provoked strong reactions among colleagues, he was prepared to draw powerfully on management texts and techniques drawn from the literature, applying them to 'cause a certain amount of chaos'; he then set up project groups to 'sort it out'. He describes his approach as not shying away from conflict ('go to the frontline . . . get involved, make lots of mistakes'), but treating issues and reactions dispassionately ('avoid getting emotional or irrational . . . business is business . . . just don't get upset about it').

In contrast to Peter's example of grassroots-level change, where resistance and negative reactions initially threatened to derail his change initiative, in

Clive's example we find top-down system-orientated change efforts, tying some colleagues' existing (although quite marginal) interest in the balanced scorecard into top-down strategic leadership narratives of organizational transformation. Analytically, we see the balanced scorecard model being applied, blended, and developed in relation to locally sensitive issues, powerfully operationalizing Clive's vision of establishing more metrics- (and financially) driven managerial practices. These efforts were supported by a suite of organizational development interventions (see Chapter 9). From his account, however, we see that establishing the balanced scorecard as a dominant model (reinforced by regularly 'hammering' its focus on metrics) was facilitated by actively disrupting alternative models, reporting mechanisms, hierarchical structures, and committees that he regarded as means of resisting change. Supported by standardized organizational techniques and mechanisms, the balanced scorecard model was used to stimulate and embed organizational-level change.

## PRODUCING UNIFYING TECHNIQUES FOR ORGANIZATIONAL INTERVENTION IN UK HEALTH CARE

Tom was a senior partner of a global management consultancy (Elmhouse Consulting). He fostered a specialist focus on organizational development before moving into management consulting. He had an enduring interest in drawing upon and mobilizing empirical evidence to inform his consulting practice. He held a Ph.D. from a leading business school.

A distinctive feature of Tom's approach to management knowledge was his interest in actively seeking out and linking empirical data with management theories. He described his knowledge orientation as constantly scanning his environment, seeking to 'steal ideas' as a routine part of his day-to-day work.

I am very explicit in making that kind of learning contract with myself that I will steal something from everyone I work with . . . I'm kind of religious about it . . . it's not a kind of vague intention that I rationalize afterwards . . . I will take part of my energy in that meeting to think about what I'm going to learn from this person. And when you have the privilege to meet an awful lot of people as you do, well you have a privilege to steal an awful lot of things. So that's one of the things I do, I nick good ideas.

Despite his disciplined receptivity to new ideas, as head of the global practice he actively sought to synthesize diverse forms of evidence into practically useful, unifying models to drive Elmhouse's work with clients. Indeed, he saw consultants' diverse pursuits of the 'search for truth' as potentially problematic for the practice, especially in delivering integrated and impactful solutions for clients.

I mean the good thing is, you know, everyone is motivated to generate knowledge . . . But an unintended consequence of that is a client can receive . . . articles on the same topic that have quite fundamental different points of view in them . . . So, there are some challenges, [Elmhouse's] knowledge is a very delicate asset that we could easily kill, so we're concerned about it.

Seeking to overcome tensions between contrasting perspectives, he established an influential academic board which included esteemed scholars and well-known 'gurus' from leading business schools, intended to powerfully contribute to and shape an authoritative book which Tom co-authored, articulating Elmhouse's evidence-based approach to consulting practice.

I did design it, I'm very invested in it . . . I personally would say that it's worked extremely well in the sense that our biggest knowledge deliverable in the last five years has been encapsulated in the book. And the book itself is a powerful thing for us, but even more powerful is the fact that we'll no longer have . . . the framework wars where different bits of the firm would each view transformation in a different way. We have one unified coherent point of view . . . everyone singing off the same hymn sheet . . . So, I think, a very powerful book.

As a colleague commented, the process of developing this book proved highly influential within Elmhouse, acting as a catalyst that stimulated increasing interest and adoption of its evidence-based approach across the firm.

It's kind of bubbled up in to, you know . . . we've compiled all of his evidence in to a body of work which we're calling the sort of 'science of organization' . . . which we put out to initially the [health care] practice, then to the body of senior partners across the firm . . . we've shown that to them, got their feedback and started spreading it out that way . . . kind of tested [advance] versions of it with them.

Interestingly, the production of this text was seen by colleagues as intrinsically tied to Tom's personal knowledge orientation and authority, thus encapsulating in key respects his 'super-inspiring' influence and style ('he's a completely different kind of guy'), powerfully drawing in similarly research-minded colleagues.

This really comes down to some quite specific individuals . . . The global knowledge leader [Tom] . . . quite likes that sort of evidence-based kind of approach . . . There are, sort of, two or three other folks in the [health care] practice in particular who've got particular biases towards empiricism and sound academic research . . . It really has come down to that great question: do individuals matter in history: yes or no? And I think this [spread of influence] really is down to specific individuals in a specific place, talking about these ideas.

As another consultant suggested, the spread, adoption, and contribution to this unifying body of knowledge among consultants was regarded as a primary driver of both career and commercial advantage, far exceeding the basic requirement to 'just be good with clients or to bring in business':

> To make a long-term, sustainable career at Elmhouse, you have to know something... that's what makes you distinctive here... You know, the question you asked, what is knowledge at Elmhouse? It's the only kind of capital that we have, right? We sell people and knowledge. And even when we sell [our] people, we're selling knowledge. Our [entire] methodology is to derive knowledge.

As Tom indicated, instead of being orientated towards notions of particular ideas as 'truthful', he actively worked to synthesize and mobilize an authoritative body of evidence-based knowledge, sidelining historical differences between competing perspectives. Yet interestingly, he sought to combine the firm's adoption of this unifying knowledge with a more politically focused approach that mobilized consultants' understanding of the political dimensions of using such knowledge in their work with clients. Knowledge, in other words, is not just something that is 'sold', but implies deeper micro-political operations that combine organizational politics, research-based texts, and methodologies (of the Elmhouse 'science of organizations'), and consultants' personal styles and impact.

> We are slowly getting to the point where our, as part of our normal offering for, let's say, a strategy [project], there would be a capability building element [that] actually means something... It's quite intensive, quite a deep level of training... a mixture between [analysing] the dynamics of politics and power and the personal impact of you as a consultant.

As the case of Tom exemplifies, we see an approach to management research that is closely related to his pragmatic philosophical position, strongly orientated towards evidence of what works in practice. An interesting aspect of his approach is what some colleagues describe as his inspiring, 'guru-like' influence within his organization—adding to his overt research focus a persuasive ability to integrate meanings in the form of persuasive, organizational stories: 'I don't think that the empirical evidence on its own would change my mind, I would need to have a story, a piece of logic... backed up by empirical data, which would change my mind.'

Analytically, we see in the work of the academic board a powerful technique that simultaneously *sources* and *mobilizes* management research. Internally, we see a synthesizing of diverse perspectives from leading management scholars, combined with an organizational process of enrolling senior colleagues across the firm in commenting on and critiquing Elmhouse's emerging authoritative text to silence 'framework wars'. Accordingly, this text functions powerfully both internally and externally to mobilize a unified 'science of organizations', influentially selling evidence-based policy and organizational ideas to governments and other organizational stakeholders.

## COMBINING RESEARCH AND POLITICS TO STIMULATE COLLABORATION ACROSS AN INTERORGANIZATIONAL HEALTH CARE SYSTEM

Our final example focuses on how management ideas are used to frame and organize a model for driving a new collaboration across multiple institutional boundaries in an NHS Collaboration for Leadership in Applied Health Research and Care (CLAHRC), one of nine such network-based organizations in England intended to mobilize academic science and research into practice in the NHS.

Simon was a senior academic with a Ph.D. in management studies, who directed this university/hospital collaboration. He had a long-standing interest in organizational change and sought to apply research-based ideas to empirical contexts in novel and interesting ways that drove wider change, and in turn provided opportunities for further empirical research: 'What I do is, I have second-mover advantage. So, I take something and apply it to the health care setting, or take something that's relatively theoretical, and empirically elaborate upon it, and that's how I move.'

He sought to transpose into practice and then diffuse management knowledge, within his region, as part of developing the CLAHRC. He saw this task as a process of not just translating research to inform the design of the CLAHRC, but gaining practical adoption and 'buy-in' from key (and locally, politically important) stakeholders.

Simon's efforts to drive change were influenced by his need to act persuasively among multiple stakeholders, spanning managerial, clinical, and policy perspectives. In order to do this, he actively sought to develop models that were overtly evidence-based, yet applied in ways that were accessible and plausible as practical approaches to change.

Models of management . . . provide you with a broad framework that you need to be reflective about as you take action. So those sort of models or literature inform their thinking, but combine it with an element of craft and intuition and improvisation. I mean it gives you legitimacy, actually it's been really useful with critical academics to spend all day going 'this is a model'. And they like it!

In creating his model for systems-wide organizational change and influence, he synthesized business school concepts, in particular, combining ideas taken from communities of practice and systems change theory. He then borrowed from other organizing frameworks to develop a new model with associated diagrams, representations, and named mechanisms as a basis for a programme of organizational change: 'So, what happened then was, I then drove the development of the rewriting . . . it became a much more organizational learning-focused model using . . . business school concepts around, you know, the research practice gap and how you breach that, you know, knowledge brokering, knowledge brokers, the diffusion people, building communities of practice.'

In directing this collaboration, he drew further upon his research-based orientation and credibility to persuade other senior academics and managers in the region to support the collaboration and its intended purpose of knowledge exchange.

Simon's efforts to create and assemble a narrative using business school texts on models of change were an important and influential aspect of his efforts to mobilize them across the interorganizational system. Moreover, these were not just theoretically driven frameworks but woven into a persuasive narrative that he crafted in relation to the national policy issues and local perspectives, and sought to sell and mobilize.

[This was not] just about local [organizational issues but] about the national things. I found the managers incredibly useful in helping me develop a narrative. So, you know, we've gone from a time of plenty to a more parsimonious financial climate and the QIPP agenda, so in trying to develop a narrative, you know, I've had to improvise and develop a narrative to place in to QIPP and with chief execs and other exec directors have been incredibly useful for that.

Interestingly this 'selling' involved actual processes of personally investing energy into and convincing others, creating demonstrable alliances and links with national and local leaders to create performances that were personally and politically invested.

So, I describe myself as an academic salesman. A lot of it was going to board meetings, standing up doing hard-hitting presentations, standing on stages with (policy experts) chief execs, the lead clinicians. That was the thing, real visible, charismatic delivery, waving your arms around . . . enthusiastic and running around the stage, and you put some energy in to the thing. It's an odd thing, but people say you've got a certain style, and that really worked at the start.

His efforts to overtly 'perform' research-based knowledge in this way are interesting because of its dramatizing 'animation' from its origins in codified knowledge to a more personally invested and dramatized form of mobilization, actively engaging and attempting to excite others across wider organizational settings. Other managers and clinicians saw his academic role (and associated research outputs) as giving him credibility, even if Simon felt a degree of uncertainty about the model's actual potential to create the changes he intended ('It took a lot out of me, because I'm not entirely a believer, and I'm not too sure if this (project) will work').

Analytically, transposing work such as this involves actors who draw upon codified research and theories, yet whose efforts actively mobilize knowledge by animating and situating it in specific settings. In the case of Simon, he drew upon well-established research on models of organizational change which he shaped (in part through discussions with senior health service managers) into powerful narratives that addressed the wider policy agenda of reform. Research-based knowledge became a compelling local narrative through being synthesized with visual artefacts, templates, diagrams, and named mechanisms. Visually representing and animating research ideas in this way created an emotionally charged and exciting vision, designed to stimulate interest and motivate willing followers: 'So that made me understand, this [engagement] is hard work . . . it was a lot of emotional work . . . I've had to improvise and develop a narrative . . . One of the things I took out of it was when you become something like a leader . . . people look to me for leadership, and it's a very odd experience.'

Of particular analytical interest in this case is the more deliberately political stance Simon adopted in positioning his activities across his interorganizational system. He combined the research and animating narratives with powerful appearances with national leaders in the health system, so producing compelling symbols and images of (professional, managerial, and political) endorsement.


## Discussion and conclusion

As these six cases illustrate, knowledge leadership mobilizes management research into practice at different organizational levels, ranging from a micro-level focus within particular organizations (Peter and Clive) and sub-units (Ben), to broader efforts to mobilize research at health system (Tom and Clive) and interorganizational (James) levels.

Although our knowledge leaders adopted a variety of mobilization tactics, in general terms we find two distinct sets of practices that reflect their degree of access to power, and their abilities to mobilize organizational resources. In our first set of Peter, James, and Ben, each occupying mid-level positions (generally regarded as specialists, with seniority in professional and/or technical expertise), their tactics emphasized their distinct access to research-based knowledge as a scarce resource. Whereas their specific approaches to accessing research, translating meaning, and mobilizing research differed significantly, in each case, these individuals utilized their privileged positions of access to place them centrally to work on research mobilization. Through generating 'bottom-up' research engagement in their settings, their activities focused on mobilizing upwards codified texts and research into practice, moving from micro- to meso-organizational levels. This first group can be characterized as essentially operating at the early stage of 'animating' and transposing research texts into organizational practices.

Our second set of knowledge leaders, Clive, Tom, and Simon—each holding senior, executive-level positions—can be seen as operating at a later stage of appropriating and assembling texts, techniques, and influences, powerfully shaping and mobilizing dominant organizational narratives. Although this second group signalled their specialist knowledge and access to distinct bodies of research, their tactics created authoritative 'assemblages' (Deleuze and Guattari 1987) of research-based ideas in the form of synthesized texts, devices, and narratives. By stimulating powerful 'top-down' and inter-organizational engagement with these textual artefacts and devices, this second group of knowledge leaders orchestrated and mobilized a powerful assemblage of strategies, change initiatives, and projects, bundled with the disruption of prior arrangements. In this way, they can be seen as operating on the meso-to-macro-organizational flow and mobilization of a circulating 'textual economy', animated through power, influence, and privileged access to resources.

In summary, these empirical findings indicate that knowledge leaders operate by bringing together and mobilizing compelling assemblages of texts, expert knowledge, and power resources accessible in their contexts. Whereas mid-level 'specialists' emphasized privileged access to research and their abilities to transpose it into organizational practices, senior-level leaders emphasized their privileged access to wider organizational resources and abilities to powerfully synthesize and activate research-based ideas within their broader assembling of actors, materials, and techniques, which they were then able to powerfully mobilize.

What might we conclude analytically from our cases? We suggest, first, that knowledge leaders deliberately seek out and select particular research-based texts, aiming to convert and transpose these into a variety of materials, devices, techniques, and practices for utilization in their settings. This transposition process is especially interesting because of the prominent centrality of research texts in combining—and rhetorically justifying—how and why a heterogeneous array of artefacts and practices is composed as an authoritative, research-based process of knowledge mobilization. Returning to our earlier review of academic literature on management knowledge, we see that knowledge leadership emphasizes much of the tacit, experiential, and relational forms of knowledge identified by practice scholars; yet its 'complex texture of doings and sayings' (Nicolini 2009, 1411) has an especially strongly *textual* dimension, emphasizing specific research texts that powerfully shape knowledge mobilization between and across macro, meso, and micro levels. Hence what starts out as a mere idea can be skilfully elaborated in the form of texts, materials, and artefacts that may then be 'activated' to mobilize influence and change among other actors.

Second, knowledge leaders tend to identify with—and indeed, are identified by others—with particular topics and types of research-based knowledge, often engaging with their chosen knowledges in ways replete with personal meanings, narratives, and experiences. Such forms of close engagement and personal identification with particular knowledges tend to be, unsurprisingly, not merely technical, but rather invested with personal emotions, meaning, and purpose. Importantly, these personal dimensions of engagement are often shaped through formative experiences in individuals' personal biographies and careers.

As we have argued previously, knowledge moves not through some inherent force, but through the personal and interpersonal engagements of actors, often passionately engaged with various emotional, political, and personal values, both within and between organizations (Fischer 2012; Fischer and Ferlie 2013). More generally, our cases indicate that these emotionally invested dimensions relate not just to the activities of knowledge leaders but tend to be an important aspect of engaging with and mobilizing knowledge across boundaries.

Similarly, the way knowledge leaders engage with particular research-based texts and materials in their settings tends to be strongly emotionally imbued, often evoking personal and symbolic meanings which connect the work of knowledge leadership with individuals' personal identities and narratives. As we have seen in our cases, leaders vary in how they manage such engagement interpersonally, varying from Clive's efforts to retain a rational composure ('avoid getting emotional or irrational . . . just don't get upset about it') to James's efforts to allow emotions to subside ('you just have to wait for them to calm down, because there's a hell of a lot of emotion'). Nonetheless, the work of knowledge leadership is personally effortful and fraught with risks to knowledge leaders' reputations, their sense of themselves, and their personal well-being. This has important implications for knowledge leaders' abilities to sustain their work of knowledge mobilization over sufficiently long periods to effectively mobilize research-based change.

Third, these 'animating' dynamics play a significant, if previously under-explored, role in how research-based texts come to be materially assembled and mobilized within and between organizations. We find the exchange and interplay of persons and material objects, animated by emotion and politics, produced meaningful texts that may circulate and appear to 'take on a life of their own'. These interplays, involving emotional and affective 'entanglements' (Fischer 2012; Fischer and McGivern 2016) with material objects stimulate energized shared actions between persons, ideas, and technologies: 'A flow of emotional energy that travels in networks of technology, people, images . . . technologies are important because they distribute and circulate affect in action nets . . . Affect flows from non-human devices to people and back again . . . act(ing) as a node in a network of affect production' (Boedker and Chua 2013, 262–3).

Indeed, as our cases reveal, the mobilization of texts in these sites often stimulated strong (both positive and negative) flows of interpersonal engagement and reaction, whether as unintended by-products of change (as seen in Peter's efforts to introduce evidence-based operational management), or through energetically stimulating excitement and willing buy-in (as seen in Simon's visible displays to mobilize ideas associated with policy leaders).

Finally, and importantly, we argue that this potential of knowledge leaders to powerfully stimulate influence across organizational boundaries should be understood in terms of the wider political and affective dynamics that activate and mobilize knowledge flows between diverse actors. As we have emphasized in this chapter, doing so does not merely take place at micro levels implied by practice perspectives, but becomes powerfully entangled within a broader political economy of ideas, strategies, and devices. In our earlier analysis of think tanks, we described how networks of influence can operate to energize relations and resources between actors, stimulating potential to 'dynamise-in' (Mazzucato 2013) research-based, systems-level change. Such knowledge flows, we suggest, connect the work of powerful knowledge leadership with wider macro-level phenomena, both stimulating and energizing the circulation of an expanding 'textual economy' of management knowledge.

# 11 Concluding discussion

## Management knowledge, politics, policy, and public services organization in times of austerity

The concluding discussion draws out some themes which have emerged across the substantive chapters previously presented. Reflecting on these chapters, we ask: What have we learnt more broadly about the nature of management knowledge in current English health care organizations? What are the forces and dynamics that influence which types of management knowledge are preferred and become embedded?

## A critique of EBMgt

Our original project took as its motivation the underexplored question of whether the EBMgt movement had developed the same traction in the health care managerial field as the earlier EBM wave had in the clinical field. EBM was indeed taken by supportive authors (Walshe and Rundall 2001; Tranfield et al. 2003) as a positive role model for EBMgt. The health care sector should in our view be seen as a 'best case' test for EBMgt, given the EBM inheritance there and the strong scientific and research culture.

However, we found empirically (at least in the six English sites we studied) that EBMgt was as yet very weakly developed. Core EBMgt 'knowledge products', such as evidence-based guidelines, randomized control trials (RCTs), meta-analyses, and systematic reviews, were all conspicuous by their absence. Nor was it clear how the preferred RCT method could usefully be applied in the field of managerial research, either in practice (again, EBMgt-orientated RCTs were largely absent, see Reay et al. 2009) or even more fundamentally in theory. This is because the importance of organizational 'context' (Pettigrew et al. 1992) was at least as important as any focal 'intervention' which is central in EBM/ EBMgt thinking. Our work is rather aligned with more sociologically informed literature—both theoretical and empirical (Sturdy 2004)—on the often contested ways in which management knowledge is created and mobilized in firms and organizations. For example, management ideas and practices may be reinterpreted (Ansari et al. 2010) as they diffuse, so that they fit better with the underlying organizational context.

Swan et al. (2016) have recently applied and developed many of these ideas within health care organizations. They work with the umbrella term 'knowledge mobilization' as a less linear and softer prism than the traditional pipeline model of EBM/EBMgt 'implementation'. The focus is here less on the evidence-based intervention and more on the wider social and organizational settings and wider systems receiving it and which may well reinterpret it. They argue there is a wider organizational ecology that should be considered as a whole, which shapes how knowledge is mobilized. We endorse these remarks.

Nevertheless, the health care organizations studied were not found to be devoid of management texts and associated knowledge bases. We indeed found alternative forms of non EBMgt-style management knowledge present, on occasion associated with high-impact and business-orientated texts (e.g. Kaplan and Norton 1996).

The health organizations studied appeared to be looking 'outwards' to a range of alternative knowledge producers for ideas in the realm of management knowledge. Specific and sectoral forms of health management knowledge were by contrast weakly apparent: for example, the old regionally based health management centres that used to produce applied health management research, often linked to their education provision for local NHS managers, had disappeared. Instead, there was a range of influences found, from management consultancies, think tanks (including non-sectoral ones), and business school faculty, including authors in major American schools. A series of texts around Lean (see Radnor et al. 2012), which had diffused out from an original base in Japanese manufacturing settings, was also found to have been influential at national level in providing techniques which might assist locally in the major QIPP change programme. The management knowledge economy of English health care should now be seen as an open rather than a closed one.

# The importance of the macro context of the political economy of public management reforming

How can such a shift be explained? Previous studies of major change processes in health care organizations (Pettigrew et al. 1992) suggested that such change was influenced by: (i) the content of the change issue; and (ii) the context, both the inner context (the organization) and the outer context (the wider system).

Our literature review chapter explored in more detail the importance of understanding the broad political economy of public management reforming in England, which we see as proceeding at a macro level and over an extended period of time. This force should be seen as a major component of the outer context. We then argued this macro-level prism adds to well-developed but more micro-level perspectives (such as the EBMgt movement and also practice-based literature) and the meso- or organizational-level focus of the RBV school in strategic management on the question of how to understand knowledge mobilization processes.

In particular, the rise of New Public Management (NPM) doctrines and associated public management reforms in the 1980s and 1990s in the UK should be seen as a significant and long-term development (Hood 1991) in the outer context, including in the health care sector (Ferlie et al. 1996). While some politically led attempts to move on to a post-NPM narrative of network governance were evident in the New Labour period (1997–2010) (Ferlie et al. 2013), many elements of NPM have in our view remained embedded in the underlying pattern of the organization of English public services.

NPM reforms typically have the effect of moving the organization of public services closer to that of the private firm which is held up as a positive role model. It therefore increases the receptivity of public policymakers and managers to general management-based ideas and knowledge and decreases the legitimacy of public administration-based knowledge. It is no accident that the UK displays a well-developed management consulting sector (Saint-Martin 2004) when compared internationally and one which has an active presence in public services reform (as we saw in one of our chapters). The UK hosts a major grouping of important business schools which were founded early and have been expanding since the 1960s—for example, Warwick Business School was set up as early as 1967—and are important deliverers of MBA programmes.

We have here updated our previous analyses of earlier English public management reform periods (Ferlie et al. 1996, 2013) to consider the legacy of the more recent 2010–15 period of the Conservative and Liberal Democrat Coalition. This period coincided with a prolonged policy of austerity in the UK public finances after the 2008 global financial crisis. So, the expectation of growth in public spending evident in the earlier New Labour period (especially between 2000 and 2008) went into reverse.

We argued that initially the Coalition government developed what can be seen as a 'proto' reform narrative around what was termed the Big Society which favoured third-sector providers over both state- and market-led solutions. Professionals were also seen in this account as more trustworthy than managers. These ideas were championed for a while by the then prime minister, David Cameron. Staff mutualization emerged as the signature policy idea within this narrative. Within the health care sector, the creation of GP-led clinical commissioning groups as membership-based organizations in an attempt to re-engage clinical professionals in management can be seen as compatible with this Big Society approach.

However, the Big Society proto-narrative failed in our view to institutionalize itself as it was trumped by wider austerity discourse, championed by the powerful Treasury. There was intense pressure on public expenditure levels throughout the 2010–15 Parliament. Although health care was partially protected when compared to (say) local government, the NHS's financial settlements remained tight throughout the period. Rather, the 2010–15 period of public management reform saw, in our view, in practice a tilt back to many NPM-style principles, including user choice, provider competition (as reflected in the 2012 Health and Social Care Act which was the Coalition government's key piece of legislation in the health policy area), productivity, and value for money. These productivity-led goals were operationalized in the ambitious QIPP change programme.

NPM reforms in public services have now been well studied (e.g. see Hood and Dixon's 2015 overview of the UK experience; also see Christensen and Laegreid's 2011 international handbook). However, we add an important extra strand to the stock of existing work on NPM: we here considered the nature of management knowledge production, diffusion, and consumption in a health care sector still heavily influenced by NPM thinking. We find a major shift from old public administration-style knowledge bases to more general management-orientated ones, with strong influence from management consultancies and some business school faculty. The intense activity of think tanks in the health policy domain also provides an arena of potential communication with the political world.

The regional level of analysis was also found to be an important element of the 'outer context' in the chapter on think tanks, as well as national-level forces. We suggested that there was a London-based 'ecosystem' of public policy and management knowledge production in operation, given that a significant cluster of think tanks were co-located close to centres of political power. We found influence from politically aligned think tanks as well as those that worked more specifically in the health sector. We then suggested some think tanks had third-sector characteristics of organization and governance which were compatible with a quadruple helix model (Carayannis and Campbell 2009) of knowledge production developing in the science policy literature which stresses the importance of an activated civil society in knowledge production, along with the more conventional triple helix model (Etzkowitz and Leydesdorff 2000) of interactions between government, business, and universities.

# The importance of micro-level agency and knowledge leadership

As our cases reveal, the role of key knowledge leaders plays a significant role in how management knowledge is engaged with and mobilized, both within and across settings. The very existence of these knowledge leaders (Fischer et al. 2016) themselves proved important in motivating others to access and use forms of management knowledge, particularly academic texts and articles.

We have argued that this work of knowledge leadership is far less a transactional task of dispassionately brokering (von Krogh et al. 2012) or translating (Lakshman 2005; Srivastava et al. 2006) 'evidence', but rather involves personal identification and meaningful engagement with certain management knowledges (Dopson et al. 2013; Fischer et al. 2016). These personal dimensions of knowledge leadership carry with them an animating dynamic in which selected management knowledges may be seen not just in terms of rational evidence, but as being brought into and 'enlivened' through locally important meanings, emotions, and politics (Fischer and McGivern 2016). As Emirbayer (1997) finds, such interconnectedness between material aspects of culture and interpersonal emotional flows is an important, yet significantly underexplored area of scholarship.

The development of meaningful, personal engagement in management knowledge can be understood in terms of individuals' formative experiences in which their early biographies and careers can bring them into long periods of contact with influential forms of knowledge. As we have previously described, some knowledge leaders recount childhood and other formative experiences in which family discussion drawing on management knowledge was an everyday aspect of their upbringing. For others, meaningful engagement with research texts and models was gained through immersion in in-depth study during master's and doctoral studies, particularly when associated with influential supervisors. Unsurprisingly, personally meaningful experiences such as these tend to support enduring interests, identifications, and emotional investments in certain management knowledges, potentially influencing how knowledge leaders craft their emerging identities, self-narratives, and roles (Fischer et al. 2016).

Identifications and personally meaningful engagements such as these matter because of what we see is the central role of knowledge leadership in mobilizing and enacting knowledge within and between organizations. Whereas knowledge leaders may adopt a variety of mobilizing tactics, their privileged access to knowledge affords the potential to stimulate, variously, bottom-up, top-down, and lateral flows of codified knowledges and texts into organizational practice. When enacting and mobilizing management knowledge in these ways, knowledge leaders combine and synthesize text-based knowledge with a wider array of narratives, techniques, templates, political strategies, and other resources—actively utilizing these to influence, (partially) disrupt, and reshape their settings.

Importantly, we find that such knowledge leadership work is a crucial intermediary in stimulating and dynamizing (Mazzucato 2013), what we describe as a 'textual economy' of management knowledge—across macro, meso, and micro organizational levels. As we have seen in the case of think tanks and other interorganizational networks, knowledge leaders may activate and mobilize knowledge not merely within local settings, but can powerfully stimulate interorganizational and systems-level flows, connecting and activating people and resources between civil society, universities, health care organizations, and government. In this way, the work of knowledge leadership underlines our earlier argument (see Chapter 7) that the crucial aspect of these interactions lies in the various ways in which they assemble and stimulate powerful 'ecosystems' between influential actors and resources (Edwards 2012).

## What should be the role of the business school as a knowledge producer?

We now deliberately move from considering the results of our empirically founded study to more normative form of argumentation. Leading business school faculties have emerged as major knowledge producers in the health care management arena (see Porter and Teisberg 2006) as in other sectors. For example, Kaplan and Norton's (1996) text was a major influence in one of our sites. However, there was little evidence in our empirical work that business schools and their faculty are active in supporting knowledge transposition work. Furthermore, we saw little activity in relation to dissemination of research or in utilizing business schools' potential convening power to assist reflection and knowledge exchange.

We noted that the knowledge leaders we studied were aware of business schools but struggled with how to access people and knowledge there. This was most starkly illustrated in the Elmhouse case: here partners were keen to engage with academics generally and the elite business schools in particular, but failed to do so. The explanation given to us for this situation was the very different timescales that academics work to as compared to consultants and the career incentive systems for faculty where publication in top journals is the main career driver. Consultants, on the other hand, have much more pragmatic aims for management knowledge, and junior consultants in particular found it very hard to find time to consider what they described as abstract, over-theoretical, and inaccessible knowledge produced by academics. The renewed emphasis on the importance of the impact of academic work and impact of case studies in shaping academic careers could help here if senior faculty in business schools adjust the performance management systems supporting their faculty accordingly.

Full-service business schools often have a vibrant executive education arm and provide a range of leadership development programmes for a huge range of organizations. They do often therefore have the capacity to provide spaces for reflection and engagement with knowledge. In our experience, it is rare that such activities focus on actual work-based problems of participants in real time, and when it happens it can lead to transformational change.

In Fischer and colleagues' (Fischer and White 2014, Fischer et al. 2015) ethnographic study of senior leadership development programmes at Oxford Saïd Business School, they found that some of the most effective interventions stimulated reflective, 'formative spaces' (Fischer 2012; McGivern and Fischer 2012) that fostered the development of participants' personal and emotional responses to management models and theories. According to their findings, business school programmes need to rebalance formal theories, tools, and heuristics with a stronger emphasis on interpersonal dimensions of leadership linked to personal insights and identities. Such personal responses provide vital areas of sensemaking which participants can meaningfully reflect on and develop over time.

Business schools and indeed other higher education settings might increase managers' access to and use of management knowledge if academics more purposefully thought about their convening power, using more creatively spaces for stimulating knowledge exchange and mobilization, such as case-study discussions, practical exercises, and research-based discussions in the service of stimulating critical enquiry and testing both knowledge and practice. It could be helpful, for example, to consider what might be the prospects of encouraging academic learning in organizational contexts where external research/empirical evidence and local case-based evidence are combined to address local puzzles. Such interventions could enable the connection of the two domains of knowledge we found, namely formal knowledge and experiential knowledge, with the aims of generating ideas and creativity. This is a very different model to that of business schools as a source of codified knowledge which is then translated uncritically into practice.

Postgraduate degrees offered by business schools and other higher education settings were found to be important opportunities for critical and reflexive learning, increasing interest in codified texts, other organizational settings and more critical approaches to leadership work. Increased engagement with codified knowledge at postgraduate level appeared to stimulate 'lateral' interest in formal/theoretical management knowledge. These findings suggest that there may be some disadvantages of uni-professional education and continuing professional development that do not adequately factor in both clinical and leadership training. Multiprofessional programmes are more likely to lead managers to venture from their core knowledge domains and epistemic communities to explore new knowledge domains as well as facilitating access to experiential knowledge from a variety of settings. We would encourage business schools to consider opportunities for convening Multiprofessional forums, not merely uni-professional learning forums, thus brokering different epistemic communities and knowledge paradigms.

In discussing the role of business schools as knowledge producers, we fully recognize that they are part of a fiercely competitive global market in which they must attract students and outstanding faculty, at the same time competing for limited space in academic journals and research monies. We also recognize the important role business schools play in producing knowledge products. However, in our view, there is a need to move away from seeing business schools as merely a physical setting producing knowledge and educating students/ participants to finding new ways of working that involve engagement, impact, and innovation. We would encourage business schools to offer filtered management knowledge products that are more accessible and orientated to puzzles relevant to organizational challenges as they present themselves in local contexts as well as future challenges. Alerting leaders to the importance of exploring the as yet unknown and helping them do so is again a potentially important contribution of a business school. Our work suggests that it is timely to rethink the purpose of a business school as well as the incentive structure for academics, enabling richer forms of engagement to take place.

## From Big Society to bullshit: the changing knowledge context since our empirical research

In 2016, shortly after we completed our empirical research, the Brexit vote in the UK, which appeared to reveal widespread public distrust of experts and expertise, and the election of President Trump in the USA, changed the discursive context in which knowledge and evidence are considered. The terms 'post-truth' (the *Oxford English Dictionary*'s 2016 'word of the year', defined as relating to or denoting circumstances in which objective facts are less influential in shaping opinion than appeals to emotion and personal belief), 'fake news', and 'bullshit' abound. Discussion of tribalism, identity politics, and social media 'echo chambers' have heightened awareness of 'confirmation bias', the tendency to interpret evidence as confirming one's existing beliefs, raising new questions about truth and evidence (Ball 2017; Davis 2017). While these issues had been discussed before (we noted, for example, that the Big Society had earlier been dubbed 'BS' (Scott 2011)), the important notion of 'post-truth' has implications for evidence-based health policy (Speed and Mannion 2017),[1] this book's findings, and management knowledge and evidence in organizations more generally.

---

[1]   See Prof Trish Greenhalgh's lecture on evidence and post-truth at the Global Evidence Summit, Cape Town, Sept 2017, available at: https://www.youtube.com/watch?time_continue=1611&v=6kAn_B4gdRY (accessed 10 December 2017).

Our empirical research highlighted the existence of competing truths and related forms of management knowledge and evidence in health care organizations, which reflected actors' personal frames and signalled their tribal, social, political, and epistemic affiliations. Knowledge and evidence were then mobilized (or not) according to their 'fit' with a blend of micro-level personal and pragmatic local contextual (Fischer et al. 2016), macro-level rational, political, social (Sturdy 2004; Ansari et al. 2010; Ferlie et al. 2016; Swan et al. 2016), and epistemic (McGivern et al. 2016) factors. Thus, actors mobilizing 'hard' management knowledge, promising to deliver financial savings and quick, measurable performance improvements, were successful in a political economy and politics of management knowledge dominated by austerity (Ferlie et al. 2016).

Thus, we have critiqued the concept of EBMgt for promoting a partial and misleading understanding of the 'truth' and 'hard facts' about management knowledge and evidence (Pfeffer and Sutton 2006c). Importantly, such formalized and rational analytic forms of expertise may be expected to have even less appeal and impact in such a post-truth world. Yet management knowledge and evidence does, in our view, need to be subjected to critical scrutiny and analysis, because the effective overmobilization of poorly considered or partisan management ideas can damage organizations, public services, and wider society.

Business schools have been critiqued for their detachment from organizational life (Starkey and Madan 2001; Bennis and O'Tool 2005) and corporate capture, having abandoned the 'higher aims' of professionals to become 'hired hands' serving business interests (Khurana 2007). Yet, particularly in the post-truth era, we see an ever more important role for business and management schools in serving the 'public interest' (Ferlie et al. 2010). Business and management schools need to conduct rigorous research open to peer review so as to challenge what some have called 'business bullshit' (Spicer 2018) and present evidence and knowledge in a convincingly open-minded, honest, and balanced way (Davis 2017). Yet business and management school academics also need to be reflective and transparent about their own political, institutional, and epistemic frames and interests. Indeed, we are aware, as business school-based academics ourselves, that we could be seen as a remote 'liberal elite', so reviled by populists, writing about management knowledge for our own purposes.

Moreover, a key lesson from the Brexit vote and the election of President Trump was that large parts of the population no longer trust the liberal elite. This was, in part, because the latter had overlooked and did not understand large parts of the less privileged population. Hence, these different social and political tribes need to engage, become less isolated, and better understand one another (Ball 2017; Davis 2017).

Likewise, business school academics can better engage with and understand practising managers and better communicate academic ideas to them, while retaining the critical, analytical, and theoretical rigour of the research and evidence underpinning their ideas. Addressing self-referential debates in closed academic circles will not by itself challenge post-truth. While most business schools are preoccupied with publishing articles in the highest-ranked academic journals, few outside academia read or can understand them. Business schools should, in our view, bring together and articulate the perspective of different tribes through dialogue. Therefore, engaging with (senior) managers, other professionals, policymakers, and the public, writing for practitioner journals, and teaching students are also necessary tasks to mobilize honest and balanced management knowledge, and evidence and challenge organizational post-truth in times of economic austerity and political populism.

# ▓ APPENDIX 1 OUR METHODS AND RESEARCH JOURNEY

The authors acknowledge funding from the UK National Institute of Health Research Health Services and Delivery Research programme (project 08/1808/242) for the work renalysed and reported in Chapters 6 to 10 (however the earlier chapters did not draw on this funded work). The views expressed are those of the authors and do not necessarily reflect those of the Health Services and Delivery Research programme, the National Institute for Health Research, NHS, or the Department of Health.

Our original research project (Dopson et al. 2013) used a range of qualitative methods. Its three-stage research design sought to explore the production of management research knowledge and how it was adopted in practice (or indeed not) in a set of English health care organizations. We deliberately recruited a variety of organizations to the study, which went well beyond a conventional focus on NHS hospitals, to reflect the greater organizational diversity apparent in the sector. We add that all the participating organizations were assessed by us and our steering committee members consulted as positive outliers in their openness to management knowledge rather than as typical of the wider population of English health care organizations. They were then selected as receptive sites and positive outliers.

In Phase 1 (Dopson et al. 2013), the unit of analysis was the individual manager. Phase 1 involved forty-five interviews with general and also clinician managers in our six local sites, who were identified as interested in using management research and knowledge. We here focused on exploring these individuals' perspectives on what motivated them to seek out new management knowledge, which search processes and sources were used, how such management knowledge was utilized in their work and, finally, what were the main influences of their 'knowledge career' on their management practice. We only draw on Phase 1 data in this book in Chapter 10.

The primary focus of Phase 2 was on the utilization of management knowledge in local health care organizations. It consisted of six in-depth and comparative case studies of management knowledge utilization processes, with the career of a concrete management knowledge 'tracer' being tracked over time in each site. Over 108 interviews with staff and key external stakeholders were carried out in this phase. The Phase 2 data are drawn on here and specifically inform the four case study-based chapters located towards the end of the book (Chapters 7 to 10).

Phase 3 was an experimental and evaluated intervention with Action Learning Sets with small groups of volunteer managers from the sites designed to facilitate greater personal reflection and uptake of evidence in personal practice. This material is being written up for submission for publication elsewhere and is not drawn on in this book.

Our six case-study sites, to which we have given pseudonyms, were as follows:

*Beechwell*: a national-level health policy unit (so it is a producer of health management knowledge) which aims to improve UK health care through policy analysis, applied research, and advice and support to the NHS field. It has several internal divisions working in distinct fields. We were interested to study health management knowledge flows between the different divisions.

*Elmhouse*: is a management consultancy with a major presence in the health care sector; therefore, it is also an important knowledge producer. Management consultancy knowledge has been widely drawn on by the NHS field (including in supporting QIPP implementation), so this is an important site.

*Firgrove*: is a recently accredited Academic Health Sciences Centre (ASHC) which brought together a medical school, NHS hospitals, and a research-intensive, multi-faculty university in a new confederation designed to shorten the 'from bench to bedside' knowledge translation cycle. It offered the opportunity to study the consumption of management knowledge in a developing and complex partnership-based organizational setting.

*Oakmore*: is a private charitable trust offering specialist services, some of which were funded by NHS commissioners, and which was undergoing a long transition from being a local traditional provider to being more 'business-like'. We saw this site as 'high impact' in terms of its consumption of generic management knowledge.

*Willowton*: was a primary care trust (PCT) operating in the primary health care field and commissioning heath care services for its local population. It had to cope with increasing resource constraints from 2009 onwards, following national expenditure decisions. Towards the end of the study, it turned into a new clinical commissioning group (CCG), following a national reorganization. This site provided an opportunity to study the absorption of different management knowledges during a period of significant organizational challenge and transition, including some tensions between alternative knowledge traditions.

## Further information on Phase 2

The basic design of Phase 2 was that of a comparative and processual study (i.e. the study of organizational processes over time), using organizational case-study methods. Specifically, the research focused on the production or consumption of management knowledge(s) in six contrasting organizations in the English health care sector, all assessed by ourselves and our steering committee members as promising sites in respect of their openness to various forms of management knowledge.

As our study objectives related to interpretive 'how' and 'why' questions more than measurement-based 'how much' questions, we drew on qualitative methods as a basic framing (Yin 1999, 2009). These methods enabled us to explore relevant organizational processes that unfolded over time and also the meaning that actors engaged in them attached to their actions. Longitudinal case-study designs are often seen as stronger than cross-sectional ones.

Qualitative designs may contain an element of both induction and deduction so that findings and concepts can emerge in the course of the study as well being identified and tested from the start, which would be normal in more quantitative and hypothesis-based studies. Some qualitative designs are purely inductive—as in the case of grounded theory (Glaser and Strauss 1967)—but others mix inductive and deductive elements, as in the case of the study. Indeed, the research team's decision to frame the study around the political economy of management knowledge came late in the process and led to further literature review work and web-based research to supplement material on the national and public policy level.

Multiple case-study designs help increase the level of external generalizability which can be achieved beyond that of a single case (Yin 1999, 2009), especially with purposeful selection of cases (Stake 2000), as was the case here. If the number of cases remains restricted, they still retain internal validity. They further provide the opportunity for structured comparisons between the cases (Stake 2000) so as to generate higher level propositions.

So Phase 2 consisted of six cases exploring the production and consumption of management knowledge in various English health care organizations. In each site, early interviews in Phase 1 had also identified a 'tracer issue' where there had been sustained and collective activity within the organization around a management text for more intensive and retrospective exploration in Phase 2.

In Phase 2, we sought to triangulate various data sources (Stake 2000). We included first of all some basic factual data on each case, including archival and other contextual data. Our analytic approach to handling 'context' revolves round the idea developed within organizational process analysis that there are both inner and outer organizational contexts (Pettigrew 1987; Pettigrew et al. 1992) to be considered. We see each case-study organization as being influenced by its outer context, such as its positioning in the wider health care sector and even broader economic and social systems. It is also influenced by inner context which includes its history, its competitive position and strategy (in the case of a for-profit organization in a market), and its relative importance on the policy agenda (in the public sector).

We then undertook semi-structured interviews (108 in Phase 2) with a range of stakeholders in each organization who had been identified as being able to comment on the tracer. The schedule was designed both to generate a narrative of the organization and also explore the history of the tracer issue selected in depth. Typically interviews lasted between forty and ninety minutes and were recorded and transcribed.

We thirdly undertook some observation of relevant key meetings and knowledge dissemination events. While observation took place across all sites, the most extensive observation took place in Willowton, given the need to keep up with rapid organizational change there. Our plan was to conduct the six cases concurrently, however, issues surrounding getting ethical approval in the more network-based Mapleshire meant that this case was started six months later.

The research within the case studies was then organized in three phases. We first worked in pairs negotiating access and undertaking 'scoping' interview work, sometimes interviewing jointly and sharing early reflections. The later writing of the initial case report, however, was led by the lead researcher in the pair. Third, all team members then read all the initial cases, discussed them in a group, and contributed to cross-case and more thematic analysis.

## Analysis of Phase 2 data

The case-study analysis started with a review of the early documentary material. The descriptive documents on the purpose, size, scope, history, and (where available) performance of the organization were initially analysed by the case leads. Six basic case-study documents (organized to the same template) were later produced following analysis from and discussions between the two team members assigned to each site.

Each of these case documents was then the subject of debate and discussion with the full research team at one of our regular and long face-to-face project meetings held towards the end of the project, to encourage comparison and the inducing of more analytic findings. We were sensitive in these discussions to the existing quality assessment frameworks available to comparative case-study researchers (Blaxter 1996; Mays and Pope 2000; Mays et al. 2001).

Cross-case analysis commenced by examining the data through the light of our original research questions. We then compared our conclusions across the six sites and moved on to examine core themes which had emerged inductively and in group meetings and discussions, and compared them across sites. At this point, we listed a small set of core themes which had emerged. We then returned to the early literature review to explore whether candidate theories discussed there enabled us to conceptualize the empirical data further. Finally, we considered how our data might extend, develop, or refute existing research.

In each site, we circulated a draft case study to key respondents for verification and comment. An executive summary and feedback event was also offered to each site. Our study steering committee proved very helpful in debating our emergent findings. A final end-of-project conference involving representatives of all the sites was successfully held at Saïd Business School, Oxford.

We faced some issues and challenges during the project. The first issue related to securing NHS ethical approval from a large number of different NHS organizations. Our project—which solely involved management research with staff—did not fit neatly into a risk-averse approval system more designed to protect NHS patients enrolled in clinical trials. As well as having to adapt the protocol to the demands of the NHS approval system, we also spent considerable time in determining the correct answers to questions of sponsorship of the project, insurance, and site-specific R&D issues. A new system of NHS 'proportionate review' has since been brought in nationally to damp down such demands and it would be interesting to track whether a similar project starting now would face a less intense process in terms of ethical approval.

A second challenge was undertaking the research during a period of intense organizational turbulence in the NHS, where many managers were pragmatically more concerned about keeping their jobs than engaging with research. Willowton, for example, was abolished in the course of the study, along with all PCTs nationally.

## The post-report research journey

We have more recently built on the text of the original report by moving in a more analytical direction and positioning the writing more in the context of wider academic debates. Specifically, we have expanded one chapter and written three new chapters in the middle of the book, reflecting our later decision to use the political economy prism to organize the book as a whole.

This further work was undertaken because we wanted to contribute more effectively to general academic debates and literature as well as to empirical literature within the

UK health sector. After group discussions undertaken after the end of the initial project to 'make sense' of our findings theoretically at a broader level, we decided to adopt the anchoring idea that we should characterize the cases within the macro-level political economy of management knowledge production and consumption. These ideas about the operation of the macro-level political economy and how it impacts on management knowledge in UK public/health services were initially worked through in an academic article (Ferlie et al. 2016) and are developed further here.

This relatively late theoretical clarification led to additional work in particular chapters beyond the text of the original report. We have developed the literature review (Chapter 2) on social science approaches to management knowledge to expand beyond the original focus on the evidence-based management movement and practice-based approaches to management knowledge. We have added in a greater focus on academic literature on macro-level diffusion processes including international and inter-sectoral flows of management texts and ideas, within a broadly institutionalist framing theoretically.

A new Chapter 3 explores alternative long-run narratives of public management reforming evident in English public services since the 1980s, picking out what we see as their strong implications for the health care sector. A new Chapter 4 updates the story of English public and health management reform to the 2010–15 period, arguing that an early Big Society proto-narrative of reform gave way to a dominant austerity discourse. The chapter introduces the history of the major NHS and national-level change programme known as QIPP which started in 2009 and has continued since. QIPP is designed to improve NHS productivity substantially but without negatively affecting service quality. QIPP is picked up in more detail in a couple of the later chapters as it exerted important effects at local level.

We also added a new chapter on the history of national-level NHS service improvement agencies (Chapter 6) to complement our initial focus on health care organizations at the local level. We downloaded and read much of the copious amount of material now available on these agencies' websites which related to their preferred approaches to organizational change, trying to trace which management models and authors were revealed as important in these texts. Such readily available web-based written material seems at present under-utilized as a research resource. We did not undertake any further interviews for this chapter.

One important theme from the Phase 2 case studies was the agency exercised by a small but important group of 'knowledge leaders'. An initial consideration of how these knowledge leaders constructed their roles was published in Fischer et al. (2015) and is further developed here in Chapter 10. This more micro-level focus on agency complements the macro-level framing of the political economy largely adopted elsewhere in the book.

# ■ **APPENDIX 2** CASE-STUDY SUMMARIES

## The Beechwell case study

Beechwell was a policy think tank with a long history of influencing English health care organizations to deliver change. Its directorate structure included a policy directorate producing knowledge through policy analysis and research and a leadership development directorate seeking to influence health care leaders through leadership and organizational development. Although orientated to different audiences in the field, a theme that unified its directorates was an underlying commitment to improving health care. Members of the organization described strong emotional investment and a sense of belonging.

Beechwell's knowledge identity centred on taking a future-orientated, horizon-scanning approach to produce knowledge that was practically useful to the wider health care system. Changes to the policy environment were significant stimulants for producing new knowledge.

### KNOWLEDGE MANAGEMENT SYSTEM

Beechwell's approach was to handle and translate existing knowledge, as well as actively producing new knowledge. Originality and creativity were valued as a means of tackling 'real world' problems. There was a strong value orientation towards pragmatism as a means of achieving change in the health care system, and finding innovative means of doing so.

Beechwell had a significant shared library facility, including extensive access to electronic journals, which was well used by directorates across the organization. However, its directorates had quite different knowledge orientations and although there was a collaboration programme to increase knowledge exchange between directorates which served as a repository for written (codified) knowledge outputs, this common knowledge management system was not a significant source of accessing and using knowledge in this case. This may have reflected directorates' contrasting knowledge activities and use. Policy tended to be rational-analytic and data driven, and used established methodologies to engage both expert opinion and practitioner experience. Leadership development was more experiential and experimental—focusing on 'aligning hearts and minds'.

### KNOWLEDGE ACTORS

Key knowledge actors at Beechwell included prominent experts who played a visible role in influencing health care policy through frequent media outputs and public events. The chief executive and directors had significant externally facing knowledge roles.

The executive tended to exercise strong hierarchical authority in stimulating knowledge activity and shaping knowledge projects (for instance, in response to developing policy contexts). Knowledge leadership tended to be diffuse, and was contested at directorate levels between different directorates.

With a flattened hierarchy offering little opportunity for promotion, individuals tended to have short stays of around two years and then leave. Being successful in the organization meant making a distinctive and often publicly visible contribution.

## HIGHLIGHTS OF FINDINGS FROM THE CASE

Beechwell was a knowledge-producing organization. Its directorates produced pragmatically useful knowledge for both health policy and practice audiences. While sharing a value rationality of advancing high-quality health services, the directorates appeared markedly separate, with different ways of seeking to influence their wider audiences and quite distinct cultural legacies and associated forms of management knowledge.

While the executive centre exercised hierarchical authority, and executive decision-making was important in steering and legitimating knowledge activity, it was not a strong source of management knowledge. Respondents expressed a sense of hierarchical distance, with direct contact being quite formalized, taking the form of presentations, with little opportunity for interaction and knowledge sharing.

Within the directorates, local knowledge leadership appeared influential, shaping respondents' knowledge work. For instance, as a means of increasing collaboration between directorates, the organization developed a number of cross-directorate themes, intended to increase potential innovation and translation across knowledge boundaries. A senior academic in the policy directorate had produced original, research-based knowledge on health care economics that had made a significant impact on the wider policy environment. Identified as strategically important by the executive and adopted by the organization as a cross-directorate strategic theme, this was the management knowledge tracer study for this case.

The theme was initially viewed by staff as a promising means of focusing joint effort around a strategic priority, potentially translatable into distinct knowledge products across each of Beechwell's directorates. However, despite initially resonating with participants across directorates, a sense of insufficient knowledge leadership meant it failed to attract 'natural synergy' and cross-directorate support. Consequently, the intended translation of this knowledge theme failed to materialize, and it was subsequently seen as having failed its purpose.

Despite its failure to translate, however, the theme did elucidate an interesting feature of this case, which was its function as an important textual—or perhaps rhetorical—device, serving to reinforce participants' sense of purpose and overarching organizational identity.

## The Elmhouse case study

Elmhouse Consulting was a management consultancy, advising clients worldwide about strategy, leadership, and change in the private and public sectors. This case focused on Elmhouse's UK health care practice.

Elmhouse's strong culture was reinforced by the careful recruitment and retention of the highest calibre consultants. Demanding and competitive, it operated an 'up or out' policy. New consultants came from elite universities and commonly stayed for two years, getting training and formative work experience before moving on to high-flying careers elsewhere. Senior 'superstar' consultants were recruited externally. Many had formative training and work experience at Elmhouse and returned after several years in senior roles in other organizations. Although highly diverse in terms of ethnicity, nationality, religion, and gender, recruitment and retention ensured consultants were of universally high standard, making it possible to 'plug and play' consultants from anywhere in the world into any project.

Consultants received comprehensive feedback after every assignment, informing compensation and promotion decisions. Promotion was also dependent upon developing a good reputation, social capital, and networks within Elmhouse and among its clients. Performance management criteria included being 'nice' and 'a person who says "yes"', sharing knowledge, and helping others. Elmhouse was a 'team-driven' culture and respondents said they liked their work and colleagues, despite the pressures they were under.

Training and development was also excellent, including challenging and developmental opportunities and work assignments, and working alongside 'inspirational' colleagues and mentors. Senior Elmhouse consultants also had an impact on the company's culture as role models and mentors.

## KNOWLEDGE MANAGEMENT SYSTEM

Elmhouse derived income from selling knowledge; knowledge generation, management, and application were of crucial importance. It invested heavily in managing knowledge to support its consultants. This included employing generalist, industry- and function-specific experts, researchers, and information specialists, and publishing bulletins. There was a global knowledge management system containing PowerPoint presentations about previous Elmhouse projects. This information was tagged and rated so the content perceived to be most valuable was prioritized. Consultants were keen to contribute to the knowledge management system because they developed their reputations (and hence promotion prospects) from their work being known and used.

When seeking knowledge and information, consultants turned first to this knowledge management system, before approaching immediate colleagues and Elmhouse consultants worldwide. If they were unable to get the knowledge they needed from either of these sources, they could finally ask 'information specialists' to look for it.

Some partners had links with elite management academics, who alerted them to new and interesting ideas, but only one respondent reported reading any academic management journals other than Elmhouse's in-house publications or the *Harvard Business Review*. Instead, consultants commonly drew upon Elmhouse's own client work-based case studies (in the knowledge management system). A partner noted that, although Elmhouse's own knowledge generation could be very good, the system was inward-looking and tended to diminish intellectual curiosity.

## KNOWLEDGE ACTORS

Key actors in this case study were the Elmhouse senior consultant who authored the monograph *The Elmhouse Model*; senior strategic health authority (SHA) managers who played an important role in commissioning Elmhouse to conduct the Quality, Improvement, Productivity, and Prevention (QIPP) project; and PCT managers and PCT-based clinicians who played a counter role by raising doubts about the Elmhouse analysis and its 'fit with reality' and perverse effects on patients in NHS practice.

## HIGHLIGHTS OF FINDINGS FROM THE CASE

Consultants were aware that too much reliance on Elmhouse's own internally produced evidence risked hermetically sealed learning, 'superficial innovation', and missing new ideas from academia. Recognizing this problem, one partner had established an 'academic board' to challenge Elmhouse's ideas and thinking. This partner commented that the outcome of such collaboration could be 'magic', but was also aware of the need to balance academic collaborators' desire to 'experiment' with new theoretical ideas with the impact on clients and the need to keep them happy.

The 'Elmhouse Model' was applied in a PCT as part of a QIPP project during 2009–10, commissioned and funded by its SHA, and this project was our tracer study. The SHA commissioned Elmhouse to rapidly identify and begin making productivity gains in its regional PCTs in line with QIPP. Senior SHA managers knew and respected Elmhouse consultants, who were viewed as 'expensive' but affordable in the circumstances.

Elmhouse's approach was to help PCTs organize services better through 'the systematic application of what's already known to be best practice'. They first analysed the PCTs' performance to establish potential quality and productivity gains from a redesign of services to meet national QIPP targets. They then set about helping the SHA with action planning, running pilot redesign projects, and developing 'golden rules' and 'prescriptions' for redesigning and delivering health care.

Elmhouse ran three structured learning events, facilitated by Elmhouse consultants, to persuade senior PCT managers of the benefits of QIPP and equip them with skills to take it forward. Using Elmhouse's PowerPoint-based template, based upon their 'prescriptions' and 'golden rules', PCTs were to demonstrate how they would make productivity gains, and discuss the plans at local (clinical) stakeholder workshops, and report back at the next event.

Views in the PCT about Elmhouse's approach were mixed. While PCT managers were impressed by individual consultants, they were more critical of Elmhouse's structured PowerPoint-based approach and how it translated into their context.

As the Elmhouse contract finished (in our site), the NHS white paper was published which proposed the abolition of SHAs and PCTs, stalling the QIPP project's progress. Some PCT managers described feeling relieved that Elmhouse had left and the pressure to implement QIPP was gone. However, other PCT managers believed that after an intense period, there was still a lot of work to do.

# The Firgrove case study

The subject of this case study, Firgrove, was an alliance of two organizations offering specialist services, operating within an academic health science centre (AHSC). AHSCs are intended to facilitate collaboration across basic and clinical sciences, along with health care practice and education, giving opportunities for rapid translation of innovation and learning into health care. Clinical-academic collaborative groups (CAGs) are intended to be the central means of innovation, by integrating health care sciences, education, and practice.

The AHSC studied was a recently formed partnership between leading NHS foundation trusts and a university which all had long traditions and international reputations for excellence in the field of health care sciences. Research-based knowledge was predominantly from health sciences, but both social-science and management knowledge appeared important—particularly in the two organizations comprising Firgrove, which both had worldwide reputations as centres of excellence in their field, and had made rapid progress within the AHSC in aligning and reorganizing their structures and services to create CAGs. Firgrove had a long history of collaboration and a strong ethos of locally designed, participatory, and negotiated services, and had developed a team-based model of CAG leadership, directed by three or four senior academics, clinicians, and managers. This was unlike more hierarchical structures adopted in the wider AHSC.

Firgrove's ethos of collaboration was strongly shaped by the chief executive and dean, and supported by the wider leadership team. Its unusually stable board (key members had held positions for a decade) featured strong relational engagement, identification with and pride in its leaders who were perceived as 'punching above their weight' in their field.

## KNOWLEDGE MANAGEMENT SYSTEM

Firgrove's openness to ideas and innovation and aspirations for development meant that creative ideas and practice were encouraged. An OD internal consultancy unit (ODIC) was one example of a local initiative which was playing an increasingly prominent role.

While a rational-analytic focus on research evidence and 'hard data' was respected as significant and important in building international prestige, respondents were also orientated to 'soft', more qualitative data involving narratives and stories, political dimensions, and more reflective approaches to management knowledge and practice. Senior managers advocated a knowledge framework of an 'extended epistemology'. Here 'very, very different ways of knowing' were used to combine 'sanitized data' which may *lose meaning* with a 'local feel' of experience and relationships that *take on meaning*. Management theories and models, case studies, uses of narrative, and organizational development frameworks were also important in providing theoretical frameworks to support management reflexivity.

Developing an integrated knowledge management system across the AHSC was a significant challenge to the new partnership, and connectivity between the different Firgrove systems was partial. Nevertheless, there was an innovative development of the electronic clinical record system as a new research tool to search and interrogate the complete dataset of qualitative clinical records. This had strong application as an expert system for identifying qualitative texts to improve clinical care and research, organizational performance, governance, and learning.

## KNOWLEDGE ACTORS

Key knowledge actors at Firgrove were the elite scholars, clinicians, and managers who were members of the senior leadership team. In particular, the chief executive and the dean were experts in academic health science collaboration, with international reputations as knowledge leaders in the field. Together with their wider team, they were seen as embodying the tripartite AHSC mission of integrating academic research, the organization and delivery of health care, and education.

The Firgrove CAG leadership structure differed from that of the wider AHSC in producing a team-based leadership model, designed to integrate management knowledge alongside clinical and academic knowledges.

An unusual knowledge actor in this case was a director in the research-based ODIC. The unit supported leadership team development across the partnership— including at board level, where the director was regarded as playing a key role in translating management knowledge into practice, particularly in developing a coaching culture.

## HIGHLIGHTS OF FINDINGS FROM THE CASE

Firgrove was a knowledge-producing partnership with a strong history of knowledge creation and translation between the academic institute and the specialist clinical service. As internationally acclaimed centres of excellence they attracted both academics and academically orientated practitioners, engaged in linking knowledge production with testing and translation in the clinical unit. Collaboration across academic and service boundaries brought together diverse knowledges—biomedical laboratory research and clinical sciences in the academic institute, with multiple and plural knowledges in the clinical service, including social sciences, social psychology, and management knowledge.

The formation of the AHSC placed even more emphasis on multidisciplinary, team-based collaboration and a distinctive feature of the new clinical-academic teams was a strongly pluralist epistemology, bringing together 'really different belief systems'. This orientation towards collaboration and knowledge pluralism was also widely reflected across the partnership, with team-based leadership at both senior management and practitioner levels bringing together academic, clinical, and managerial leaders. Management knowledge appeared an important and valued source of knowledge in supporting this organizational approach, and the work of the internal ODIC unit had gained increasing prominence. Its method of 'facilitating conversations'—drawing upon Schein's (1969, 193) process consultation—had been significantly adopted in building collaboration and trouble-shooting problems—at senior management as well as service levels.

Our tracer study was the development of a strategic initiative to build a coaching culture advanced by the ODIC unit. This was adopted at board level, and used to develop 'coaching conversations' in the senior management team. The ODIC unit's methods were widely accepted, and seen as pragmatically important in building collaboration. However, the codified (text-based) knowledge it sought to promote was only partially adopted, with participants regarding it as an example of a management fad.

## The Oakmore case study

Oakmore Healthcare was a long established and independently run specialist medical charity. Its headquarters and largest number of beds occupy the original site, a large estate in a Midlands city. The rest of its beds were spread between several other sites elsewhere in the UK. Over the years many prominent local families had been involved with the charity; some were still acting as governors, trustees, and board members.

The charity was run by a board of executive and non-executive directors. The CEO, a clinician, had joined the organization ten years previously and since then Oakmore had followed a policy of expansion. The specialist services offered by Oakmore were not readily available elsewhere and most of its referrals came from NHS commissioners. Demand for its services had ensured Oakmore was in a good financial position, its charitable status allowing profits to be ploughed back into improvement and expansion of its facilities. However, at the time of the study, the recession had adversely affected referral numbers and the organization was reviewing its strategy and considering new ways of responding to current demand.

### KNOWLEDGE MANAGEMENT SYSTEM

Knowledge management systems around clinical practice had been in place at Oakmore for many years. Its doctors had statutory professional requirements to refresh and update their clinical knowledge and hospitals also had statutory-obligations to ensure staff were adequately trained in various practical and clinical areas. Oakmore also had a strong cultural tradition of encouraging the acquisition and use of knowledge. Originally this was primarily medical knowledge as, when founded, the organization was in the vanguard of innovation in its field. It had also established an academic research centre in partnership with another acknowledged centre of excellence, offering clinical placements to staff from other institutions.

A more recent focus on systems for acquiring and using management knowledge dated from the arrival of the CEO, who, as well as pursuing a career in medicine, had always been fascinated by management and brought a new, business–orientated focus to the organization. The process of turning a 'slightly old-fashioned trading charity' into a dynamic and expanding organization had required the recruitment of an experienced top management team with a strong knowledge base. As well as considerable management experience in public and/or private organizations, all but one of the non-clinical senior managers interviewed had completed various formal management courses before coming to Oakmore. Since the advent of a more business-orientated approach, Oakmore's list of clinical publications dating from the early 1970s had been augmented by an increasing number of papers relating to management.

Part of the new focus on management knowledge was the development of performance management systems, notably Kaplan and Norton's 'balanced scorecard', introduced as a relatively objective measure of service quality. This was our management knowledge tracer. Translated into a matrix format, key performance indicators (KPIs) for each ward and department were available online to all management staff. Some data were also available directly to customers, mostly NHS commissioners, to help them understand the rationale behind the care packages they were purchasing.

The other key knowledge management system at Oakmore was an extensive and carefully crafted management training programme. It was important in promoting cultural change, as staff who chose to participate were also signalling their acceptance of the new management ethos. This, together with using the performance management systems and accepting promotion to managerial positions within the organization, contributed to influencing other staff to adopt the same value system.

## KNOWLEDGE ACTORS

The CEO's strategy was to change the culture of the organization through the top-down introduction and application of management knowledge. This was achieved by employing people with a management background at senior level; by coopting non-executive directors with a track record in the commercial sector to provide a counter-balance to the more traditional views of some other board members about how a charity should behave; and through an extensive training programme for all staff.

At senior management level, the acquisition and utilization of management knowledge is celebrated and seen as hugely important for running the organization effectively. For most clinical/managerial respondents, whether doctors or nurses, the idea of acquiring management knowledge and skills was something that they had come to after establishing a clinical career. Management was often seen as an inevitable part of moving into more senior positions. There was nonetheless a degree of enthusiasm among clinician respondents in this study for their new managerial roles, though some did talk of tensions experienced in reconciling the needs of their patients with the managerial needs of the organization.

## HIGHLIGHTS OF CASE FINDINGS

Over ten years Oakmore, while maintaining its reputation as a leader in its clinical specialist field, had undergone a remarkable transformation into a modern and expanding health care organization run on the lines of a profitable business (though with profits reinvested in patient care).

Crucial to this transformation was the leadership of the CEO, who may be seen as the archetype of a successful clinical/managerial hybrid, though preferring now to identify with management, rather than clinical colleagues. Oakmore's CEO was an avid scholar, reading and writing journal articles, seeking out the latest management texts, and putting together a like-minded team of senior managers. Thus, the impetus for change has been driven from the top and linked closely to acquired management knowledge.

This new managerial approach, while originally received with some suspicion by some long-serving staff members, seemed to have become largely accepted and acceptable throughout the organization. It appeared that much of the credit for this could be attributed to the effective way in which the extensive and accessible training programme was able to tailor its courses to the needs and values of staff and the perceived utility of the KPIs generated by the use of the balanced scorecard methodology.

# The Mapleshire case study

Mapleshire CLAHRC was situated within a university research department, partnered by NHS trusts drawn from three counties, an NHS SHA and a local authority, and financed by matched funding from its partners and the National Institute for Health Research (NIHR).

The CLAHRC was made up of academic research staff and a small number of managers and administrators. Its first director was a senior social scientist with a track record in health services research. Four of the six work programmes involved clinical research. The other two comprised the implementation programme, tasked with translating research findings into practice, and IFCaSS (a pseudonym), which was our tracer study. IFCaSS had three distinct areas of work: encouraging *involvement* of others with the CLAHRC; promoting *fusion* by sharing data and analytical perspectives and extracting common themes from the research projects; and fostering the *communication, sharing,* and *spread* of information.

A number of influential people from the partner organizations were seconded to the CLAHRC for one day a week as CLAHRC Collaborators (a pseudonym). They were to be advocates for the CLAHRC and facilitate dissemination of research knowledge within their organizations. In addition, some hundreds of interested people, CLAHRC Supporters (a pseudonym), were signed up to receive regular online updates and access to workshops with other stakeholders.

Progress was slow initially. Many different funding bodies made contractual issues complicated. Lack of promotion and publication opportunities led to high turnover of academic staff. Collaborators' roles lacked clarity and some had problems with meeting time commitments. Interacting effectively with the large and diffuse Supporters group also proved difficult. Clinical research projects were slow getting under way. Three years into the project, the original director left and a new director with a background in the NHS and management, rather than academia, was appointed.

## KNOWLEDGE MANAGEMENT SYSTEM

Mapleshire CLAHRC was created as a knowledge management system, using theoretical insights from social sciences and health services research to promote the translation of research findings into practice through the development of new social networks and Community of Practices (COPs).

The Collaborators were crucial to the strategy. Coming from different (often clinical) backgrounds, they were envisaged as boundary spanners, linking the worlds of research and practice. Their status and expertise were expected to enable them to act as 'knowledge brokers', ensuring that findings would have practical value and relevance to local needs. The Supporters were to develop social networks by enhancing and enlarging existing COPs and extending their sphere of influence. They would form a virtual community with privileged access to knowledge through web- and print-based publications and opportunities to meet through workshops and conferences.

Inputs to the Mapleshire knowledge management system were to come from Collaborators; from feedback from those affected by research projects; and from commissioners and researchers through links with members of the CLAHRC team. The backgrounds and experience of the team also provided knowledge to feed into and refresh the system by passing on acquired expertise from previous employment and through utilizing management theory in their work. However, with a dearth of emergent findings from clinical research projects, outputs focused mainly on raising the profile of the CLAHRC through various media. These included a website, circulated newsletters, and tweets; academic papers discussing the principles on which the CLAHRC was based; workshops to facilitate development of wider COPs; and a large conference bringing together academics, researchers, and practitioners.

## KNOWLEDGE ACTORS

Key knowledge actors at Mapleshire's inception were the original director (a social scientist) and the director of the university research centre within which it was based. Their long track record covered aspects of sociology, social policy, academic health services, and management research.

## HIGHLIGHTS OF FINDINGS FROM THE CASE

The role of the IFCaSS programme, our tracer in this case, was 'to ensure that relevant stakeholders are involved in our work, connections are made across each of the research themes, and outputs are produced that meet the needs of health service users and carers, providers, commissioners, and the third sector'.

IFCaSS was comprised mainly of academics, involved in different aspects of its work. Health economists looked at finance in relation to the clinical research programmes, social science researchers were to facilitate the development of COPs and to write up cross-project findings, and some part-time fellows were tasked with raising the profile of the CLAHRC with key stakeholder groups. IFCaSS was also responsible for the ongoing support of the Collaborators, and recruiting and informing the large group of Supporters through IT and other communications media.

The original manager of both IFCaSS and the implementation programme, arguably the two most complex of the six CLAHRC programmes, came from an academic background, had no management experience, and struggled to cope. Later the programmes were separated and a new professional manager, solely for IFCaSS, seemed to be providing leadership.

The IFCaSS programme was successful in meeting the objectives of *communication, sharing,* and *spread* of information, with large numbers of Supporters registering interest. Facilitating *involvement* was more difficult. Workshops encouraged face-to-face contacts to develop, but participation was limited. Research outputs were slow in emerging and clinical researchers were reluctant to share early data, so *fusion,* achieving a synthesis of outputs from the various projects, also proved problematic.

Some of the problems with involvement and fusion were likely to decrease with time. The new leadership was building a more cohesive team and staff were becoming more skilled.

Overall, progress towards the original objectives of Mapleshire CLAHRC was slow. Cultural differences between members of the clinical work programmes who came from different academic backgrounds had been underestimated, and there was also a gap between theoretical and practical approaches to management. In addition, many staff appointed to managerial positions were primarily academics without specific management training. It may be that a different cultural climate and management style following the advent of the new director may impact on the way in which the original vision, based on academic theories of COPs and social networks, will play out in practice.

## The Willowton case study

Willowton Primary Care Trust (PCT) was a commissioning organization responsible for managing a large health care budget and purchasing a variety of health services for a diverse urban population. It had to meet national performance targets and standards, safeguard public funds, and manage contracts with external health providers. It aimed to improve the quality of the health care delivered to the local population as well as population health through gathering local information to underpin commissioning decisions. It worked closely with the local authority to plan service provision, especially those crossing health/social care boundaries, and was committed to partnership working with community agencies.

Willowton PCT underwent major upheaval and turbulence following the restructuring of health care commissioning and primary care management in England in 2011. During the time of our study it was working to support the development and progress of a local, GP-led clinical commissioning consortium which would take over in 2013. Arising at a time of fiscal restraint with deficits in the local health economy, this wide-scale restructuring resulted in staff redundancies and redeployment and an organizational merger with neighbouring PCTs.

Prior to these structural changes, Willowton PCT had supported staff in undertaking further academic qualifications, and proactively appropriated a number of ideas aimed at quality improvement and innovation. Senior leadership had also enabled the creation of a unit to promote research activity and engaged with external organizations, such as universities. A development and research network was also established across several GP practices. Within this network the emphasis was on work-based learning and action research that engaged with 'real world' problems, both clinical and organizational. Academic alliances that could assist with the evaluation of innovative projects and initiatives were seen to benefit the PCT by providing a counterbalance to its performance management and audit culture, its preoccupation with data capture, reporting, and outcome measures being viewed by some as a constraint on creativity and risk taking.

### KNOWLEDGE MANAGEMENT SYSTEM

The PCT was informally involved in a constant process of policy filtering, knowledge interpretation, and local translation, acting as a mediator between governmental-regional authority, the local population, and professional groupings; however, 'hard knowledge' had become increasingly important and 'business skills' highly valued in the 'new climate' of health care, and clinical leaders found the legal, organizational, and financial knowledge required was unfamiliar terrain compared to a validated biomedical knowledge base.

There was no singular knowledge management system or systematized approach to knowledge sharing at the PCT. One barrier was the different IT systems and software used by the organizations with which the PCT interacted. The use of multiple spreadsheets instead of computerized databases meant that data gathering and cross-organizational knowledge exchange could be cumbersome and problematic. An off-site library was reportedly little used and, on an individual basis, knowledge search strategies tended to occur on a project-specific, need-to-know basis.

## KNOWLEDGE ACTORS

The CEO and directors comprising the original senior leadership team at Willowton PCT had cultivated relationships with external, specialist organizations to facilitate knowledge acquisition and personal learning and supported the principle of organizational learning and 'grassroots' approaches to service improvement. Attempts had also been made to cascade new knowledge and evidence using internal seminars.

The leader of the research unit, a clinical director with an academic background, was perceived as a source of theoretical management/organizational knowledge. Responsible for forging partnerships with several universities and applying for external research grants, this clinical director acted as a knowledge broker between academic-research and practitioner communities. In addition, through stakeholder learning events and a personal professional network, the clinical director facilitated dialogue and perspective exchange between different occupational groupings to bring about change in the local primary care community.

Personal credibility, plus access to some independent funding as well as some further financial assistance and oversight from the PCT executive, had enabled the clinical director to go beyond the 'stick approach' associated with the PCT's performance management function and adopt a 'softer' approach to leadership. The clinical director's ability to challenge and enthuse other professionals was seen as a praiseworthy, non-hierarchical form of leadership which had resulted in an expanding network or community of practice.

## HIGHLIGHTS OF FINDINGS FROM THE CASE

The management knowledge tracer was an 'initiative for integrated care' (IIC), premised upon a 'whole systems' and 'action research' approach, a methodology outlined theoretically in several publications authored by the clinical director of the ARU.

The initiative attempted to establish 'connected learning spaces inside a local health community'. These were multidisciplinary opportunities for learning, critical reflection, and dialogue designed to become mechanisms for generating solutions to tangible problems, to be applied or trialled in other parts of the health care system. The underlying philosophy was that constantly evolving health care systems necessitate an adaptable and dynamic approach to change. 'Whole systems engagement' and learning was seen as a developmental process facilitating connections between individuals to bring about small, incremental improvements to practice. The 'bottom-up' model was designed to ensure that the participants and contributors identified and set the priorities for action.

As financial management imperatives came to the fore, however, the initiative became increasingly marginalized, and different approaches to organizational change conflicted. Consequently, the project was 'summarily executed' for six months; a planned summer workshop was cancelled and email communications to stakeholders ended.

It seemed that the 'whole systems' approach was a philosophy and methodology requiring a strong leader to promote its value, both to multiple professional and public audiences and within the PCT. A critical issue for sustainability was demonstrating the project's success, particularly quantitatively, and aligning it with corporate PCT strategy. However, 'hard' outcomes had been limited and difficult to track, there had been a lack of formal feedback about the project's progress and achievements, and respondents struggled to see how the IIC's 'softer' processes and lessons could be evaluated and channelled into existing performance measures and metrics. The lack of 'hard' outcomes and alignment with corporate priorities was identified by some individuals within the PCT as a barrier to securing wider endorsement for the project.

# ■ REFERENCES

Abrahamson, E. 1991. 'Managerial Fads and Fashions: The Diffusion and Reflection of Innovations'. *Academy of Management Review,* 16(3): 586–612.

Abrahamson, E. 1996. 'Management Fashion'. *Academy of Management Review,* 21(1): 254–85.

Abrahamson, E., and Eisenman, M. 2001. 'Why Management Scholars Must Intervene Strategically in the Management Knowledge Market'. *Human Relations,* 54(1): 67–75.

Accelerated Access Review. 2016. *Accelerated Access Review: Final Report.* An independently chaired report supported by the Wellcome Trust. London: HMSO, see also <www/gov.uk/dh>.

Allcock, C., Dormon, F., Taunt, R., and Dixon, J. 2015. *Constructive Comfort: Accelerating Change in the NHS.* London: Health Foundation.

Allen, P., Keen, J., Wright, J., Dempster, P., Townsend, J., Hutchings, A., Street, A., and Verzulli, R. 2012. 'Investigating the Governance of Autonomous Public Hospitals in England: Multi-Site Case Study of NHS Foundation Trusts'. *Journal of Health Services Research and Policy,* 17(2): 94–100.

Alvesson, M. 2001. 'Knowledge Work: Ambiguity, Image and Identity'. *Human Relations,* 54: 863–86.

Alvesson, M. 2004. *Knowledge Work and Knowledge-Intensive Firms.* Oxford: Oxford University Press.

Alvesson, M., and Robertson, M. 2006. 'The Brightest and the Best: The Role of Elite Identity in Knowledge Intensive Companies'. *Organization,* 13: 195–224.

Ansari, Shahzad M., Fiss, P. C., and Zajac, E. J. 2010. 'Made to Fit: How Practices Vary as they Diffuse'. *Academy of Management Review,* 35(1): 67–92.

Appleby, J., Galea, A., and Murray, R. 2014. *The NHS Productivity Challenge: Experience from the Front Line.* London: King's Fund.

Argyris, C. 1976. 'Single-Loop and Double-Loop Models in Research on Decision Making'. *Administrative Science Quarterly,* 21: 363–75.

Armbrüster, T. 2006. *The Economics and Sociology of Management Consulting.* Cambridge: Cambridge University Press.

Arndt, M., and Bigelow, B., 2009. 'Evidence-Based Management in Health Care Organizations: A Cautionary Note'. *Health Care Management Review,* 34(3): 206–13.

Axelsson, R. 1998. 'Towards an Evidence Based Health Care Management'. *International Journal of Health Planning and Management,* 13(4): 307–17.

Ball, J. 2017. *Post-Truth: How Bullshit Conquered the World.* London: Biteback.

Balogun, J., and Johnson, G. 2004. 'Organizational Restructuring and Middle Manager Sensemaking'. *Academy of Management Journal,* 47: 523–49.

Barends, E., Have, S. Ten, and Huisman, F. 2012. 'Learning from Other Evidence-Based Practices: The Case of Medicine'. In D. M. Rousseau (ed.), *The Oxford Handbook of Evidence-Based Management* Oxford: Oxford University Press [Accessed online Dec. 2017].

Barney, J., 1991. 'Firm Resources and Sustained Competitive Advantage'. *Journal of Management,* 17(1): 99–120.

Barney, J. B. 2001. 'Is the Resource-Based "View" a Useful Perspective for Strategic Management Research? Yes'. *Academy of Management Review,* 26(1): 41–56.

Barney, J. B., Ketchen, D. J., and Wright, M. 2011. 'The Future of Resource-Based Theory'. *Journal of Management,* 37(5): 1299–315.

Bartunek, J., Rousseau, D., Rudolph, J., and Depalma, J. 2006. 'On the Receiving End: Sensemaking, Emotion, and Assessments of an Organizational Change Initiated by Others'. *Journal of Applied Behavioral Science,* 42: 182–206.

Bate, S. P., Bevan, H., and Robert, G. 2004a. *Towards a Million Change Agents: A Review of the Social Movements Literature: Implications for Large Scale Change in the NHS.* Leeds: NHS Modernisation Agency.

Bate, P., Robert, G., and Bevan, H. 2004b. 'The Next Phase of Healthcare Improvement: What can we Learn from Social Movements?' *Quality and Safety in Health Care,* 13(1): 62–6.

Beck, U. 2000. *The Brave New World of Work.* Cambridge: Polity Press.

Benford, R., and Snow, D. 2000. 'Framing Processes and Social Movements: An Overview and Assessment'. *Annual Review of Sociology,* 26: 611–39.

Bennis, W., and O'Tool, J. 2005. 'How Business Schools Lost their Way'. *Harvard Business Review,* 83: 96–103.

Berglund, J., and Werr, A. 2000. 'The Invincible Character of Management Consulting Rhetoric: How One Blends Incommensurates While Keeping them Apart'. *Organization,* 7: 633–55.

Berta, W., Teare, G. F., Gilbart, E., Ginsburg, L. S., Lemieux-Charles, L., Davis, D., and Rappolt, S. 2010. 'Spanning the Know–Do Gap: Understanding Knowledge Application and Capacity in Long-Term Care Homes'. *Social Science and Medicine,* 70(9): 1326–34.

Berwick, D. M. 1996. 'A Primer on Leading the Improvement of Systems'. *BMJ: British Medical Journal,* 312(7031): 619.

Berwick Report. 2013. *A Promise to Learn, a Commitment to Act.* London: HMSO.

Bevan, G., Karanikolos, M., Exley, J., Nolte, E., Connolly, S., and Mays, N. 2014. *The Four Health Systems of the United Kingdom: How do they Compare?* London: Nuffield Trust.

Bevir, M., and Rhodes, R. 2006. *Governance Stories.* Abingdon: Routledge.

Bierly, P. E., Damanpour, F., and Santoro, M. D. 2009. 'The Application of External Knowledge: Organizational Conditions for Exploration and Exploitation'. *Journal of Management Studies,* 46(3): 481–509.

Billis, D. 2010a. 'From Welfare Bureaucracies to Welfare Hybrids'. In D. Billis (ed.), *Hybrid Organizations and the Third Sector: Challenges for Practice, Theory and Policy.* Basingstoke: Palgrave Macmillan, 3–24.

Billis, D. 2010b. 'Towards a Theory of Hybrid Organizations'. In D. Billis (ed.), *Hybrid Organizations and the Third Sector: Challenges for Practice, Theory and Policy.* Basingstoke: Palgrave Macmillan, 46–69.

Black, N. 2001. 'Evidence Based Policy: Proceed with Care'. *British Medical Journal, 323*(7307): 275.

Blackler, F. 1995. 'Knowledge, Knowledge Work and Organizations: An Overview and Interpretation'. *Organization Studies,* 16(6): 1021–46.

Blackler, F., and Regan, S. 2009. 'Intentionality, Agency, Change: Practice Theory and Management'. *Management Learning,* 40(2): 161–76.

Blaxter, M., on behalf of the BSA Medical Sociology Group. 1996. 'Criteria for the Evaluation of Qualitative Research'. *Medical Sociology News*, 22: 68–71.

Blond, P. 2010. *Red Tory: How Left and Right Have Broken Britain and How We Can Fix it.* London: Faber & Faber.

Blond, P., Antonacopoulou, E., and Pabst, A. 2015. *In Professions We Trust.* London: Res Publica.

Boedker, C., and Chua, W. F. 2013. 'Accounting as an Affective Technology: A Study of Circulating, Agency and Entrancement'. *Accounting Organizations and Society*, 38: 245–67.

Borins, S. 2011. 'Making Narrative Count: A Narratological Approach to Public Management Innovation'. *Journal of Public Administration Research and Theory*, 22(1): 165–89.

Bourdieu, P. 1990. *The Logic of Practice.* Cambridge: Polity Press.

Briner, R. B., and Denyer, D. 2012. 'Systematic Review and Evidence Synthesis as a Practice and Scholarship Tool'. In D.M. Rousseau (ed.), *The Oxford Handbook of Evidence-Based Management.* Oxford: Oxford University Press [Accessed Dec. 2017].

Briner, R., Denyer, D., and Rousseau, D. 2009. 'Evidence Based Management: Concept Cleanup Time?' *Academy of Management Perspectives*, 23(4): 19–32.

British Medical Association. 2016. *Privatisation and Independent Sector Provision of NHS Healthcare.* London: BMA.

Brown, J., and Duguid, P. 1991. 'Organizational Learning and Communities-of-Practice: Toward a Unified View of Working, Learning, and Innovation'. *Organization Science,* 2(1): 40–57.

Buchanan, D. A., Fitzgerald, L., and Ketley, D., eds. 2007. *The Sustainability and Spread of Organizational Change.* London: Routledge.

Burke, C., and Morley, M. 2016. 'On Temporary Organizations: A Review, Synthesis and Research Agenda'. *Human Relations*, 69: 1235–58.

Burton, C. R., and Rycroft-Malone, J. 2014. 'Resource Based View of the Firm as a Theoretical Lens on the Organisational Consequences of Quality Improvement'. *International Journal of Health Policy and Management,* 3(3): 113–15.

Cabinet Office. 2007. *Capability Review of the Department of Health.* London: Cabinet Office.

Cabinet Office. 2012a. 'Launch of Big Society Capital—the World's First Ever Social Investment Market Builder'. Press release, 4 Apr. <https://www.gov.uk/government/news/launch-of-big-society-capital-the-world-s-first-ever-social-investment-market-builder> [Accessed Feb. 2017].

Cabinet Office. 2012b. *Public Bodies.* London: HMSO.

Cabinet Office. 2015. 'Social Investment Tax Relief'. <https://www.gov.uk/government/col lections/social-investment-tax-relief> [Accessed Feb. 2017].

Carayannis, E. G., and Campbell, D. F. 2009. 'Mode 3 and Quadruple Helix: Toward a 21st Century Fractal Innovation Ecosystem'. *International Journal of Technology Management*, 46: 201–34.

Cartwright, N. 2007. 'Are RCTs the Gold Standard?' *BioSocieties*, 2(1): 11–20.

Cartwright, N., and Hardie, J. 2012. *Evidence-Based Policy: A Practical Guide to Doing it Better.* Oxford: Oxford University Press.

Casebeer, A., Reay, T., Dewald, J., and Pablo, A. 2010. 'Knowing through Doing: Unleashing Dynamic Capabilities in the Public Sector'. In K. Walshe, G. Harvey, and P. Jas (eds), *Connecting Knowledge and Performance in Public Services.* Cambridge: Cambridge University Press, 251–75.

Centre for Health Economics, University of York. 2017. 'Efficiency and Productivity: Publications'. <https://www.york.ac.uk/che/research/health-policy/efficiency-and-productivity/#tab-2> [Accessed Oct. 2017].

Charlesworth, A., Roberts, A., and Lafond, S. 2016. 'NHS Finances Under the Coalition'. In M. Exworthy, R. Mannion, and M. Powell (eds), *Dismantling the NHS? Evaluating the Impact of Health Reforms*. Bristol: Policy Press, 39–64.

Checkland, K., Coleman, A., McDermott, I., and Peckham, S. 2016. 'Clinically Led Commissioning: Past, Present and Future?'. In Exworthy, M., Mannion. R. and Powell, M. (eds), Dismantling the NHS? Evaluating the Impact of Health Reforms. Bristol: Policy Press, Chapter 8, 149–70.

Christensen, T., and Laegreid, P. 2011. *The Ashgate Research Companion to New Public Management*. Farnham: Ashgate.

Clark, B. R. 1998. *Creating Entrepreneurial Universities: Organizational Pathways of Transformation*. Issues in Higher Education. New York: Elsevier Science.

Clark, T., and Salaman, G. 1998. 'Telling Tales: Management Gurus' Narratives and the Construction of Managerial Identity'. *Journal of Management Studies*, 35(2): 137–61.

Cochrane. 2016. 'Strategy to 2020'. <https://community.cochrane.org/sites/default/files/uploads/inline-files/centres___branches_structure___function_review_-_final_-_june_2016.pdf>.

Cohen, W. M., and Levinthal, D. A. 1990. 'Absorptive Capacity: A New Perspective on and Innovation Learning'. *Administrative Science Quarterly*, 35(1): 128–52.

Competition and Markets Authority. 2014. *Private Healthcare Market Investigation: Final Report*. London: Queen's Printer and Controller of HMSO. <https://assets.publishing.service.gov.uk/media/533af065e5274a5660000023/Private_healthcare_main_report.pdf> [Accessed Feb. 2017].

Contu, A., and Willmott, H. 2000. 'Comment on Wenger and Yanow. Knowing in Practice: A "Delicate Flower" in the Organizational Learning Field'. *Organization*, 7(2): 269–76.

Contu, A., and Willmott, H. 2003. 'Re-embedding Situatedness: The Importance of Power Relations in Learning Theory'. *Organization Science*, 14(3): 283–96.

Corradi, G., Gherardi, S., and Verzelloni, L. 2010. 'Through the Practice Lens: Where is the Bandwagon of Practice-Based Studies Heading?' *Management Learning*, 41: 265–83.

Courts and Tribunals Judiciary. 2013. <https://www.judiciary.gov.uk/wp-content/uploads/JCO/Documents/Judgments/lewisham-hospital-summary.pdf>.

Craig, D. 2006. *Plundering the Public Sector: How New Labour are Letting Consultants Run off with £70 Billion of our Money*. London: Constable.

Crilly, T., Jashapara, A., and Ferlie, E. 2010. *Research Utilisation and Knowledge Mobilisation: A Scoping Review of the Literature*. National Institute for Health Research Service Delivery and Organisation programme. <https://www.journalslibrary.nihr.ac.uk/programmes/hsdr/081801220/#>.

Croft, C., and Currie, G. 2016. 'Enhancing Absorptive Capacity of Healthcare Organizations: The Case of Commissioning Service Interventions'. In J. Swan, S. Newell, and D. Nicolini (eds) *Mobilizing Knowledge in Healthcare: Challenges for Management and Organization*. Oxford: Oxford University Press, 65–81.

Crowdjustice. 2016. <https://www.crowdjustice.co.uk/case/nhs>. [Accessed Aug. 2016].

Currie, G., and White, L. 2012. 'Inter-Professional Barriers and Knowledge Brokering in an Organizational Context: The Case of Healthcare'. *Organization Studies*, 33(10): 1333–61.

Czarniawska-Joerges, B. 1990. 'Merchants of Meaning: Management Consultants in the Swedish Public Sector'. In B. Turner (ed.), *Organizational Symbolism*. New York: de Gruyter, 139–50.

Darlenski, R. B., Neykov, N. V., Vlahov, V. D., and Tsankov, N. K. 2010. 'Evidence-Based Medicine: Facts and Controversies'. *Clinics in Dermatology*, 28(5): 553–7.

Dart, R. 2004. 'The Legitimacy of Social Enterprise'. *Nonprofit Management and Leadership*, 14(4): 411–24.

Darzi, A. 2008. *High Quality Care for All: NHS Next Stage Review Final Report.* London: HMSO.

Davies, C., Wetherell, M., and Barnett, E. 2006. *Citizens at the Centre: Deliberative Participation in Healthcare Decisions.* Bristol: Policy Press.

Davis, E. 2017. *Post-Truth: Why We Have Reached Peak Bullshit and What We Can Do About It.* London: Little, Brown.

Day, P., and Klein, R. 1997. *Steering But Not Rowing? The Transformation of the Department of Health—A Case Study.* Bristol: Policy Press.

Deleuze, G., and Guattari, F. 1987. *A Thousand Plateaus: Capitalism and Schizophrenia.* Minneapolis: University of Minnesota.

Demos. 2017. <https://www.demos.co.uk/wp-content/uploads/2017/03/2015-signed-accounts.pdf>.

Department of Health 2010a. *Equity and Excellence: Liberating the NHS. London.* Cm 7881. London: HMSO. <https://www.gov.uk/government/uploads/system/uploads/attachment_data/file/213823/dh_117794.pdf> [Accessed Oct. 2017].

Department of Health. 2010b. *Revision to the NHS Operating Framework for 2010/2011.* London: Department of Health.

Department of Health. 2012. 'Overview of the Health and Social Care Act', factsheet. <https://www.gov.uk/government/uploads/system/uploads/attachment_data/file/138257/A1.-Factsheet-Overview-240412.pdf> [Accessed Feb. 2017].

Department of Health and Social Security. 1983. *NHS Management Enquiry Report* (Griffiths Report), DA(83)38. London: DHSS.

Department of Trade and Industry. 2002. *Social Enterprise: A Strategy for Success.* London: HMSO. Retrieved from: <http://www.faf-gmbh.de/www/media/socialenterprisestrategyforsucess.pdf> [Accessed July. 2018].

Dewulf, A., Gray, B., Putnam, L., Lewicki, R., Aarts, N., Bouwen, R., and Van Woerkum, C. 2009. 'Disentangling Approaches to Framing in Conflict and Negotiation Research: A Meta-Paradigmatic Perspective'. *Human Relations*, 62: 155–93.

Dixon, J. 2015. Blog, 16 July, <http://www.health.org.uk/blog/nhs-improvement-can-monitortda-adapt-future#sthash.ZABCxS2t.dpuf> [Accessed Jan. 2016].

Dopson, S., Bennett, C., Fitzgerald, L., Ferlie, E., Fischer, M. D., Ledger, J., McCulloch, J., and McGivern, Gerry. 2013. *Health Care Managers' Access and Use of Management Research: Final Report.* Southampton: National Institute for Health Research.

Dopson, S., and Fitzgerald, L., eds. 2005. *Knowledge to Action? Evidence-Based Health Care in Context.* Oxford: Oxford University Press.

Dopson, S., FitzGerald, L., Ferlie, E., Gabbay, J., and Locock, L. 2002. 'No Magic Targets! Changing Clinical Practice to Become More Evidence Based'. *Health Care Management Review*, 27(3): 35–47.

Dopson, S., Locock, L., Chambers, D., and Gabbay, J. 2001. 'Implementation of Evidence-Based Medicine: Evaluation of the Promoting Action on Clinical Effectiveness Programme'. *Journal of Health Services Research and Policy*, 6(1): 23–31.

Dopson, S., Locock, L., Gabbay, J., Ferlie, E., and Fitzgerald, L. 2003. 'Evidence-Based Medicine and the Implementation Gap'. *Health*, 7: 311–30.

Drucker, P. F. 2007. *The Essential Drucker: Selections from the Management Works of Peter F. Drucker.* Amsterdam and London: Butterworth-Heinemann.

Dunleavy, P., 1995. 'Policy Disasters: Explaining the UK's Record'. *Public Policy and Administration*, 10(2): 52–70.

Dunleavy, P., Margetts, H., Bastow, S., and Tinkler, J. 2006. 'New Public Management is Dead—Long Live Digital-Era Governance'. *Journal of Public Administration Research and Theory*, 16(3): 467–94.

Dunn, P., McKenna, H., and Murray, R. 2016. *Deficits in the NHS*. London: King's Fund.

Edwards, M. 2012. 'Introduction: Civil Society and the Geometry of Human Relations'. In M. Edwards (ed.), *The Oxford Handbook of Civil Society*. Oxford: Oxford University Press [Accessed online].

Elkjaer, B. 2003. 'Social Learning Theory: Learning as Participation in Social Processes'. In M. Easterby-Smith and M. Lyles (eds), *The Blackwell Handbook of Organizational Learning and Knowledge Management*. Oxford: Blackwell Publishing, 38–53.

Elwyn, G., Taubert, M., and Kowalczuk, J. 2007. 'Sticky Knowledge: A Possible Model for Investigating Implementation in Healthcare Contexts'. *Implementation Science*, 2(1): 44.

Emirbayer, Mustafa. 1997. 'Manifesto for a Relational Sociology'. *American Journal of Sociology*, 103(2): 281–317.

Engwall, L. 2010. 'Business Schools and Consultancies'. In M. Kipping and T. Clark (eds), *The Oxford Handbook of Management Consulting*. Oxford: Oxford University Press, 364–85.

Enthoven, A. 1985. *Reflections of the Management of the NHS*. Occasional Paper 5. London: Nuffield Provincial Hospitals Trust.

Erskine, J., Hunter, D. J., Small, A., Hicks, C., McGovern, T., Lugsden, E., Whitty, P., Steen, N., and Eccles, M. P. 2013. 'Leadership and Transformational Change in Healthcare Organisations: A Qualitative Analysis of the North East Transformation System'. *Health Services Management Research*, 26(1): 29–37.

Etzioni, A. 1994. *Spirit of Community*. New York: Touchstone.

Etzioni, A. 1998. 'Introduction'. In A. Etzioni (ed.), *The Essential Communitarian Reader*. Lanham, MD: Rowman & Littlefield, ix–xxiv.

Etzkowitz, H. 2006. 'The New Visible Hand: An Assisted Linear Model of Science and Innovation Policy'. *Science and Public Policy*, 33: 310–20.

Etzkowitz, H., and Klofsten, M. 2005. 'The Innovating Region: Toward a Theory of Knowledge-Based Regional Development'. *R&D Management*, 35: 243–55.

Etzkowitz, H., and Leydesdorff, L. 2000. 'The Dynamics of Innovation: From National Systems and "Mode 2" to a Triple Helix of University–Industry–Government Relations'. *Research Policy*, 29(2): 109–23.

Evans, D. 2003. 'Hierarchy of Evidence: A Framework for Ranking Evidence Evaluating Health Care Interventions'. *Journal of Clinical Nursing*, 12: 77–84.

Fabian Society. 2017. <http://www.fabians.org.uk/wp-content/uploads/2017/02/Fabian-Society-annual-report-2016.pdf>. London: Fabian Society.

Feinstein, A. R., and Horwitz, R. I. 1997. 'Problems in the "Evidence" of "Evidence-Based Medicine"'. *American Journal of Medicine*, 103(6): 529–35.

Ferlie, E. 2014. 'Resource Based View: A Promising New Theory for Healthcare Organizations: Comment on "Resource Based View of the Firm as a Theoretical Lens on the Organisational Consequences of Quality Improvement"'. *International Journal of Health Policy and Management*, 3(6): 347–8.

Ferlie, E. 2016. *Analysing Health Care Organizations*. Abingdon: Routledge.

Ferlie, E., and McGivern, G. 2014. 'Bringing Anglo-Governmentality into Public Management Scholarship: The Case of Evidence-Based Medicine in UK Health Care'. *Journal of Public Administration Research and Theory*, 24(1): 59–83.

Ferlie, E., Ashburner, L., FitzGerald, L., and Pettigrew, A. 1996. *The New Public Management in Action*. Oxford: Oxford University Press.

Ferlie, E., Fitzgerald, L., Wood, M., and Hawkins, C. 2005. 'The Nonspread of Innovations: The Mediating Role of Professionals'. *Academy of Management Journal*, 48(1): 117–34.

Ferlie, E., McGivern, G., and Morales, A. 2010. 'A Public Interest School of Management: Creating and Sustaining Divergence in the Business School Field'. *British Journal of Management*, 21: S60–70.

Ferlie, E., Fitzgerald, L., McGivern, G., Dopson, S., and Bennett, C. 2011. 'Public Policy Networks and "Wicked Problems": A Nascent Solution?' *Public Administration*, 89: 307–24.

Ferlie, E., Crilly, T., Jashapara, A., and Peckham, A. 2012. 'Knowledge Mobilisation in Healthcare: A Critical Review of Health Sector and Generic Management Literature'. *Social Science and Medicine*, 74(8): 1297–304.

Ferlie, E., FitzGerald, McGivern, G., Dopson, S., and Bennett, C. 2013. *Making Wicked Problems Governable? The Case of Managed Networks in Health Care*. Oxford: Oxford University Press.

Ferlie, E., Crilly, T., Jashapara, A., Trenholm, S., Peckham, A., and Currie, G. 2015. 'Knowledge Mobilization in Healthcare Organizations: A View from the Resource-Based View of the Firm'. *International Journal of Health Policy and Management*, 4(3): 127–30.

Ferlie, E., Ledger, J., Dopson, S., Fischer, M. D., Fitzgerald, L., McGivern, G., and Bennett, C. 2016. 'The Political Economy of Management Knowledge: Management Texts in English Healthcare Organizations'. *Public Administration*, 94(1): 185–203.

Fincham, R. 1999. 'The Consultant–Client Relationship: Critical Perspectives on the Management of Organizational Change'. *Journal of Management Studies*, 36: 335–51.

Fincham, R., Clark, T., Handley, K., and Sturdy, A. 2008. 'Configuring Expert Knowledge: The Consultant as Sector Specialist'. *Journal of Organizational Behavior*, 29(8): 1145–60.

Fine, D. J. 2006. 'Toward the Evolution of a Newly Skilled Managerial Class for Healthcare Organizations'. *Frontiers of Health Services Management*, 22(3): 31–54.

Fischer, M. D. 2012. 'Organizational Turbulence, Trouble and Trauma: Theorizing the Collapse of a Mental Health Setting'. *Organization Studies*, 33(9): 1153–73.

Fischer, M. D., and Ferlie, E. 2013. 'Resisting Hybridisation between Modes of Clinical Risk Management: Contradiction, Contest, and the Production of Intractable Conflict'. *Accounting Organizations and Society*, 38(1): 30–49.

Fischer, M. D., and McGivern, G. 2016. 'Affective Overflows in Clinical Riskwork'. In M. Power (ed.), *Riskwork: Essays on the Organizational Life of Risk Management*. Oxford: Oxford University Press, 232–52.

Fischer, M. D., and White, A. 2014. 'Designed to Lead? Advancing Evidence-Based Design of Transformative Leadership Journeys'. *Developing Leaders Quarterly* 17: 34–8.

Fischer, M. D. Ferlie, E., French, C., Fulop, N., and Wolfe, C. 2013. *The Creation and Survival of an Academic Health Science Organization: Counter-Colonization through a New Organizational Form?* Saïd Business School Working Paper Series, WP 2013–26. Oxford: University of Oxford.

Fischer, M. D., Morris, T., and Dopson, S. 2015. 'Counter-Programmatic Space and Its Role in Leadership Development: A Study of Senior Leadership Programmes at University of Oxford

Saïd Business School'. Asia-Pacific Researchers in Organisation Studies and European Group for Organizational Studies Conference. Sydney, Australia.

Fischer, M. D., Dopson, S., Fitzgerald, L., Bennett, C., Ferlie, E., Ledger, J., and McGivern, G. 2016. 'Knowledge Leadership: Mobilizing Management Research by Becoming the Knowledge Object'. *Human Relations*, 69(7): 1563–85.

Foss, N. 2005. *Strategy, Economic Organization, and the Knowledge Economy: The Coordination of Firms and Resources*. Oxford: Oxford University Press.

Francis Report. 2013. *Report of the Mid Staffordshire NHS Foundation Trust Public Inquiry: Executive Summary*. London: HMSO.

Freidson, E. 1970. *Professional Dominance: The Social Structure of Medical Care*. New York: Atherton Press.

Freidson, E. 2001. *Professionalism, the Third Logic*. Chicago: University of Chicago Press.

French, C. E., Ferlie, E., and Fulop, N. J. 2014. 'The International Spread of Academic Health Science Centres: A Scoping Review and the Case of Policy Transfer to England'. *Health Policy*, 117(3): 382–91.

Gabbay, J., and Le May, A. 2004. 'Evidence-Based Guidelines or Collectively Constructed "Mindlines"? Ethnographic Study of Knowledge Management in Primary Care'. *British Medical Journal*, 7473: 1013–16.

Gabbay, J., and Le May, A. 2011. *Practice-Based Evidence for Healthcare: Clinical Mindlines*. Abingdon: Routledge.

Gains, F., and Stoker, G. 2011. 'Special Advisers and the Transmission of Ideas from the Policy Primeval Soup'. *Policy and Politics*, 39(4): 485–98.

Gainsbury, S. 2016. *Feeling the Crunch: NHS Finances to 2020*. London: Nuffield Trust. <https://www.nuffieldtrust.org.uk/files/2017-01/feeling-the-crunch-nhs-finances-to-2020-web-final.pdf> [Accessed Dec. 2017].

Galbreath, J. 2005. 'Which Resources Matter the Most to Firm Success? An Exploratory Study of Resource-Based Theory'. *Technovation*, 25(9): 979–87.

Geiger, D. 2009. 'Revisiting the Concept of Practice: Toward an Argumentative Understanding of Practicing'. *Management Learning*, 40(2): 129–44.

General Medical Council. 2013. *Good Medical Practice*. London: Medical Guidance. <https://www.gmc-uk.org/static/documents/content/Good_medical_practice_-_English_1215.pdf> [Accessed Dec. 2017].

Gherardi, S. 2001. 'From Organizational Learning to Practice-Based Knowing'. *Human Relations*, 54(1): 131.

Gherardi, S. 2004. 'Translating Knowledge While Mending Organisational Safety Culture'. *Risk Management*, 6(2): 61–80.

Gibbons, M. 2000. 'Mode 2 Society and the Emergence of Context-Sensitive Science'. *Science and Public Policy*, 27(3): 159–63.

Gibson, C. B., and Birkinshaw, J. 2004. 'The Antecedents, Consequences, and Mediating Role of Organizational Ambidexterity'. *Academy of Management Journal*, 47(2): 209–26.

Gill, M. 2015. 'Elite Identity and Status Anxiety: An Interpretative Phenomenological Analysis of Management Consultants'. *Organization*, 22(3), 306–25.

Gkeredakis, E., Swan, J., Powell, J., Nicolini, D., Scarbrough, H., Roginski, C., Taylor-Phillips, S., et al. 2011. 'Mind the Gap'. *Journal of Health Organization and Management*, 25(3): 298–314.

Glaser, B., and Strauss, A. 1967. *The Discovery of Grounded Theory: Strategies for Qualitative Research.* Chicago: Aldine.

Greenhalgh, T. 1999. 'Narrative Based Medicine: Narrative Based Medicine in an Evidence Based World'. *BMJ* (Clinical Research Ed.), 318(7179): 323–5.

Greenhalgh, T. 2002. 'Intuition and Evidence: Uneasy Bedfellows?' *British Journal of General Practice*, 52(478): 395–400.

Greenhalgh, T., and Wieringa, S. 2011. 'Is it Time to Drop the "Knowledge Translation" Metaphor? A Critical Literature Review'. *Journal of the Royal Society of Medicine*, 104(12): 501–9.

Greenhalgh, T., Howick, J., and Maskrey, N. 2014. 'Evidence Based Medicine: A Movement in Crisis?' *BMJ* 348: g3725.

Greer, S. 2004. *Four Way Bet: How Devolution has Led to Four Different Models for the NHS.* Constitution Unit Report. London: University College London.

Greer, S. L., and Jarman, H. 2007. *The Department of Health and the Civil Service: From Whitehall to Department of Delivery to Where?* London: Nuffield Trust.

Griffiths, R. 1983. *NHS Management Enquiry.* London: HMSO.

Gross, A., and Poor, J. 2008. 'The Global Management Consulting Sector'. *Business Economics*, 43: 59–68.

Haas, E. B. 1990. *When Knowledge is Power: Three Models of Change in International Organizations.* Berkeley and Los Angeles: University of California Press.

Haas, P. 1992. 'Introduction: Epistemic Communities and International Policy Coordination'. *International Organization*, 46(1): 1–35.

Haas, M., Criscuolom, P., and George, G. 2015. 'Which Problems to Solve? Online Knowledge Sharing and Attention Allocation in Organizations'. *Academy of Management Journal*, 58: 680–711.

Hall, K., Alcock, P., and Millar, R. 2012. 'Start up and Sustainability: Marketisation and the Social Enterprise Investment Fund in England'. *Journal of Social Policy*, 41(04): 733–49.

Halligan, J. 2013. 'NPM in Anglo Saxon Countries'. In T. Christensen and P. Laegreid (eds), *The Ashgate Research Companion to the NPM.* Farnham: Ashgate, 83–96.

Ham, C., Kipping, R., and McLeod, H. 2003. 'Redesigning Work Processes in Health Care: Lessons from the National Health Service'. *Milbank Quarterly*, 81(3): 415–39.

Hammer, M., and Champy, J. 1993. *Reengineering the Corporation.* New York: Harper Collins.

Hammersley, M. 2005. 'The Myth of Research-Based Practice: The Critical Case of Educational Inquiry'. *International Journal of Social Research Methodology: Theory and Practice*, 8(4): 317–30.

Handley, K., Sturdy, A., Fincham, R., and Clark, T. 2006. 'Within and beyond Communities of Practice: Making Sense of Learning through Participation, Identity and Practice'. *Journal of Management Studies*, 43(3): 641–53.

Harris, R. G. 2001. 'The Knowledge-Based Economy: Intellectual Origins and New Economic Perspectives'. *International Journal of Management Reviews*, 3(1): 21–40.

Harrison, S. 1998. 'The Politics of Evidence-Based Medicine in the United Kingdom'. *Policy and Politics*, 26(1): 15–31.

Hartley, J., and Rashman, L. 2010. 'The Role of Leadership in Knowledge Creation and Transfer for Organizational Learning and Improvement'. In K. Walshe, G. Harvey, and P. Jas (eds), *Connecting Knowledge and Performance in Public Services.* Cambridge: Cambridge University Press, 145–72.

Harvey, G., Jas, P., Walshe, K., and Skelcher, C. 2010. 'Absorptive Capacity: How Organizations Assimilate and Apply Knowledge to Improve Performance'. In K. Walshe, G. Harvey, and P. Jas (eds), *Connecting Knowledge and Performance in Public Services*. Cambridge: Cambridge University Press, 226–50.

Harvey, G., Skelcher, C., Spencer, E., Jas, P., and Walshe, K. 2010. 'Absorptive Capacity in a Non-Market Environment'. *Public Management Review*, 12(1): 77–97.

Haynes, R. B., Devereaux, P. J., and Guyatt, G. H. 2002. 'Clinical Expertise in the Era of Evidence-Based Medicine and Patient Choice'. *BMJ Evidence-Based Medicine*, 7: 36–8.

Health and Social Care Act. 2012. England. London: The Stationery Office. <http://www.legislation.gov.uk/ukpga/2012/7/introduction/enacted>.

Health Foundation. 2015. <http://www.health.org.uk/sites/health/files/AnnualReportFinancial Statements2015.pdf>.

Health Foundation and King's Fund. 2015. *Making Change Possible: A Transformation Fund for the NHS. Research Report 2015*. London: Health Foundation. <https://www.kingsfund.org.uk/sites/files/kf/field/field_publication_file/making-change-possible-a-transformation-fund-for-the-nhs-kingsfund-healthfdn-jul15.pdf> [Accessed Feb. 2017].

Health Policy and Economic Research Unit. 2010. *The QIPP Initiative (England) and Addressing the Recession—Briefing*. London: BMA.

Heifetz, R., and Laurie, D. L. 1997. 'The Work of Leadership'. *Harvard Business Review*, Jan./Feb.: 124–34.

Heusinkveld, S., and Visscher, K. 2012. 'Practice What you Preach: How Consultants Frame Management Concepts as Enacted Practice'. *Scandinavian Journal of Management*, 28: 285–97.

Hill, M., and Hupe, P. 2009. *Implementing Public Policy*, 2nd edn. London: Sage.

Hilton, K., and Lawrence-Pietroni, C. 2013. *Leaders Everywhere: The Story of NHS Change Day— A Learning Report*. Leeds: NHS IQ.

Hinings, C. R., Casebeer, A., Reay, T., Golden-Biddle, K., Pablo, A., and Greenwood, R. 2003. 'Regionalizing Healthcare in Alberta: Legislated Change, Uncertainty and Loose Coupling'. *British Journal of Management*, 14: S15–S30.

HM Government. 1979. *Report of The Royal Commission on the NHS*. Cmnd 7615 (Merrison Report). London: HMSO.

HM Government. 2010a. *Equity and Excellence: Liberating the NHS*. Cm 7881. London: HMSO.

HM Government. 2010b. *Spending Review*. Cm 7942. London: HM Treasury.

HM Government. 2011. *Open Public Services*. Cm 8145. London: HMSO.

HM Government. 2016a. <https://www.gov.uk/government/organisations#non-ministerial-departments> [Accessed Feb. 2016].

HM Government. 2016b. <https://www.gov.uk/government/organisations#department-of-health> [Accessed Feb. 2016].

HM Government. 2016c. <https://www.gov.uk/government/organisations#ministry-of-justice> [Accessed Feb. 2016].

HM Government. 2016d. <https://www.gov.uk/government/organisations#home-office> [Accessed Feb. 2016].

HM Government. 2016e. 'Social Investment: A Force for Social Change. 2016 Strategy'. London: HMSO. <https://www.gov.uk/government/uploads/system/uploads/attachment_data/file/507215/6.1804_SIFT_Strategy_260216_FINAL_web.pdf> [Accessed Feb. 2017].

HM Government. 2017. <https://www.gov.uk/government/uploads/system/uploads/attachment_data/file/579892/List_of_special_advisers_in_post_as_at_21_December_2016.pdf>.

HM Treasury. 2010. *Budget 2010*. HC 61. London: HMSO.

Hodgkinson, G. P. 2012. 'The Politics of Evidence-Based Decision Making'. In D. M. Rousseau (ed.), *The Oxford Handbook of Evidence-Based Management*. Oxford: Oxford University Press, Oxford Handbooks Online. <http://www.oxfordhandbooks.com/view/10.1093/oxfordhb/9780199763986.001.0001/oxfordhb-9780199763986?result=154> [Accessed Dec. 2017].

Holder, H., Robertson, R., Ross, S., Bennett, L., Gosling, J., and Curry, N. 2015. *Risk or Reward? The Changing Role of CCGs in General Practice*. London: King's Fund and Nuffield Trust.

Holliday, I. 2000. 'Is the British State Hollowing out?'. *Political Quarterly*, 71(2): 167–76.

Hood, C. 1991. 'A Public Management for All Seasons?'. *Public Administration,* 69(1): 3–19.

Hood, C., and Dixon. R. 2015. *A Government that Works Better and Costs Less*. Oxford: Oxford University Press.

Houghton, J., and Sheehan, P. 2000. *A Primer on the Knowledge Economy*. Working Paper. Melbourne: Victoria University. <http://vuir.vu.edu.au/59> [Accessed Dec. 2017].

House of Commons Public Accounts Committee. 2013. *Department of Health: Progress in Making Efficiency Savings*. HC 865, 39th Report of Session 2012/2013. London: HMSO.

Hughes, D. 1996. 'NHS Managers as Rhetoricians: A Case of Culture Management?' *Sociology of Health and Illness,* 18(3): 291–314.

Huy, Q. N. 2011. 'How Middle Managers' Group-Focus Emotions and Social Identities Influence Strategy Implementation'. *Strategic Management Journal,* 32: 1387–410.

Iles, V., and Sutherland, K. 2001. *Organisational Change: A Review for Health Care Managers, Professionals and Researchers*. London: National Coordinating Centre for NHS Service Delivery and Organization R&D.

Ioannidis, J. P. A. 2016. 'Evidence-Based Medicine has been Hijacked: A Report to David Sackett'. *Journal of Clinical Epidemiology,* 73: 82–6.

Jarzabkowski, P. 2004. 'Strategy as Practice: Recursiveness, Adaptation, and Practices-in-Use'. *Organization Studies,* 25(4): 529–60.

Jelley, R. B., Carroll, W. R., and Rousseau, D. M. 2012. 'Reflections on Teaching Evidence-Based Management'. In D. M. Rousseau (ed.), *The Oxford Handbook of Evidence-Based Management*. Oxford: Oxford University Press [Accessed online Dec. 2017].

Jenkins, K., Caines, K., and Jackson, A. 1988. *The Next Steps: Report to the Prime Minister*. London: HMSO.

Johnson, G., Langley, A., Melin, L., and Whittington, R. 2007. *Strategy as Practice: Research Directions and Resources*. Cambridge: Cambridge University Press.

Joss, R., and Kogan, M. 1995. *Advancing Quality: Total Quality Management in the National Health Service*. Buckingham: Open University Press.

Kahneman, D. 2003. 'A Perspective on Judgement and Choice: Mapping Bounded Rationality'. *American Psychologist,* 58(9): 697–720.

Kahneman, D. 2011. *Thinking, Fast and Slow.* New York: Farrar, Straus & Giroux.

Kaplan, R. S. and Norton, D. P. 1996. *The Balance Scorecard: Translating Strategy into Action.* Cambridge, MA: Harvard University Press.

Kaplan, S. 2008. 'Framing Contests: Strategy Making under Uncertainty'. *Organization Science,* 19: 729–52.

Kash, B. A, Spaulding, A., Gamm, L., and Johnson, C. E. 2013. 'Health Care Administrators' Perspectives on the Role of Absorptive Capacity for Strategic Change Initiatives: A Qualitative Study'. *Health Care Management Review,* 38(4): 339–48.

Keane, M., and Berg, C. 2016. 'Evidence-Based Medicine: A Predictably Flawed Paradigm'. *Trends in Anaesthesia and Critical Care,* 9: 49–52.

Kennedy Information (2008) *The Global Consulting Marketplace: Key Data, Forecasts and Trends*: Fitzwilliam, NH: Kennedy Information Inc.

Kerr, D., Bevan, H., Gowland, B., Penny, J., and Berwick, D. 2002. 'Redesigning Cancer Care'. *British Medical Journal,* 324(7330): 164.

Ketley, D., and Bevan, H. 2007. 'Changing by Numbers'. In D. A. Buchanan, L. Fitzgerald, and D. Ketley (eds), *The Sustainability and Spread of Organizational Change.* London: Routledge, 1–21.

Khurana, R. 2007. *From Higher Aims to Hired Hands: The Social Transformation of American Business Schools and the Unfulfilled Promise of Management as a Profession.* Princeton: Princeton University Press.

Kieser, A. 2002. 'On Communication Barriers between Management Science, Consultancies and Business Organizations'. In T. Clark and R. Fincham (eds), *Critical Consulting: New Perspectives on the Management Advice Industry.* Oxford: Blackwell, 206–27.

Kilo, C. M. 1998. 'A Framework for Collaborative Improvement: Lessons from the Institute for Healthcare Improvement's Breakthrough Series'. *Quality Management in Healthcare,* 6(4): 1–14.

King's Fund. 2014. *How is Health and Social Care Performing: Quarterly Monitoring Report.* London: King's Fund.

King's Fund. 2015a. *Devolution: What It Means for Health and Social Care in England.* London: King's Fund.

King's Fund. 2015b. *Mental Health under Pressure.* Briefing. London: King's Fund. <https://www.kingsfund.org.uk/sites/files/kf/field/field_publication_file/mental-health-under-pressure-nov15_0.pdf> [Accessed Feb. 2017].

King's Fund. 2016a. <http://www.kingsfund.org.uk/projects/nhs-in-a-nutshell/nhs-budget> [Accessed Aug. 2016].

King's Fund. 2016b. *Quarterly Monitoring Report,* 20. London: King's Fund.

Kirkpatrick, I., Lonsdale, C., and Neogy, I. 2016. 'Management Consulting in Health'. In E. Ferlie, K. Montgomery, and A. R. Pedersen (eds), *The Oxford Handbook of Health Care Management.* Oxford: Oxford University Press, 517–38.

Kitchener, M. 1999. 'All Fur Coat and No Knickers: Contemporary Organisational Change in United Kingdom Hospitals'. In D. Brock, M. Powell, and C. R. Hinings, *Restructuring the Professional Organization: Accounting, Law and Medicine.* London: Routledge, 183–99.

Klein, R. 2013. *The New Politics of the NHS,* 7th edn. London: Radcliffe Publishing.

Knorr-Cetina, K. 1999. *Epistemic Cultures: How the Sciences Make Knowledge*. Cambridge, MA: Harvard University Press.

Knudsen, H. K., and Roman, P. M. 2004. 'Modeling the Use of Innovations in Private Treatment Organizations: The Role of Absorptive Capacity'. *Journal of Substance Abuse Treatment*, 26(1): 353–61.

Kothari, A., Edwards, N., Hamel, N., and Judd, M. 2009. 'Is Research Working for you? Validating a Tool to Examine the Capacity of Health Organizations to Use Research'. *Implementation Science*, 4(1): 46.

Kotter, J. P. 1995. 'Leading Change: Why Transformation Efforts Fail'. *Harvard Business Review*, 73: 59.

Kovner, A. R., Elton, J. J., and Billings, J. 2000. 'Evidence-Based Management/Commentaries/ Reply'. *Frontiers of Health Services Management*, 16(4): 3–46.

Kravitz, R. L., Duan, N., and Braslow, J. 2004. 'Evidence-Based Medicine, Heterogeneity of Treatment Effects, and the Trouble with Averages'. *Milbank Quarterly 82* (4): 661–87. [Erratum appears in *Milbank Quarterly*, 84(4) (2006): 759–60.]

Lakshman, C. 2005. 'Top Executive Knowledge Leadership: Managing Knowledge to Lead Change at General Electric'. *Journal of Change Management*, 5(4): 429–46.

Landry, R., Amara, N., and Lamari, M. 2001. 'Utilization of Social Science Research Knowledge in Canada'. *Research Policy*, 30: 333–49.

Lane, J. E. 2000. *New Public Management: An Introduction*. London: Routledge.

Langley, G. J., Nolan, K. M., and Nolan, T. W. 1996. *The Improvement Guide: A Practical Approach to Enhancing Organizational Performance*. San Francisco, CA: Jossey-Bass.

Learmonth, M. 2006. 'Is there Such a Thing as "Evidence-Based Management"?: A Commentary on Rousseau's 2005 Presidential Address'. *Academy of Management Review*, 31(4): 1089–91.

Learmonth, M. 2008. 'Speaking out: Evidence-Based Management: A Backlash Against Pluralism in Organizational Studies?' *Organization*, 15(2): 283–91.

Learmonth, M., and Harding, N. 2006. 'Evidence-Based Management: The Very Idea'. *Public Administration*, 84(2): 245–66.

Ledger, J. 2014. 'Competing Knowledges in Turbulent Times: The Use of Management Knowledge in Commissioning Organisations in the English NHS'. Doctoral thesis, King's College London.

Le Grand, J., and the Mutuals Task Force. 2012. *Public Services Mutuals: The Next Steps*. London: Cabinet Office.

Leigh-Star, S., and Griesemer, J. 1989. 'Institutional Ecology, "Translations" and Boundary Objects: Amateurs and Professionals in Berkeley's Museum of Vertebrate Zoology, 1907–39'. *Social Studies of Science*, 19: 387–420.

Lewin, A. Y., Massini, S., and Peeters, C. 2011. 'Microfoundations of Internal and External Absorptive Capacity Routines'. *Organization Science*, 22(1): 81–98.

Locock, L. 2001. *Maps and Journeys: Redesign in the NHS*. Birmingham: University of Birmingham Health Services Management Centre.

Locock, L. 2003. 'Healthcare Redesign: Meaning, Origins and Application'. *Quality and Safety in Health Care*, 12(1): 53–7.

London School of Economics Centre for Civil Society. 2009. 'What is Civil Society?', <http://www.lse.ac.uk/collections/CCS/introduction/what_is_civil_society.htm>.

Lundin, R., and Söderholm, A. 1995. 'A Theory of the Temporary Organization'. *Scandinavian Journal of Management,* 11: 437–55.

Lundvall, B. Ä., and Johnson, B. 1994. 'The Learning Economy'. *Journal of Industry Studies,* 1(2): 23–42.

McDonald, D. 2014. *The Firm: The Inside Story of McKinsey.* London: Oneworld.

Macfarlane, F., Exworthy, M., Wilmott, M., and Greenhalgh, T. 2011. 'Plus ça change, plus c'est la même chose: Senior NHS Managers' Narratives of Restructuring'. *Sociology of Health and Illness,* 33(6): 914–29.

McGann, J. G., Viden, A., and Rafferty, J., eds. 2014. *How Think Tanks Shape Social Development Policies.* Philadelphia: University of Pennsylvania Press.

McGann, J. G., and Weaver, R. K., eds. 2009. *Think Tanks and Civil Societies: Catalysts for Ideas and Action.* New Brunswick, NJ: Transaction Publishers.

McGivern, C. 1983. 'Some Facets of the Relationship between Consultants and Clients in Organizations'. *Journal of Management Studies,* 20: 367–86.

McGivern, G., and Dopson, S. 2010. 'Inter-Epistemic Power and Transforming Knowledge Objects in a Biomedical Network'. *Organization Studies,* 31(12): 1667–86.

McGivern, G., & Fischer, M. D. 2012. 'Reactivity and Reactions to Regulatory Transparency in Medicine, Psychotherapy and Counselling'. *Social Science & Medicine,* 74(3): 289–96.

McGivern, G., Dopson, S., Ferlie, E., Fischer, M., Fitzgerald, L., Ledger, J., and Bennett, C. 2017. 'The Silent Politics of Temporal Work: A Case Study of a Management Consultancy Project to Redesign Public Health Care'. *Organization Studies* [online first].

McGivern, G., Dopson, S., Ferlie, E., Bennett, C., Fischer, M., Fitzgerald, L., and Ledger, J., 2016. ' "Epistemic Fit" and the Mobilisation of Management Knowledge in Health Care'. In J. Swan, S. Newell, and D. Nicolini, (eds) *Mobilizing Knowledge in Health Care: Challenges for Management and Organization.* Oxford: Oxford University Press, 23–40.

McKenna, C. 2006. *The World's Newest Profession: Management Consulting in the Twentieth Century.* Cambridge: Cambridge University Press.

McKinsey & Co. 2009. *Achieving World Class Productivity in the NHS 2009/10–2013/14: Detailing the Size of the Opportunity.* London: Department of Health. <http://www.nhshistory.net/mckinsey%20report.pdf> [Accessed Oct. 2017].

McNulty, T., and Ferlie, E. 2002. *Reengineering Health Care: The Complexities of Organizational Transformation.* Oxford: Oxford University Press.

McNulty, T., and Ferlie, E. 2004. 'Process Transformation: Limitations to Radical Organizational Change within Public Service Organizations'. *Organization Studies,* 25(8): 1389–412.

Management Consultancies Association. 2016. *The Definitive Guide to UK Consulting Industry 2015.* London: Management Consultancies Association.

Margetts, H., and Dunleavy, P. 2013. 'The Second Wave of Digital-Era Governance: A Quasi-Paradigm for Government on the Web'. *Philosophical Transactions of the Royal Society A,* 371 (1987): 20120382.

Marinetto, M. 2003. 'Governing Beyond the Centre: A Critique of the Anglo-Governance School'. *Political Studies,* 51(3): 592–608.

Martin, G. P., Armstrong, N., Aveling, E. L., Herbert, G., and Dixon-Woods, M. 2015. 'Professionalism Redundant, Reshaped, or Reinvigorated? Realizing the "Third Logic" in Contemporary Health Care'. *Journal of Health and Social Behavior,* 56(3): 378–97.

Martin, G. P., Sutton, E., Willars, J., and Dixon-Woods, M. 2013. 'Frameworks for Change in Healthcare Organisations: A Formative Evaluation of the NHS Change Model'. *Health Services Management Research*, 26(2–3): 65–75.

Mays, N., Dixon, A., and Jones, L. 2011. *Understanding New Labour's Market Reforms of the English NHS*. London: King's Fund.

Mays, N., and Pope, C. 2000. 'Quality in Qualitative Research'. In C. Pope and N. Mays (eds), *Qualitative Research in Health Care*, 2nd edn. London: BMJ Books, 89–101.

Mays, N., Roberts, E., and Popay, J. 2001. 'Synthesising Research Evidence'. In N. Fulop, P. Allen, A. Clarke, N. Black, (eds), *Studying the Organization and Delivery of Health Services: Research Methods*. London: Routledge, 188–220.

Mazzucato, M. 2013. *The Entrepreneurial State: Debunking Public vs Private Sector Myths*. London: Anthem Press.

Michael Young Foundation. 2016. *Annual Report*. <http://apps.charitycommission.gov.uk/Accounts/Ends45/0000274345_AC_20161231_E_C.PDF>.

Miettinen, R., Samra-Fredericks, D., and Yanow, D. 2009. 'Re-Turn to Practice: An Introductory Essay'. *Organization Studies*, 30(12): 1309–27.

Milewa, T., and Barry, C. 2005. 'Health Policy and the Politics of Evidence'. *Social Policy and Administration*, 39(5): 498–512.

Mintzberg, H., Ahlstrand, B., and Lampel, J. 2009. *Strategy Safari*, 2nd edn. Harlow: FT Prentice Hall.

Moore, M. H. 1995. *Creating Public Value: Strategic Management in Government*. Cambridge, MA: Harvard University Press.

Moore, M., and Bennington, J., eds. 2011. *Public Value: Theory and Practice*. Basingstoke: Palgrave Macmillan.

Moran, M. 2003. *The British Regulatory State: High Modernism and Hyper-Innovation*. Oxford: Oxford University Press.

Morrell, K. 2008. 'The Narrative of "Evidence Based" Management: A Polemic'. *Journal of Management Studies*, 45(3): 613–35.

Mueller, F., and Whittle, A. 2011. 'Translating Management Ideas: A Discursive Devices Analysis'. *Organization Studies*, 32(2): 187–210.

Mykhalovskiy, E., and Weir, L. 2004. 'The Problem of Evidence-Based Medicine: Directions for Social Science'. *Social Science and Medicine*, 59(5): 1059–69.

National Audit Office. 2011. *Delivering Efficiency Savings in the NHS*. Briefing Paper for the House of Commons Health Committee. London: National Audit Office.

National Audit Office. 2012. *Department of Health: Progress in Making NHS Efficiency Savings*. London: HMSO, HC 686, Session 2012/2013.

National Audit Office. 2016. *Use of Consultants and Temporary Staff*. London: National Audit Office.

Neath, A. 2007. 'Tracking Sustainability: Lessons from the Patient Booking Timeline'. In D. A. Buchanan, L. Fitzgerald, and D. Ketley (eds), *The Sustainability and Spread of Organizational Change*. London: Routledge, 104–25.

NESTA. 2016. *Annual Report 2015/16*. <http://apps.charitycommission.gov.uk/Showcharity/RegisterOfCharities/ContactAndTrustees.aspx?RegisteredCharityNumber=1120797&SubsidiaryNumber=0)>.

Newell, S., and Marabelli, M. 2016. 'Knowledge Mobilization in Healthcare Network: The Power of Everyday Practices'. In J. Swan, S. Newell, and D. Nicolini (eds), *Mobilizing Knowledge in*

*Healthcare: Challenges for Management and Organization.* Oxford: Oxford University Press, 132–50.

Newman, J. 2001. *Modernizing Governance: New Labour, Policy and Society.* London: Sage.

NHS Commissioning Board. 2012. *Towards Establishment: Creating Responsive and Accountable Clinical Commissioning Groups.* Leeds: NHS Commissioning Board.

NHS Digital. 2016. 'Non-NHS Organizations: Independent Sector Healthcare Providers' [Dataset]. <https://digital.nhs.uk/organisation-data-service/data-downloads/non-nhs> [Accessed Feb. 2017].

NHS England. 2014. *Five Year Forward View.* London: NHS England.

NHS England. 2016a. <https://www.england.nhs.uk/2016/07/operational-performance>.

NHS England. 2016b. <https://www.england.nhs.uk/2016/12/hiv-prevention-pregramme>.

NHS III. 2009. <http://www.institute.nhs.uk/commissioning/tackling_tough_choices/an_intro duction_to_public_value.html> [Accessed Jan. 2016].

NHSIQ. 2013. *An Introduction to the NHS Change Model.* Leeds: NHSIQ.

NHSIQ. 2014. *Bringing Lean to Life.* Leeds: NHSIQ.

NHSIQ. 2016. <http://www.nhsiq.nhs.uk/capacity-capability/nhs-change-day.aspx#sthash. jblJF0Tu.dpuf>.

Nicholson, D. 2009. *NHS Executive's Annual Report for 2008/09.* London: Department of Health.

Nicolini, D. 2006. 'The Work to Make Telemedicine Work: A Social and Articulative View'. *Social Science and Medicine,* 62(11): 2754–67.

Nicolini, D. 2009. 'Zooming In and Out: Studying Practices by Switching Theoretical Lenses and Trailing Connections'. *Organization Studies,* 30(12): 1391–1418.

Nicolini, D. 2011. 'Practice as the Site of Knowing: Insights from the Field of Telemedicine'. *Organization Science,* 22(3): 602–20.

Nicolini, D., Gherardi, S., and Yanow, D., eds. 2003. *Knowing in Organizations: A Practice-Based Approach.* New York: M. E. Sharpe.

Nicolini, D., Mengis, J., Meacheam, D., Waring, J., and Swan, J. 2016. 'Recovering the Performative Role of Innovations in the Global Travel of Healthcare Practices: Is There a Ghost in the Machine?' In J. Swan, S. Newell, and D. Nicolini (eds), *Mobilizing Knowledge in Healthcare: Challenges for Management and Organization.* Oxford: Oxford University Press, 177–98.

Niemietz, C. 2017. *A Piggy Bank for Health Care.* Discussion Paper 83. London: IEA.

Nikolova, N., and Devinney, T. 2012. 'The Nature of the Client-Consultant Interaction: A Critical Overview'. In M. Kipping and T. Clark (eds), *The Oxford Handbook of Management Consulting.* Oxford: Oxford University Press, 389–410.

Nonaka, I., and Teece, D. 2001. *Managing Industrial Knowledge: Creation, Transfer and Utilization.* London: Sage.

Norman, J. 2010. *The Big Society: The Anatomy of the New Politics.* Buckingham: University of Buckingham Press.

Nowotny, H., Scott, P., and Gibbons, M. 2003. 'Introduction: "Mode 2" Revisited: The New Production of Knowledge'. *Minerva,* 41(3): 179–94.

Nuffield Trust. 2015. *Viewpoint: What Do Leaders Want from NHS Improvement?,* London: Nuffield Trust.

Nuffield Trust, Health Foundation, and King's Fund. 2015. *Impact of the 2015 Spending Review on Health and Social Care: Written Evidence for the Health Select Committee, on Behalf of the*

*Nuffield Trust, the Health Foundation and The King's Fund.* <https://www.nuffieldtrust.org.uk/files/2017-01/2015-spending-review-inquiry-joint-submission-web-final.pdf> [Accessed July 2018].

Oborn, E., Barrett, M., and Racko, G. 2013. 'Knowledge Translation in Healthcare: Incorporating Theories of Learning and Knowledge from the Management Literature'. *Journal of Health Organization and Management*, 27(4): 412–31.

Oborn, E., Prince, K., and Barrett, M. 2016. 'Knowledge Mobilization across Inter-Organizational Healthcare Innovation Partnerships: A Network Ambidexterity Perspective'. In J. Swan, S. Newell, and D. Nicolini (eds), *Mobilizing Knowledge in Healthcare: Challenges for Management and Organization*. Oxford: Oxford University Press, 107–31.

Olivas-Lujan, M. 2008. 'Evidence-Based Management: A Business Necessity for Hispanics', *Business Journal of Hispanic Research,* 2(2): 10–26.

Oliver, D. 2014. 'Stop Wasting Taxpayers' Money on Management Consultancy for the NHS'. *BMJ: British Medical Journal* (online), 349.

O'Mahoney, J., Heusinkveld, S., and Wright, C. 2013. 'Commodifying the Commodifiers: The Impact of Procurement on Management Knowledge'. *Journal of Management Studies*, 50: 204–35.

O'Mahoney, J., and Markham, C. 2013. *Management Consultancy*. Oxford: Oxford University Press.

O'Mahoney, J., and Sturdy, A. 2016. 'Power and the Diffusion of Management Ideas: The Case of McKinsey & Co'. *Management Learning*, 47(3): 247–65.

Orlikowski, W. J., and Scott, S. V. 2008. 'Sociomateriality: Challenging the Separation of Technology, Work and Organization'. *Academy of Management Annals*, 2(1): 433–74.

Orr, J. E. 1996. *Talking About Machines: An Ethnography of a Modern Job.* Ithaca, NY: ILR Press/ Cornell University Press.

Orr, J. E. 1998. 'Images of Work'. *Science, Technology, and Human Values*, 23(4): 439–55.

Osborne, D., and Gaebler, T. 1992. *Reinventing Government: How the Entrepreneurial Spirit is Transforming Government.* Reading, MA: Adison Wesley Public Comp.

Osborne, S. P., ed. 2010. *The New Public Governance: Emerging Perspectives on the Theory and Practice of Public Governance.* Abingdon: Routledge.

Packwood, T., Pollitt, C., and Roberts, S. 1998. 'Good Medicine? A Case Study of Business Process Re-Engineering in a Hospital'. *Policy and Politics*, 26(4): 401–15.

Page, J., Pearson, J., Panchamnia, N., Thomas, P., and Traficante, J. 2014. *Leading Change in the Civil Services.* London: Institute for Government.

Painter, M. J., and Peters, B. G., eds. 2010. *Tradition and Public Administration.* Basingstoke: Palgrave Macmillan.

Panchamia, N., and Thomas, P. 2010. *Public Services Agreements and the Prime Minister's Delivery Unit.* London: Institute for Government.

Penrose, E. 1959. *The Theory of the Growth of the Firm.* New York: John Wiley.

Peters, T. J., and Waterman, R. H. 1982. *In Search of Excellence: Lessons from America's Best-Run Companies.* New York: Harper & Row.

Pettigrew, A. 1987. 'Context and Action in the Transformation of the Firm'. *Journal of Management Studies,* 24(6): 649–70.

Pettigrew, A., Ferlie, E., and McKee, L. 1992. *Shaping Strategic Change.* London: Sage.

Pfeffer, J. and Sutton, R. I. 2006a. 'A Matter of Fact'. *People Management 12* (19): 24–30.

Pfeffer, J., and Sutton, R. 2006b. 'Evidence Based Management'. *Harvard Business Review*, 84(1): 62.

Pfeffer, J., and Sutton, R. I. 2006c. *Hard Facts, Dangerous Half-Truths, and Total Nonsense: Profiting from Evidence-Based Management*. Boston, MA: Harvard Business School Press.

Pfeffer, J., and Sutton, R. I. 2007. 'Suppose We Took Evidence-Based Management Seriously: Implications for Reading and Writing'. *Academy of Management Learning and Education*, 6(1): 153–5.

Piening, E. P. 2013. 'Dynamic Capabilities in Public Organizations: A Literature Review and Research Agenda'. *Public Management Review*, 15(2): 209–45.

Pollitt, C. 2013. 'The Evolving Narratives of Public Management Reform: 40 Years of Reform White Papers in the UK'. *Public Management Review*, 15(6): 899–922.

Pollitt, C., and Bouckaert, G. 2011. *Public Management Reform: A Comparative Analysis—New Public Management, Governance, and the Neo-Weberian State*. London: Oxford University Press.

Pollitt, C., Talbot, C., Caulfield, J., and Smullen, A. 2004. *Agencies: How Governments Do Things through Semi Autonomous Organizations*. Basingstoke: Palgrave Macmillan.

Porter, M. E., and Teisberg, E. O. 2006. *Redefining Health Care: Creating Value-Based Competition on Results*. Cambridge, MA: Harvard University Press.

Powell, M. 1999. 'New Labour and the Third Way in the British National Health Service'. *International Journal of Health Services*, 29(2): 353–70.

Powell, M., ed. 2007. *Understanding the Mixed Economy of Welfare*. Bristol: Policy Press.

Powell, M., and Miller, R. 2016. 'Seventy Years of Privatizing the British National Health Service?' *Social Policy and Administration*, 50(1): 99–118.

Powell, W. W., and Snellman, K. 2004. 'The Knowledge Economy'. *Annual Review of Sociology*, 30: 199–220.

Putnam, R. D. 2000. *Bowling Alone: The Collapse and Revival of American Community*. New York: Simon & Schuster.

Quilter-Pinny, H., and Gorsky, M. 2017. *Devo Then; Devo Now*. London: IPPR.

Radnor, Z. J., Holweg, M., and Waring, J. 2012. 'Lean in Healthcare: The Unfilled Promise?' *Social Science and Medicine*, 74(3): 364–71.

Rashman, L., Withers, E., and Hartley, J. 2009. 'Organizational Learning and Knowledge in Public Service Organizations: A Systematic Review of the Literature'. *International Journal of Management Reviews*, 11(4): 463–94.

Reay, T., Berta, W., and Kohn, M. K., 2009. 'What's the Evidence on Evidence-Based Management?' *Academy of Management Perspectives*, 23(4): 5–18.

ResPublica. 2017. <http://apps.charitycommission.gov.uk/Showcharity/RegisterOfCharities/ContactAndTrustees.aspx?RegisteredCharityNumber=1120797&SubsidiaryNumber=0>.

Rhodes, R. A. 1997. *Understanding Governance: Policy Networks, Governance, Reflexivity and Accountability*. Buckingham: Open University Press.

Rhodes, R. A. 2007. 'Understanding Governance: Ten Years On'. *Organization Studies*, 28(8): 1243–64.

Rhodes, R. A., and Wanna, J. 2007. 'The Limits to Public Value, or Rescuing Responsible Government from the Platonic Guardians'. *Australian Journal of Public Administration*, 66(4): 406–21.

Roberts, A., Marshall, L., and Charlesworth, A. 2012. *A Decade of Austerity? The Funding Pressures Facing the NHS from 2010/11 to 2021/22*. London: Nuffield Trust. <https://www.

nuffieldtrust.org.uk/research/a-decade-of-austerity-the-funding-pressures-facing-the-nhs-from-2010-11-to-2021-22> [Accessed Oct. 2017].

Robertson, R., Holder, H., Ross, S., Naylor, C., and Machaquerio, S. 2016. *Clinical Commissioning: GPs in Charge?* London: King's Fund and Nuffield Trust.

Rochester, C., and Zimmick, M. 2012. 'That Was the Year That Was—Farewell to 2011'. Blog, Voluntary Action History Society. <http://www.vahs.org.uk/2012/01/rochester-zimmeck-review-2011> [Accessed Nov. 2016].

Rose, D. 2012. 'The Firm That Hijacked the NHS'. *Daily Mail,* 12 Feb.

Rosenberg Hansen, J., and Ferlie, E. 2016. 'Applying Strategic Management Theories in Public Sector Organizations: Developing a Typology'. *Public Management Review,* 18(1): 1–19.

Rouleau, L. 2005. 'Micro-Practices of Strategic Sensemaking and Sensegiving: How Middle Managers Interpret and Sell Change Every Day'. *Journal of Management Studies,* 42: 1413–41.

Rousseau, D. M. 2006. 'Presidential Address: Is There Such a Thing as "Evidence-Based Management"?' *Academy of Management Review,* 31(2): 256–69.

Rousseau, D. M., ed. 2012. *The Oxford Handbook of Evidence-Based Management.* Oxford: Oxford University Press. [Accessed online Dec. 2017].

Rousseau, D. M., and McCarthy, S. 2007. 'Educating Managers from an Evidence-Based Perspective'. *Academy of Management Learning and Education,* 6(1): 84–101.

Rousseau, D., Manning, J., and Denyer, D. 2009. 'Evidence in Management and Organizational Science: Assembling the Field's Full Weight of Scientific Knowledge through Syntheses'. *Academy of Management Annals,* 2(1): 475–515.

RSA (2016). <https://www.thersa.org/globalassets/pdfs/governance/rsa-impact-report-2016.pdf>.

Sackett, D. L., Richardson, W. S., Rosenberg, W., et al. 2000. *Evidence-Based Medicine: How to Practice and Teach EBM,* 2nd edn. Edinburgh: Churchill Livingstone.

Sackett, D. L., and Rosenberg, W. M. C. 1995. 'On the Need for Evidence-Based Medicine'. *Health Economics,* 4(4): 249–54.

Sahlin, K., and Wedlin, L. 2008. 'Circulating Ideas: Imitation, Translation and Editing'. In R. Greenwood, C. Oliver, R. Suddaby, and K. Sahlin (eds), *The SAGE Handbook of Organizational Institutionalism.* London: SAGE, 218–42.

Sahlin-Andersson, K. 1996. 'Imitating by Editing Success: The Construction of Organizational Fields'. In B. Czarniawska and G. Sevon (eds), *Translating Organizational Change.* Berlin: De Gruyter, 69–92.

Sahlin-Andersson, K., and Engwall, L. 2002a. 'Carriers, Flows and Sources of Management Knowledge'. In K. Sahlin-Andersson and L. Engwall (eds), *The Expansion of Management Knowledge.* Stanford, CA: Stanford Business Books, 3–32.

Sahlin-Andersson, K., and Engwall, L. 2002b. 'The Dynamics of Management Knowledge Expansion'. In K. Sahlin-Andersson and L. Engwall (eds), *The Expansion of Management Knowledge.* Stanford, CA: Stanford Business Books, 277–96.

Sahlin-Andersson, K., and Engwall, L., eds. 2002c. *The Expansion of Management Knowledge: Carriers, Flows, and Sources.* Stanford, CA: Stanford University Press.

Saint-Martin, D. 1998. 'The New Managerialism and the Policy Influence of Consultants in Government: An Historical-Institutionalist Analysis of Britain, Canada and France'. *Governance,* 11(3): 319–56.

Saint-Martin, D. 2004. *Building the New Managerialist State: Consultants and the Politics of Public Sector Reform in Comparative Perspective.* Oxford: Oxford University Press.

Saint-Martin, D. 2012. 'Management Consultants and Governments'. In M. Kipping and T. Clark (eds), *The Oxford Handbook of Management Consulting.* Oxford: Oxford University Press, 447–66.

Sandberg, J., and Tsoukas, H. 2011. 'Grasping the Logic of Practice: Theorizing through Practical Rationality'. *Academy of Management Review,* 36(2): 338–60.

Scarbrough, H., ed. 1996. *The Management of Expertise.* Basingstoke and London: Macmillan.

Schatzki, T. R. 2006. 'On Organizations as They Happen'. *Organization Studies,* 27(12): 1863–73.

Schatzki, T. R., Knorr-Cetina, K., and Von Savigny, E., eds. 2001. *The Practice Turn in Contemporary Theory.* London: Routledge.

Schein, E. 1969. *Process Consultation: Its Role in Organizational Development.* Reading, MA: Addison Wesley.

Scherer, A. G. 1998. 'Pluralism and Incommensurability in Strategic Management and Organization Theory: A Problem in Search of a Solution'. *Organization,* 5(2): 147–68.

Scherer, A. G., and Steinmann, H. 1999. 'Some Remarks on the Problem of Incommensurability in Organization Studies'. *Organization Studies,* 20(3): 519–44.

Schön, D. 1983. *The Reflective Practitioner: How Practitioners Think in Action.* London: Temple Smith.

Schoonmaker, M. G., and Carayannis, E. G. 2013. 'Mode 3: A Proposed Classification Scheme for the Knowledge Economy and Society'. *Journal of the Knowledge Economy,* 4: 556–77.

Scott, M. 2011. 'Reflections on "The Big Society"'. *Community Development Journal,* 46(1): 132–7.

Scott, W. R., Ruef, M., Mendel, P., and Caronna, C. 2001. *Institutional Change and Health Care Organizations: From Professional Dominance to Managed Care.* Chicago: University of Chicago Press.

Selznick, P. 2015. *TVA and the Grass Roots.* London: Forgotten Books, reprint.

Shaw, S. E., Russell, J., Greenhalgh, T., and Korica, M. 2014. 'Thinking about Think Tanks in Health Care: A Call for a New Research Agenda'. *Sociology of Health and Illness,* 36(3): 447–61.

Sheaff, R., and Allen, P. 2016. 'Provider Plurality and Supply Side Reform'. In M. Exworthy, Mannion, and M. Powell (eds), *Dismantling the NHS? Evaluating the Impact of Health Reforms.* Bristol: Policy Press, 211–32.

Smith Review. 2015. *Review of Centrally Funded Improvement and Leadership Development Functions.* Leeds: NHS England, Paper 4.

Speed, E., and Mannion, R. 2017. 'The Rise of Post-Truth Populism in Pluralist Liberal Democracies: Challenges for Health Policy'. *International Journal of Health Policy and Management,* 6(5): 249.

Spicer, A. 2018. *Business Bullshit.* Abingdon: Routledge.

Srivastava, A., Bartol, K. M., and Locke, E. A. 2006. 'Empowering Leadership in Management Teams: Effects on Knowledge Sharing, Efficacy and Performance'. *Academy of Management Journal,* 49(6): 1239–51.

Stake, R. E. 2000. 'Case Studies'. In N. Denzin and Y. Lincoln (eds), *Handbook of Qualitative Research,* 2nd edn. London: Sage, 435–54.

Starbuck, W. H. 1992. 'Learning by Knowledge Intensive Firms'. *Journal of Management Studies,* 29(6): 713–40.

Starkey, K., and Madan, P. 2001. 'Bridging the Relevance Gap: Aligning Stakeholders in the Future of Management Research'. *British Journal of Management,* 12: S3–S26.

Stehr, N. 1994. *Knowledge Societies.* London: Sage.

Stone, D. 1996. *Capturing the Political Imagination: Think Tanks and the Policy Process.* London: Frank Cass.

Stone, D. 2000. 'Think Tanks across Nations: The New Networks of Knowledge'. *NIRA Review,* 7(1): 34–9.

Stone, D. 2007. 'Recycling Bins, Garbage Cans or Think Tanks? Three Myths Regarding Policy Analysis Institutes'. *Public Administration,* 85(2): 259–78.

Sturdy, A. 2004. 'The Adoption of Management Ideas and Practices: Theoretical Perspectives and Possibilities'. *Management Learning,* 35(2): 155–79.

Sturdy, A. 2011. 'Consultancy's Consequences? A Critical Assessment of Management Consultancy's Impact on Management'. *British Journal of Management,* 22: 517–30.

Sturdy, A., Clark, T., Fincham, R., and Handley, K. 2009. 'Between Innovation and Legitimation— Boundaries and Knowledge Flow in Management Consultancy'. *Organization,* 16(5): 627–53.

Suddaby, R., and Greenwood, R. 2001. 'Colonizing Knowledge: Commodification as Dynamic of Jurisdictional Expansion in Professional Service Forms'. *Human Relations,* 54: 933–53.

Swan, J., Newell, S., Scarbrough, H., and Hislop, D. 1999. 'Knowledge Management and Innovation: Networks and Networking'. *Journal of Knowledge Management,* 3(4): 262–75.

Swan, J., Nicolini, D., and Newell, S., eds. 2016. *Mobilizing Knowledge in Healthcare: Challenges for Management and Organization.* Oxford: Oxford University Press.

Teece, D. J., Pisano, G., and Shuen, A. 1997. 'Dynamic Capabilities and Strategic Management'. *Strategic Management Journal,* 18(7): 509–33.

Thomas, R., Sargent, L., and Hardy, C. 2011. 'Managing Organizational Change: Negotiating Meaning and Power-Resistance Relations'. *Organization Science,* 22: 22–41.

Thorlby, R., and Arora, S. 2016. 'The English Health Care System, 2015'. In E. Mossialos and M. Wenzl (eds), *2015 International Profiles of Health Care Systems.* New York and Washington, DC: The Commonwealth Fund, 49–58.

Thrift, N. 2005. *Knowing Capitalism.* London: Sage.

Times Higher Education. 2017. <https://www.timeshighereducation.com/world-university-ran kings/2017/world-ranking#!/page/0/length/25/sort_by/rank/sort_order/asc/cols/stats>.

Timmermans, S. 2008. 'Professions and Their Work: Do Market Shelters Protect Professional Interests?' *Work and Occupations,* 35(2): 164–88.

Timmermans, S., and Berg, M. 2003. *The Gold Standard: The Challenge of Evidence-Based Medicine and Standardization in Health Care.* Philadelphia: Temple University Press.

Todorova, G., and Durisin, B. 2007. 'Absorptive Capacity: Valuing a Reconceptualization'. *Academy of Management Review,* 32(3): 774–86.

Toolky, J., 1992. 'The "Pink-Tank" on the Education Reform Act'. *British Journal of Educational Studies,* 40(4): 335–49.

Tortoriello, M. 2015. 'The Social Underpinnings of Absorptive Capacity: The Moderating Effects of Structural Holes on Innovation Generation Based on External Knowledge'. *Strategic Management Journal,* 36(4): 586–97.

Tranfield, D., Denyer, D., and Smart, P. 2003. 'Towards a Methodology for Developing Evidence-Informed Management Knowledge by Means of Systematic Review'. *British Journal of Management,* 14(3): 207–22.

Traynor, M. 2003. 'Introduction'. *Health: An Interdisciplinary Journal for the Social Study of Health, Illness and Medicine,* 7(3): 265–6.

Trenholm, S., and Ferlie, E. 2013. 'Using Complexity Theory to Analyse the Organisational Response to Resurgent Tuberculosis across London'. *Social Science and Medicine,* 93: 229–37.

Trenholm, S., Lee, R., Ferlie, E., and Tulloch, T. 2016. *From Words to Wards: Operationalizing Michael Porter's Theory of Value Based Health Care in an English Hospital Setting.* Working paper, King's College London: School of Management and Business.

Tsoukas, H. 2009. 'A Dialogical Approach to the Creation of New Knowledge in Organizations'. *Organization Science,* 20: 941–57.

Tversky, A., and Kahneman, D. 1974. 'Judgment Under Uncertainty: Heuristics and Biases'. *Science,* 185(4157): 1124–31.

Van Elk, S. 2016. 'Austerity and Value Based Health Care: A Discursive Approach'. PhD upgrade document, King's College London: School of Management and Business.

Verheijen, T. 2010. 'The New Member States of the European Union: Constructed and Historical Traditions and Reform Trajectories'. In M. Painter and B. G. Peters (eds), *Tradition and Public Administration.* Basingstoke: Palgrave Macmillan, 217–33.

Viitala, R. 2004. 'Towards Knowledge Leadership'. *Leadership and Organization Development Journal,* 25(6): 528–44.

Vining, A. R. 2011. 'Public Agency External Analysis Using a Modified "Five Forces" Framework'. *International Public Management Journal,* 14(1): 63–105.

Virgin Care. 2016. <http://www.virgincare.co.uk/about-us>. [Accessed Nov. 2016].

von Krogh, G., Nonaka, I., and Rechsteiner, L. 2012. 'Leadership in Organizational Knowledge Creation: A Review and Framework'. *Journal of Management Studies,* 49(1): 240–77.

Walshe, K., and Davies, H. T. O. 2010. 'Research, Influence and Impact: Deconstructing the Norms of Health Services Research Commissioning'. *Policy and Society,* 29(2): 103–11.

Walshe, K., and Davies, H. T. O. 2013. 'Health Research, Development and Innovation in England from 1988 to 2013: From Research Production to Knowledge Mobilization'. *Journal of Health Services Research and Policy,* 18(3):_suppl., 1–12.

Walshe, K., and Rundall, T. G. 2001. 'Evidence-Based Management: From Theory to Practice in Health Care'. *Milbank Quarterly,* 79(3): 429–57.

Wanless Report. 2002. *Securing our Future Health: Taking a Long-Term View.* London: Public Enquiry Unit, HM Treasury. <http://www.dh.gov.uk/en/Publicationsandstatistics/Publications/PublicationsPolicyAndGuidance/DH_4009293>.

Warren, M. E. 2012. 'Civil Society and Democracy'. In M. Edwards, *The Oxford Handbook of Civil Society.* Oxford: Oxford University Press, 66–78.

Weaver, R. K. 1989. 'The Changing World of Think Tanks'. *PS: Political Science and Politics,* 22(3): 563–78.

Weaver, R. K., ed. 2002. *Think Tanks and Civil Societies: Catalysts for Ideas and Action.* New Brunswick, NJ: Transaction.

Weaver, R. K., and McGann, J. G. 2009. 'Think Tanks and Civil Societies in a Time of Change'. In J. G. McGann and R. K. Weaver (eds), *Think Tanks and Civil Societies: Catalysts for Ideas and Action.* New Brunswick, NJ: Transaction Publishers, 1–36.

Weick, K. E., 1995. *Sensemaking in Organizations.* London: SAGE.

Weiss, C. H. 1979. 'The Many Meanings of Research Utilization'. *Public Administration Review,* 39(5): 426–31.

Wenger, E. 1998. *Communities of Practice: Learning, Meaning, and Identity*. Cambridge: Cambridge University Press.

Wenger, E. 2000. 'Communities of Practice and Social Learning Systems'. *Organization*, 7(2): 225–46.

Wernerfelt, B. 1984. 'A Resource-Based View of the Firm'. *Strategic Management Journal*, 5(2): 171–80.

Werr, A. 2012. 'Knowledge Management and Management Consulting'. In M. Kipping and T. Clark (eds), *The Oxford Handbook of Management Consulting*. Oxford: Oxford University Press, 247–66.

Whittington, R. 2006. 'Completing the Practice Turn in Strategy Research'. *Organization Studies*, 27(5): 613–34.

Williams, I., and Shearer, H. 2011. 'Appraising Public Value: Past, Present and Futures'. *Public Administration*, 89(4): 1367–84.

Willmott, P., and Young, M. 1957. *Family and Kinship in East London*. London: Routledge Kegan Paul.

Wright, C., Sturdy, A., and Wylie, N. 2012. 'Management Innovation through Standardization: Consultants as Standardizers of Organizational Practice'. *Research Policy*, 41(3): 652–62.

Yin, R. 1999. 'Enhancing the Quality of Case Studies in Health Services Research'. *Health Services Research*, 34(3): 1209–24.

Yin, R. 2009. *Case Study Research: Design and Methods*, 4th edn. Thousand Oaks, CA: Sage.

Zahra, S. A., and George, G. 2002. 'Absorptive Capacity: A Review, Reconceptualization, and Extension'. *Academy of Management Review*, 27(2): 185–203.

Zald, M. N. 2005. 'The Strange Career of an Idea and Its Resurrection: Social Movements in Organizations'. *Journal of Management Inquiry*, 14(2): 157–66.

Zald, M. N., and Berger, M. A. 1978. 'Social Movements in Organizations: Coup d'etat, Insurgency, and Mass Movements'. *American Journal of Sociology*, 83(4): 823–61.

# ■ INDEX